THE ANNALS

© 1986 *by* The American Academy *of* Political *and* Social Science

ERICA GINSBURG, *Assistant Editor*

All rights reserved. No part of this volume may be reproduced or utilized in any form or by any means, electronic or mechanical, including photocopying, recording or by any information storage and retrieval system, without permission in writing from the publisher.

Editorial Office: 3937 Chestnut Street, Philadelphia, Pennsylvania 19104.

For information about membership* (individuals only) and subscriptions (institutions), address:

SAGE PUBLICATIONS, INC.
275 South Beverly Drive
Beverly Hills, CA 90212 USA

From India and South Asia, write to:	*From the UK, Europe, the Middle East and Africa, write to:*
SAGE PUBLICATIONS INDIA Pvt. Ltd.	SAGE PUBLICATIONS LTD
P.O. Box 4215	28 Banner Street
New Delhi 110 048	London EC1Y 8QE
INDIA	ENGLAND

SAGE Production Editor: JACQUELINE SYROP

**Please note that members of The Academy receive THE ANNALS with their membership.*

Library of Congress Catalog Card Number 85-063002
International Standard Serial Number ISSN 0002-7162
International Standard Book Number ISBN 0-8039-2695-2 (Vol. 484, 1986 paper)
International Standard Book Number ISBN 0-8039-2694-4 (Vol. 484, 1986 cloth)
Manufactured in the United States of America. First printing, March 1986.

The articles appearing in THE ANNALS are indexed in *Book Review Index; Public Affairs Information Service Bulletin; Social Sciences Index; Monthly Periodical Index; Current Contents; Behavioral, Social Management Sciences;* and *Combined Retrospective Index Sets.* They are also abstracted and indexed in *ABC Pol Sci, Historical Abstracts, Human Resources Abstracts, Social Sciences Citation Index, United States Political Science Documents, Social Work Research & Abstracts, Peace Research Reviews, Sage Urban Studies Abstracts, International Political Science Abstracts, America: History and Life,* and/or *Family Resources Database.*

Information about membership rates, institutional subscriptions, and back issue prices may be found on the facing page.

Advertising. Current rates and specifications may be obtained by writing to THE ANNALS Advertising and Promotion Manager at the Beverly Hills office (address above).

Claims. Claims for undelivered copies must be made no later than three months following month of publication. The publisher will supply missing copies when losses have been sustained in transit and when the reserve stock will permit.

Change of Address. Six weeks' advance notice must be given when notifying of change of address to insure proper identification. Please specify name of journal. Send change of address to: THE ANNALS, c/o Sage Publications, Inc., 275 South Beverly Drive, Beverly Hills, CA 90212.

VOLUME 484 MARCH

THE ANNALS

of The American Academy *of* Political *and* Social Science

RICHARD D. LAMBERT, *Editor*
ALAN W. HESTON, *Associate Editor*

THE LAW AND MENTAL HEALTH: RESEARCH AND POLICY

Special Editor of this Volume

SALEEM A. SHAH

*Chief
Center for Studies of Antisocial
and Violent Behavior
National Institute of Mental Health
Rockville
Maryland*

SAGE PUBLICATIONS   *BEVERLY HILLS   LONDON   NEW DELHI*

The American Academy of Political and Social Science

3937 Chestnut Street   Philadelphia, Pennsylvania 19104

Board of Directors

ELMER B. STAATS	RANDALL M. WHALEY
MARVIN E. WOLFGANG	HENRY W. SAWYER, III
LEE BENSON	WILLIAM T. COLEMAN, Jr.
RICHARD D. LAMBERT	ANTHONY J. SCIRICA
THOMAS L. HUGHES	FREDERICK HELDRING
LLOYD N. CUTLER	

Officers

President
MARVIN E. WOLFGANG

Vice-Presidents
RICHARD D. LAMBERT, *First Vice-President*
STEPHEN B. SWEENEY, *First Vice-President Emeritus*

Secretary	*Treasurer*	*Counsel*
RANDALL M. WHALEY	ELMER B. STAATS	HENRY W. SAWYER, III

Editors, THE ANNALS

RICHARD D. LAMBERT, *Editor*   ALAN W. HESTON, *Associate Editor*

THORSTEN SELLIN, *Editor Emeritus*

Assistant to the President
MARY E. HARRIS

Origin and Purpose. The Academy was organized December 14, 1889, to promote the progress of political and social science, especially through publications and meetings. The Academy does not take sides in controverted questions, but seeks to gather and present reliable information to assist the public in forming an intelligent and accurate judgment.

Meetings. The Academy holds an annual meeting in the spring extending over two days.

Publications. THE ANNALS is the bimonthly publication of The Academy. Each issue contains articles on some prominent social or political problem, written at the invitation of the editors. Also, monographs are published from time to time, numbers of which are distributed to pertinent professional organizations. These volumes constitute important reference works on the topics with which they deal, and they are extensively cited by authorities through-out the United States and abroad. The papers presented at the meetings of The Academy are included in THE ANNALS.

Membership. Each member of The Academy receives THE ANNALS and may attend the meetings of The Academy. Membership is open only to individuals. Annual dues: $26.00 for the regular paperbound edition (clothbound, $39.00). Add $9.00 per year for membership outside the U.S.A. Members may also purchase single issues of THE ANNALS for $6.95 each (clothbound, $10.00).

Subscriptions. THE ANNALS (ISSN 0002-7162) is published six times annually—in January, March, May, July, September, and November. Institutions may subscribe to THE ANNALS at the annual rate: $50.00 (clothbound, $66.00). Add $9.00 per year for subscriptions outside the U.S.A. Institutional rates for single issues: $10.00 each (clothbound, $15.00).

Second class postage paid at Philadelphia, Pennsylvania, and at additional mailing offices.

Single issues of THE ANNALS may be obtained by individuals who are not members of The Academy for $7.95 each (clothbound, $15.00). Single issues of THE ANNALS have proven to be excellent supplementary texts for classroom use. Direct inquiries regarding adoptions to THE ANNALS c/o Sage Publications (address below).

All correspondence concerning membership in The Academy, dues renewals, inquiries about membership status, and/or purchase of single issues of THE ANNALS should be sent to THE ANNALS c/o Sage Publications, Inc., 275 South Beverly Drive, Beverly Hills, CA 90212. *Please note that orders under $20 must be prepaid.* Sage affiliates in London and India will assist institutional subscribers abroad with regard to orders, claims, and inquiries for both subscriptions and single issues.

THE EIGHTY-NINTH ANNUAL MEETING OF THE AMERICAN ACADEMY OF POLITICAL AND SOCIAL SCIENCE

APRIL 18 AND 19, 1986
FRANKLIN PLAZA HOTEL
PHILADELPHIA, PENNSYLVANIA

The annual meeting of The Academy is attended by many distinguished scholars, statesmen, authors, and professionals in diverse fields, including representatives of many embassies, academic institutions, and cultural, civic, and scientific organizations.

This 89th Annual Meeting will be addressed at each session by prominent scholars and officials and will be devoted to the topic of

REVITALIZING THE INDUSTRIAL CITY

Members of the Academy are cordially invited to attend and will receive full information. Information on Academy membership can be found in each volume of THE ANNALS.

- Proceedings of the 89th Annual Meeting will be published in the November 1986 volume of THE ANNALS.

- All members and attendees who have published a book may participate in the exhibits at the hotel. Contact Harve C. Horowitz & Associates, 10369 Currycomb Court, Columbia, MD 21044, tel. (301) 997-0763.

FOR DETAILS ABOUT THE ANNUAL MEETING WRITE TO
THE AMERICAN ACADEMY OF POLITICAL AND SOCIAL SCIENCE
BUSINESS OFFICE • 3937 CHESTNUT STREET
PHILADELPHIA, PENNSYLVANIA 19104

CONTENTS

PREFACE .... *Saleem A. Shah*	9
CARE AND TREATMENT OF THE MENTALLY ILL IN THE UNITED STATES: HISTORICAL DEVELOPMENTS AND REFORMS .... *Joseph P. Morrissey and Howard H. Goldman*	12
CIVIL COMMITMENT OF THE MENTALLY ILL: AN OVERVIEW .... *Mark J. Mills*	28
LEGAL INTERVENTION IN CIVIL COMMITMENT: THE IMPACT OF BROADENED COMMITMENT CRITERIA .... *Mary L. Durham and Glenn L. Pierce*	42
INDEXING CIVIL COMMITMENT IN PSYCHIATRIC EMERGENCY ROOMS .... *Steven P. Segal, Margaret A. Watson, and L. Scott Nelson*	56
HOW DID *TARASOFF* AFFECT CLINICAL PRACTICE? .... *William J. Bowers, Daniel J. Givelber, and Carolyn L. Blitch*	70
OREGON'S PSYCHIATRIC SECURITY REVIEW BOARD: A COMPREHENSIVE SYSTEM FOR MANAGING INSANITY ACQUITTEES .... *Jeffrey L. Rogers, Joseph D. Bloom, and Spero M. Manson*	86
A REVIEW OF RESEARCH ON THE INSANITY DEFENSE .... *Richard A. Pasewark*	100
THE INSANITY DEFENSE: PROBLEMS AND PROSPECTS FOR STUDYING THE IMPACT OF LEGAL REFORMS .... *Henry J. Steadman and Joseph P. Morrissey*	115
POPULATIONS, PRACTICES, AND PROBLEMS IN FORENSIC PSYCHIATRIC FACILITIES .... *Charlotte A. Kerr and Jeffrey A. Roth*	127
LAW AND PSYCHIATRY: SCANDINAVIA IN THE 1980s ...... *Leif Öjesjö*	144
BOOK DEPARTMENT	155
INDEX	196

BOOK DEPARTMENT CONTENTS

INTERNATIONAL RELATIONS AND POLITICS

DOUGHERTY, JAMES E. *The Bishops and Nuclear Weapons: The Catholic Pastoral Letter on War and Peace*; and
JOHNSON, JAMES TURNER. *Can Modern War Be Just?* Gordon L. Shull 155

FRANCK, THOMAS M. *Nation against Nation: What Happened to the U.N. Dream and What the U.S. Can Do About It.* Albert L. Weeks 156

FRASER, T. G. *Partition in Ireland, India and Palestine, Theory and Practice.* Wallace Sokolsky 157

GURTOV, MELVIN and RAY MAGHROORI. *Roots of Failure: United States Policy in the Third World.* Paul W. van der Veur 158

MacFARLANE, S. NEIL. *Superpower Rivalry and Third World Radicalism: The Idea of National Liberation.* Winston Langley 159

MASHAW, JERRY L. *Due Process in the Administrative State.* Francis M. Wilhoit 160

RA'ANAN, URI and ROBERT L. PFALTZGRAFF, eds. *International Security Dimensions of Space.* Daniel C. Turack 161

STEIN, JONATHAN B. *From H-Bomb to Star Wars: The Politics of Strategic Decision Making*; and
KARSTEN, PETER, PETER HOWELL, and ART ALLEN. *Military Threats: A Systematic Historical Analysis of the Determinants of Success.* Theresa C. Smith 161

AFRICA, ASIA, AND LATIN AMERICA

CAMP, RODERIC A. *The Making of a Government: Political Leaders in Modern Mexico.* William P. Tucker 163

CLUTTERBUCK, RICHARD. *Conflict and Violence in Singapore and Malaysia 1945-1983.* Justus M. van der Kroef 163

EICKELMAN, CHRISTINE. *Women and Community in Oman*; and
PRIDHAM, B. R., ed. *Contemporary Yemen: Political and Historical Background.* William Spencer 164

GOODMAN, DAVID S., ed. *Groups and Politics in the People's Republic of China.* Frankie Fook-lun Leung 165

ISAACS, HAROLD R. *Re-encounters in China: Notes of a Journey in a Time Capsule.* S. Y. Teng 166

OBOLER, REGINA SMITH. *Women, Power, and Economic Change: The Nandi of Kenya.* Mario D. Zamora 167

SPIEGEL, STEVEN L. *The Other Arab-Israeli Conflict: Making America's Middle East Policy, from Truman to Reagan.* Donald E. Webster 168

WICKREMERATNE, L. ANANDA. *The Genesis of an Orientalist: Thomas William Rhys Davids in Sri Lanka.* Mick Moore 169

WOLF, MARGERY. *Revolution Postponed: Women in Contemporary China.* Susan Naquin 170

WOLPERT, STANLEY. *Jinnah of Pakistan.* Theodore P. Wright, Jr. 171

EUROPE

BANAC, IVO. *The National Question in Yugoslavia: Origins, History, Politics.* Pedro Ramet 171

BLOCH, SIDNEY and PETER REDDAWAY. *Soviet Psychiatric Abuse—The Shadow over World Psychiatry.* K. G. Summersett 172

PUGH, PATRICIA. *Educate, Agitate, Organize: 100 Years of Fabian Socialism*; and RADICE, LISANNE. *Beatrice and Sidney Webb: Fabian Socialists.* Paul W. van der Veur 173

UNITED STATES

BALLARD, ALLEN B. *One More Day's Journey: The Story of a Family and a People.* Ronald Provencher 174

DANIEL, PETE. *Breaking the Land: The Transformation of Cotton, Tobacco, and Rice Cultures since 1880.* Paul A. Varg 175

EDEL, MATTHEW, ELLIOTT D. SCLAR, and DANIEL LURIA. *Shaky Palaces: Homeownership and Social Mobility in Boston's Suburbanization.* Mark I. Gelfand 176

GLENNON, ROBERT JEROME. *The Iconoclast as Reformer: Jerome Frank's Impact on American Law.* David E. Alsobrook 177

RUBIN, BARRY. *Secrets of State: The State Department and the Struggle over U.S. Foreign Policy.* Arthur Gallant 178

SARKESIAN, SAM C. *America's Forgotten Wars: The Counterrevolutionary Past and Lessons for the Future.* Robin W. Winks 180

SOCIOLOGY

GOULDNER, ALVIN W. *Against Fragmentation.* Walter E. Ashley 180

POPENOE, DAVID. *Private Pleasure: Public Plight.* Nelson Wikstrom 181

ROSEN, KENNETH T. *Affordable Housing.* Harry W. Reynolds, Jr. 182

STARK, RODNEY and WILLIAM S. BAINBRIDGE. *The Future of Religion: Secularization, Revival and Cult Formation.* Harry E. Yeide, Jr. 183

TILLY, CHARLES. *Big Structures, Large Processes, Huge Comparisons.* Richard A. Wright 184

ECONOMICS

BEHREND, HILDE. *Problems of Labor and Inflation*; and WEITZMAN, MARTIN. *The Share Economy.* Michael D. Bradley 185

BORDO, MICHAEL D. and ANNA J. SCHWARTZ. *A Retrospective on the Classical Gold Standard, 1821-1931.* Gary Roth 186

CLINE, WILLIAM R. *Exports of Manufactures from Developing Countries*; and GRUNWALD, JOSEPH and KENNETH FLAMM. *The Global Factory: Foreign Assembly in International Trade.* Mira Wilkins 187

LUBIN, NANCY. *Labour and Nationality in Soviet Central Asia.* Michael K. Lenker 188

SMITH, V. KERRY, ed. *Environmental Policy under Reagan's Executive Order: The Role of Benefit-Cost Analysis*; and MILBRATH, LESTER W. *Environmentalists: Vanguard for a New Society.* Philip A. Viton 189

PREFACE

This issue of *The Annals* brings together a number of articles pertaining to various interactions between the legal and mental health systems. As the topic is very broad and covers an immense range of interesting as well as controversial topics, the focus here will be limited to some recent developments regarding the civil and criminal commitment of the mentally ill, some empirical research pertaining to these developments and related issues in the field of mental health law, and a variety of associated public policy concerns and dilemmas. This preface will provide a very brief introduction to and context for the articles that follow.

The state's exercise of its power to intervene coercively in the lives of individuals—including interventions that may result in loss of liberty—is justified in reference to its police power and *parens patriae* authorities and associated responsibilities. The state possesses a plenary power to make and enforce laws and regulations for the protection of the public health, safety, and welfare. This broad and inherent power to protect the public is referred to as the police power and is prototypically exemplified in uses of the criminal sanction. The *parens patriae* rationale for coercive interventions invokes the state's sovereign power of guardianship over persons who are unable to care for themselves, such as children and the mentally disabled. In some contrast to the rationale for exercise of the police power, the primary—although not sole—purpose of *parens patriae* interventions, at least in theory, is benevolent: to provide care, protection, and treatment.

Criminal commitments of the mentally ill comprise diversion to the mental health system—typically to security hospitals or security units that are part of regular state mental hospitals—of persons who have been charged with crimes and who, because of their mental disorder, need to be evaluated and/or treated in reference to certain specific legal issues and associated determinations and dispositions. In short, such commitments occur in the course of legal proceedings that originated because of criminal charges placed against the individual. The articles by Professor Rogers and his colleagues, by Dr. Pasewark, and by Dr. Steadman and Dr. Morrissey address a variety of issues that pertain to criminal commitments and related specific issues. Ms. Kerr and Dr. Roth report in their article on a survey of facilities and programs for mentally disordered offenders and note the various categories of criminally committed patients that typically are to be found in such programs.

Civil commitment of the mentally ill involves legal proceedings that—even though concerned with persons believed to pose a danger to themselves or others or who are gravely disabled because of mental disorder—are primarily concerned with the confinement, care, and treatment of such persons. While some police power is also involved—for example, in response to fears that the person may be dangerous to others—a major purpose and objective is remedial and therapeutic. The distinctions between criminal and civil legal proceedings have become increasingly narrow and even blurred as many of the procedural as well as substantive due-process safeguards provided in the criminal process have increasingly been afforded to those facing civil commitments. Dr. Mills's article provides an overview of these and several related developments pertaining to civil commitment of the mentally ill, and Dr. Segal and his associates report on research on clinical assessments and detention decisions in psychiatric emergency rooms.

The historical record indicates that until about the middle of the nineteenth century in America the primary—perhaps even sole—concern in the handling and confinement of the so-called furiously insane was to protect the community. During those times the socially disruptive and dangerous mentally ill were handled much like criminals: they were subjected to various incapacitative and punitive measures in efforts to control and restrain them. The opinion of Chief Justice Shaw in the case of Josiah Oakes in Massachusetts in 1845 provides probably the first formal legal articulation of remedial and therapeutic—as distinct from strictly custodial— objectives for involuntary confinement of the mentally ill. It was this remedial and therapeutic—*parens patriae*—rationale that led to the subsequent development of civil commitment proceedings for involuntary hospitalization of the mentally ill. In the opening article of this issue of *The Annals*, Dr. Morrissey provides a very nice historical background and context for the various cycles of reform in public mental health care in the United States.

As is often the case with many other controversial and vexing social issues and the development or modification of various public policies, careful attention to the available base of empirical evidence and knowledge is not too easily given in the usual political process. In certain areas, such as those addressed in this volume, shocking incidents and related media and public responses often seem to exert considerably more leverage than the knowledge available to inform and guide policymaking. The testimony of various interest groups, lobbies, and witnesses often includes assertions and beliefs that are not well supported, or that draw very selectively on the available information, or that may even fly in the face of existing facts. In this general context, Dr. Pasewark reviews the extant body of empirical research on various aspects of the insanity defense and he notes some of the glaring misconceptions that exist.

Even when laws and other changes in public policies have been very carefully considered, have taken account of available knowledge of the issues, and have very thoughtfully been drafted, there is seldom any systematic empirical assessment of the manner in which the laws were implemented and whether the desired changes were actually achieved. Typically, however, there tend to be rather glaring discrepancies between the law on the books and the law in practice. In this regard, a noteworthy development during the past two decades has been the increasing attention that has been given to legal impact studies and related research. The articles by Dr. Durham and Mr. Pierce and by Dr. Bowers and his colleagues report two recent research endeavors in this general area. The results of such research can provide very useful feedback to key policymakers, program administrators, and other interested groups about the changes that have taken place as well as those that have not. The results can also show the extent to which further refinements and adjustments may be called for if the stated policy objectives are to be achieved more adequately.

The foregoing problems and dilemmas pertaining to interactions between the legal and mental health systems are certainly not unique to the United States. Thus,

Dr. Öjesjö provides an interesting cross-national perspective in his report of recent developments in this general area in the Scandinavian countries, especially Sweden.

Although the debates and disputations concerning the many controversial and difficult issues in the area of law and mental health interaction will doubtless continue, a very promising development during the past two decades has been the markedly increased attention being given to this area by researchers from a variety of disciplines. Illustrative of this is the disciplinary range, as well as the interdisciplinary collaboration, reflected in the articles that have been contributed to the present volume. Finally, it will be noted that in contrast to the huge volume of esoteric knowledge—that is, knowledge that is highly specialized and discipline bound—that is reported in very specialized journals, the contributions in this volume focus on what has been referred to as exoteric knowledge—knowledge that is more broadly oriented and designed to be advantageous to the public.

SALEEM A. SHAH

Care and Treatment of the Mentally Ill in the United States: Historical Developments and Reforms

By JOSEPH P. MORRISSEY and HOWARD H. GOLDMAN

ABSTRACT: Three major cycles of reform in public mental health care in the United States—the moral treatment, mental hygiene, and community mental health movements—are described as a basis for assessing the shifting boundaries between the mental health, social welfare, and criminal justice systems. Historical forces that led to the transinstitutionalization of the mentally ill from almshouses to the state mental hospitals in the nineteenth and twentieth centuries have now been reversed in the aftermath of recent deinstitutionalization policies. Evidence is suggestive that the mentally ill are also being caught up in the criminal justice system, a circumstance reminiscent of pre-asylum conditions in the early nineteenth century. These trends shape the current mental health service delivery system and the agenda for policy-relevant research on issues involving the legal and mental health fields.

Joseph P. Morrissey is a research scientist with the New York State Office of Mental Health and adjunct professor of sociology with the State University of New York, Albany. He has published widely on the sociology of mental hospitalization and mental health service delivery, including The Enduring Asylum *(1981).*

Howard H. Goldman holds an appointment with the Department of Psychiatry, School of Medicine, University of Maryland at Baltimore. His numerous publications include Review of General Psychiatry *(editor, 1984) and several coauthored articles and books on mental health care policy including* The Enduring Asylum *(1981) and* The Chronically Mentally Ill *(1982).*

THE history of public intervention on behalf of the mentally ill in America reveals a cyclical pattern of institutional reforms.[1] The hallmark of each reform was a new environmental approach to treatment and an innovative type of facility or locus of care. The first cycle of reform, in the early nineteenth century, introduced moral treatment and the asylum;[2] the second cycle, in the early twentieth century, was associated with the mental hygiene movement and the psychopathic hospital;[3] and the third cycle, in the mid-twentieth century, was spawned by the community mental health movement and the community mental health center.[4] Although each reform was the result of a unique set of sociohistorical circumstances, a number of striking parallels can be discerned in the reforms' goals, evolution, and outcomes.

Each reform began with the promise that early treatment in the new setting would prevent the personal and societal problems associated with long-term mental disability. The reforms were launched, however, with little or no appreciation of the practical limits to which their core beliefs could be pushed. Consequently, each reform movement and its special facility flourished for a few decades and then faltered in the face of changing and unanticipated circumstances.

First championed as a generic solution for the treatment of the mentally ill, each intervention ultimately proved viable only with acute or milder—not chronic—forms of mental disorder. In each cycle, early optimism soon faded into despair over the increasing numbers of chronic patients who were considered incurable and who began to accumulate in acute-treatment settings. The public's reluctance to allocate sufficient resources for an ever expanding population in need of mental health care, coupled with disappointment over the inability to meet exaggerated expectations, led to a period of pessimism, retrenchment, and neglect, especially of the chronically ill.

The residue of each reform set the stage for the next generation of innovators, with little cumulative impact on the problems to which the reforms were addressed. By shifting attention from one locus of care to another, from community to institution and back again, and from isolated to centralized to decentralized services, each reform movement expanded and diversified the

---

1. Joseph P. Morrissey, Howard H. Goldman, and Lorraine V. Klerman, *The Enduring Asylum: Cycles of Institutional Reform at Worcester State Hospital* (New York: Grune & Stratton, 1980); Joseph P. Morrissey and Howard H. Goldman, "Cycles of Reform in the Care of the Chronically Mentally Ill," *Hospital and Community Psychiatry,* 35:785-93 (1984).

2. Gerald N. Grob, *The State and the Mentally Ill: A History of Worcester State Hospital in Massachusetts, 1830-1920* (Chapel Hill: University of North Carolina Press, 1966); David J. Rothman, *The Discovery of the Asylum* (Boston: Little, Brown, 1971); Gerald N. Grob, *Mental Institutions in America: Social Policy to 1875* (New York: Free Press, 1973).

3. See, for example, David J. Rothman, *Conscience and Convenience: The Asylum and Its Alternatives in Progressive America* (Boston: Little, Brown, 1980); Gerald N. Grob, *Mental Illness and American Society, 1875-1940* (Princeton, NJ: Princeton University Press, 1983); Barbara Sicherman, *The Quest for Mental Health in America, 1880-1917* (New York: Arno Press, 1980).

4. See, for example, the final report of the Joint Commission on Mental Illness and Health, *Action for Mental Health* (New York: Basic Books, 1961); David Musto, "Whatever Happened to Community Mental Health?" *Public Interest,* 39:53-79 (1975); Harry A. Foley and Steven S. Sharfstein, *Madness and Government: Who Cares for the Mentally Ill?* (Washington, DC: American Psychiatric Press, 1983).

American mental health system into today's pluralistic patchwork of public and private, acute and chronic, voluntary and involuntary service settings. Yet each reform failed to prevent chronicity or to alter the care of the severely mentally ill in any fundamental way.

In many respects, these reform cycles served to redefine the boundaries of the social welfare, mental health, and criminal justice systems and to shift responsibility for dependent populations from one institutional setting to another. In this sense, transinstitutionalization has been part of the institutional care of the mentally ill in America for the past two centuries.[5] Clearly, its appearance in the 1970s in the aftermath of rapid reductions in the state mental hospital census does not make it the new phenomenon that many observers would have us believe. Indeed, the events of the 1970s and 1980s with regard to the care and treatment of the mentally ill can be seen as the reversal of nineteenth-century transinstitutionalization processes.

In this article, the care and treatment of the mentally ill in the United States will be reviewed in the context of the three reform cycles. Particular emphasis will be placed on the interface between mental health, social welfare, and criminal justice as background for understanding the current problems and prospects of the mental health service delivery system and for contemporary research issues in the fields of the law and mental health.

MORAL TREATMENT AND THE ASYLUM

The first major effort to improve the care of the mentally ill in America occurred in the early nineteenth century as part of a broad-based social reform movement aimed at bettering the condition of the less fortunate members of society.[6] The belief that human beings could be perfected by manipulating their social and physical environment, the reformist zeal of Evangelical Protestantism, and a spirit of noblesse oblige were prominent features of this humanitarian movement. In this ideological climate, the work of Philippe Pinel in France and William Tuke in England provided both the rationale and the organizational model for public intervention on behalf of the insane in this country. The moral treatment that they championed contributed to the growing acceptance of a medical-psychological, rather than a theological, model of mental illness and led to the establishment of asylums for treatment. Influential laypeople such as Horace Mann in Massachusetts were in the front ranks of this reform movement.

Moral treatment was essentially environmental in nature, encompassing a set of beliefs and practices akin to today's concepts of milieu therapy.[7] The core

---

5. The concept of transinstitutionalization calls attention to patient/inmate flows from one institutional setting to another, whereas, in principle, deinstitutionalization refers to patient/inmate flows from institutional to noninstitutional settings. See, for example, Henry J. Steadman and Joseph P. Morrissey, "The Impact of Deinstitutionalization on the Criminal Justice System," in *The Decentralization of Social Control*, ed. J. Lowman and T. S. Palys (London: Gower, forthcoming); Leona Bachrach, *Deinstitutionalization: An Analytical Review and Sociological Perspective* (Rockville, MD: National Institute of Mental Health, 1976); Carol Warren, "New Forms of Social Control: The Myth of Deinstitutionalization," *American Behavioral Scientist*, 6:724-40 (1981).

6. Grob, *State and the Mentally Ill*, pp. 3-42; idem, *Mental Institutions in America*, pp. 1-34.

7. Norman Dain, "The Chronic Mental Patient in 19th-Century America," *Psychiatric Annals*, 10:323-27 (1980).

belief was that new cases of insanity could be cured by segregating the so-called distracted into small, pastoral asylums where they could receive humane care and instruction. The regimen called for the creation of a warm, familial atmosphere with medical treatment, occupational therapy, religious exercises, amusements and games, kind treatment by a staff headed by a resident superintendent, and in large measure a repudiation of all threats of physical violence.

Adopted first by private facilities such as the Friends Asylum in Pennsylvania, about 1817, and the Hartford Retreat in Connecticut, about 1824, moral treatment was soon advocated for use in state-supported asylums for the indigent insane, many of whom still languished unattended in local almshouses and jails. Superintendents of the early asylums often claimed success rates of 90 percent or more with patients who had been ill less than a year, and their optimism fueled the humanitarian zeal of a new generation of social reformers. Dorothea Lynde Dix, who was attracted to the cause of the insane poor in the 1840s, became the principal spokesperson and lobbyist for the construction and expansion of public asylums throughout the United States.[8] Ironically, even as this new wave of asylum building got under way, the social reality that supported the idea of a moral asylum was rapidly fading.[9]

The therapeutic ideals of these hospitals remained viable only to the extent that their patients and staff shared common religious, ethnic, and cultural values; that their caseloads were held to a relatively small size so that intimate staff-patient relationships could be developed and sustained; that their admissions consisted of recent cases, as opposed to long-term or chronic ones; that their sense of purpose was championed by charismatic superintendents and influential laypeople; and that their governmental sponsors were willing to appropriate adequate funds for their operation. Beginning in the mid-nineteenth century, each of these supports was undermined by social, economic, and intellectual forces beyond the control of hospital superintendents. Slowly but inexorably, public mental hospitals were transformed from small, therapeutic asylums into large, custodial institutions.

During the late 1840s and early 1850s, with the advent of industrialization and the influx of impoverished immigrant groups, pauperism, or public dependency, for the first time became a major social problem in America.[10] As population growth accelerated, so too did the demands for institutional care. State legislatures responded to these pressures by expanding asylum capacity or erecting larger facilities. Admissions began to be drawn disproportionately from the ranks of immigrant groups and from mentally disordered persons who had been incarcerated in local welfare and penal institutions. Many of these persons constituted the oldest and most advanced cases of mental illness and had the least chance of recovery. Typically, such patients were not eligible for discharge into the community because the law provided for their release only when the original cause of commitment ceased to exist. In addition to these legal constraints over admission and discharge

8. Dorothea Dix, *On Behalf of the Insane Poor* (New York: Arno Press, 1975).

9. Rothman, *Discovery of the Asylum*, pp. 237-95.

10. Grob, *Mental Institutions in America*, pp. 174-220.

policies, superintendents were faced with an administrative and financial structure that limited their control over maximum institutional size.[11]

Consequently the state-supported asylums began to be filled with ever increasing numbers of chronic cases that overcrowded existing facilities and undermined therapeutic practices. Under these circumstances, cure rates dropped off precipitously, and in both the public and the professional views, insanity increasingly became associated with pauperism and incurability.[12]

These incipient social and intellectual currents did not converge into an explicit public policy for dealing with problems of mental illness in a rapidly industrializing and urbanizing society until the 1870s. The intervening years were a period of reassessment and exploration for alternatives to large public asylums. One of the most imaginative proposals was the idea of building small cottages to replace large centralized institutions. Originally suggested in the 1850s by John Galt, superintendent of the Virginia State Asylum at Williamsburg, the proposal was resurrected after the Civil War by Merrick Bemis, superintendent of the Worcester Asylum in Massachusetts, who was deeply influenced by the renowned colony for the insane in the Belgian town of Gheel.[13]

Bemis advocated the decentralization of state asylums so that they could sustain their role in caring for all social classes and ethnic groups while providing humane custody for the chronically ill in family-like residences under the supervision of attendant staff. In 1869 he persuaded the Worcester trustees to adopt a Gheel-like cottage plan as the architectural design for a new facility that would replace the antiquated and overcrowded building of the original asylum. Opposed by fellow superintendents who saw the new type of institution as a threat to the central role of the psychiatrist as stipulated by the basic precepts of moral treatment, and by conservative members of the legislature who were persuaded it would be more costly to operate, approval of Bemis's plan was rescinded. Shortly thereafter, a large congregate care facility was erected and the original buildings were converted into a separate asylum for the chronically insane.

While variants of the cottage plan caught hold in some other states—most notably at the Illinois State Asylum in Kankakee and the county asylums in Wisconsin and Pennsylvania—its rejection in Massachusetts set a national precedent of building new congregate care facilities as the need arose.[14] Ultimately the Massachusetts experience also influenced the growth of a centralized administrative structure in each state to govern the ever expanding number of facilities.

By the 1870s, therefore, the functions of state asylums had been clearly delineated. Their central purpose was defined by state legislatures in terms of custodial care and community protection; treatment was of secondary importance. Emphasis was placed on the custody of the largest number of patients at the lowest

---

11. Ibid., pp. 193-95.
12. Albert Deutsch, *The Mentally Ill in America: A History of Their Care and Treatment from Colonial Times,* 2nd ed. rev. (New York: Columbia University Press, 1949).
13. Grob, *State and the Mentally Ill,* pp. 198-228; N. Dain, "Chronic Mental Patient"; Leo Srole, "Gheel, Belgium: The Natural Therapeutic Community, 1475-1975," in *New Trends of Psychiatry in the Community,* ed. G. Serban and B. Astrachan (Cambridge, MA: Ballinger, 1977).
14. Grob, *Mental Institutions in America,* pp. 320-39.

possible cost. The small, pastoral retreat that offered hope and humane care had been transformed into a general-purpose solution to the welfare burdens of a society undergoing rapid industrialization and stratification along social class and ethnic lines.

The legal climate surrounding commitment also changed markedly from the earlier decades. As Rothman points out,

> As superintendents in the post-Civil War decades reduced their claims of cures and as horror stories about institutional conditions grew more prevalent, many jurisdictions began to impose more stringent requirements. Massachusetts, for example, demanded that a certificate of insanity be signed by two doctors and that a court hearing take place, with a judicial finding that the individual was insane. Some states, like Illinois, even insisted upon a jury trial before allowing involuntary commitment.[15]

The legislation enacted during the latter part of the nineteenth century that often allowed for indefinite commitments of the mentally ill to state mental hospitals constituted the basic legal framework until the civil libertarian reforms of the 1960s and 1970s.

The transformation from therapeutic to custodial institutions was reinforced by the growing pessimism and therapeutic nihilism that began to envelop psychiatric theory and practice. With the deaths or retirement of the early moral therapists, the new generation of psychiatrists passively accepted the social role of these facilities while actively attending to their own professionalization.[16] In time, both hospital staff and local communities came to believe that the majority of patients committed to state asylums were destined to reside there for life. With overcrowding and staff shortages, a uniform routine was imposed on all patients, which ultimately led to an insidious process of institutionalization, or total dependency on the asylum.[17]

Other trends dating from the 1850s were also solidified. As the state asylums became filled with lower-class patients, well-to-do families resorted to private facilities for the care of their mentally ill members. Private resources were increasingly used to build facilities for paying patients; public resources were allocated for the establishment of separate asylums for the indigent mentally ill. Private-sector facilities tended to specialize in providing treatment to wealthier, quiet, primarily voluntary patients, while the state asylums were left to provide long-term custodial care to poor, disturbed, involuntary patients. As the care system evolved over the next century, a two-class system emerged and became firmly entrenched.[18]

MENTAL HYGIENE AND THE PSYCHOPATHIC HOSPITAL

Despite the seemingly irreversible course that state policies and programs had followed, the voices calling for institutional reform had not been completely silenced. As early as the 1870s, American psychiatrists had come under attack from their British counterparts

---

15. Rothman, *Conscience and Convenience*, pp. 326-27. For a more extended introduction to the history of commitment laws in the United States, see Deutsch, *Mentally Ill in America*, pp. 418-41.

16. Grob, *Mental Institutions in America*, pp. 132-73.

17. For modern accounts of the institutionalization process, see Erving Goffman, *Asylums* (New York: Doubleday, 1961); Ernest Gruenberg, "The Social Breakdown Syndrome and Its Prevention," in *American Handbook of Psychiatry,* 2nd ed., ed. S. Arieti (New York: Basic Books, 1974), vol. 2.

18. Morrissey, Goldman, and Klerman, *Enduring Asylum*, pp. 281-305.

for the deteriorating conditions in state asylums, the overreliance on physical restraint to maintain order, and the general stagnation of the profession. These criticisms were met by denial and countercharges from asylum medical superintendents. Gradually, however, these essentially intraprofessional disputes were transformed into a progressive social reform movement with a broad base outside of psychiatry. Neurologists, social workers, and lay reformers began to publicize some of the shortcomings that characterized American psychiatry in an effort to break the stranglehold of medical superintendents over the care of the insane.

Therapeutic pessimism soon gave way to the optimism of a new scientific psychiatry associated with turn-of-the-century figures such as Adolf Meyer. The work of Meyer and his students, reinforced by the development of psychoanalysis, restored hope that the mentally ill could be effectively treated. The public was outraged by exposés of conditions in mental hospitals, but the 1908 publication of *A Mind That Found Itself*, Clifford Beers's account of his experiences as a mental patient, added a note of optimism to the prevailing criticism.[19]

In 1909 Beers sought the support of Meyer and William James, the noted Harvard philosopher-psychologist, to help him found the National Committee for Mental Hygiene. This reform organization revived the notion of the treatability of mental disorder, especially by early intervention with acute cases.[20] Mental hygienists advocated creating a psychopathic hospital, an acute treatment or reception facility affiliated with university training and research institutes. Building upon the earlier concept of moral treatment and several later innovations in psychiatric care, the first psychopathic hospitals opened in Albany, Ann Arbor, Baltimore, and Boston.[21]

The reform spread and spawned other new mental health agencies such as psychiatric dispensaries and child guidance clinics. However, these new facilities were unable to eliminate chronic illness. They provided high-quality care and evaluations for many, but most patients who needed extended care were shortly sent on to the state hospitals. In this sense, the psychopathic hospitals were unable to reform American mental health care fundamentally. As the movement matured, its original goal of improving mental hospital care fell by the wayside. In its place, reformers began to champion the relevance of psychiatry to the care of the feebleminded, eugenics, control of alcoholism, management of abnormal children, treatment of criminals, prevention of prostitution and dependency, and the problems of industrial productivity.

As part of the received wisdom in the mental health field, it has been fashionable to think of the decades between 1890 and 1950 as the Dark Ages in the state care of the mentally ill. Recent historical scholarship, however, has begun to penetrate the myth that institutional care in this period was uniformly stagnant, repressive, and monolithic.[22] While psychiatrists pushed the bound-

---

19. The origins of the mental hygiene movement are portrayed with insight in Norman Dain, *Clifford W. Beers: Advocate for the Insane* (Pittsburgh, PA: University of Pittsburgh Press, 1980).

20. Albert Deutsch, "The History of Mental Hygiene," in *One Hundred Years of American Psychiatry*, ed. J. K. Hall, G. Zilboorg, and H. A. Bunker (New York: Columbia University Press, 1944).

21. Rothman, *Conscience and Convenience*, pp. 324-75; Grob, *Mental Illness and American Society*, pp. 144-78.

22. Grob, *Mental Illness and American Society*, pp. 179-200.

aries of their specialty outward into the community and attempted to broaden its functions and roles under the aegis of the mental hygiene movement, profound changes were also occurring within the state asylum system.

In 1890 New York's State Care Act established the precedent for states to assume full financial responsibility for the care and treatment of the mentally ill. This legislation was designed to remedy the quality-of-care deficiencies associated with asylums operated by municipalities and counties and to absolve these governmental units of the maintenance costs of asylum operation. It represented the culmination of efforts to rationalize public provisions for the mentally ill under a centralized regulatory structure; it also legitimized psychiatry's exclusive claims for care and management of this population.[23] Consistent with this development, the official designation for these institutions was soon changed from state asylums to state mental hospitals.

Local officials, however, began to recognize the advantages in redefining insanity to include aged and senile individuals. By transferring such patients from local almshouses to the state hospitals, fiscal burdens associated with their care were shifted from local to state auspices. The result was a dramatic transformation in the mix of patients served by state mental hospitals.

Prior to 1900, chronic or incurable patients and the aged senile were sent to county and local almshouses; state asylums had concentrated largely on acute cases institutionalized for fewer than 12 months.[24] After the states monopolized provisions for the mentally ill, state mental hospitals gradually assumed responsibility for senile patients as well as for individuals suffering from a variety of diseases and conditions that required custodial care on a life-long basis rather than treatment by specific psychiatric therapies. Concomitantly, the almshouse declined in significance as a public institution.

As Grob points out, "What occurred, in effect, was not a deinstitutionalization movement, but rather a transfer of patients between different types of institutions. The shift, moreover, was less a function of medical or humanitarian concerns than a consequence of financial considerations."[25] Between 1903 and 1950, the number of patients in state mental hospitals increased by 240 percent—from 150,000 to 512,000—a rate of growth nearly twice as large as the rate of increase in the U.S. population as a whole.

While the small number of psychopathic hospitals had little direct impact on the changing volume and composition of state mental hospital caseloads, other outgrowths of the mental hygiene movement such as psychiatric social work, clinical psychology, and pastoral counseling were gradually melded to the staff complement of these institutions. To a large extent, however, the state hospitals were caught up in a vast holding operation. In the absence of specific treatments, mental disorders remained chronic illnesses, and state mental hospitals remained predominantly chronic-care facilities providing long-term custody of the poor and disabled.

During these years, the state mental hospitals were portrayed as a throwback to an unenlightened and immature stage of psychiatric practice. The exhilaration of forging a marriage between the new scientific psychiatry and social activism deflected the attention of many psychia-

23. Ibid., pp. 89-92.
24. Ibid., p. 196.

25. Ibid., p. 181.

trists from the custodial and managerial origins of their profession. As the preoccupations of organized psychiatry shifted from state hospitals to practices in private offices and outpatient clinics, recognition of a core reality was lost. That is, despite their very real shortcomings and failures, state mental hospitals did provide minimum levels of care—not otherwise available—for individuals unable to survive by themselves.[26] It would take another generation, a new cycle of institutional reform, and the near-cataclysmic emptying of state mental hospitals for this fundamental truth to be fully appreciated by mental health policymakers.

COMMUNITY MENTAL HEALTH AND THE CMHC

World War II marked the transition from the mental health hygiene movement to the third cycle of reform. The finding that so many young Americans were mentally unfit for military duty, coupled with front-line successes of brief interventions in the treatment of so-called war neurosis, stimulated renewed interest in prevention and new optimism for the treatment of mental illness.[27]

The community mental health movement was born out of this enthusiasm for brief treatment techniques, which avoided the removal of patients to faraway hospitals. The psychiatrists returning to state mental hospitals from military service experimented with brief hospitalization and new psychosocial treatment techniques, and by the mid-1950s they made extensive use of the new psychotropic medications.[28] At the same time, innovative state mental hospitals opened aftercare clinics to serve increasing numbers of discharged mental patients, and general hospitals opened acute psychiatric inpatient units.[29] Again reformers offered the promise that with early intervention and treatment, especially with the new drug therapies, chronicity and long-term disability could be prevented and the state mental hospital rendered obsolete.[30]

This also was a period of significant federal government activity.[31] In 1946 the National Mental Health Act had created the National Institute of Mental Health to stimulate research and training efforts. The Mental Health Study Act of 1955 created the Joint Commission on Mental Illness and Health to analyze and evaluate the needs and resources of the mentally ill in the United States and make recommendations for a national mental health program. The final report of the joint commission in 1961, *Action for Mental Health*, promoted the concept of community mental health care. This concept became the "bold new approach" adopted by President Kennedy in the Community Mental Health Centers Act of 1963, which created the elaborate system of

26. Ibid., p. 107.
27. See, for example, John Spiegel and Roy Grinker, *Men under Stress* (Philadelphia: Blakiston, 1945); David Mechanic, *Mental Health and Social Policy* (Englewood Cliffs, NJ: Prentice-Hall, 1969).

28. John A. Talbott, "Twentieth-Century Developments in American Psychiatry," *Psychiatric Quarterly*, 54:207-19 (1982).
29. *Decentralization of Psychiatric Services and Continuity of Care*, Proceedings of the Thirty-eighth Annual Conference of the Milbank Memorial Fund, 26-27 Sept. 1961 (New York: Milbank Memorial Fund, 1962); Lawrence Linn, *Frontiers in General Hospital Psychiatry* (New York: International University Press, 1961).
30. Richard D. Lyons, "How Release of Mental Patients Began," *New York Times*, 30 Oct. 1984.
31. Foley and Sharfstein, *Madness and Government;* Joint Commission on Mental Illness and Health, *Action for Mental Health*.

community mental health centers (CMHCs) in the mid-1960s.

The near-term accomplishments of the community mental health movement seemingly rival the success claims advanced for the early asylums. Between 1955 and 1980, for example, the resident population of state mental hospitals was reduced by more than 75 percent, or by approximately 420,000 occupied beds, and since the mid-1960s more than 700 CMHCs, serving catchment areas representing 50 percent of the U.S. population, have been created.[32] Upon closer scrutiny, however, it is clear that shifts in the locus of care did not solve the problem of chronic mental illness. In many communities, the CMHCs extended services to new populations of previously untreated individuals, largely ignoring the populations traditionally served by state mental hospitals.[33] At the same time, the promise of the centers especially for reducing the census of state mental hospitals and saving resources helped to promote a policy of deinstitutionalization.[34]

DEINSTITUTIONALIZATION AND TRANSINSTITUTIONALIZATION

While the process of deinstitutionalization occurred at a different pace in various states, two important consistencies can be identified. The first is that deinstitutionalization occurred in two distinct phases; the second is that, in each state, the transition was occasioned by the coalescing of diverse interest groups.

In the first phase, policies governing the use of state mental hospitals were based on a benign form of hospital phase-down that led to the opening of the back doors of these institutions for the release of long-stay patients and for the early discharge of newly admitted patients. This phase was marked by a gradual census decline, an increased rate of both first admissions and readmissions, and a declining length of stay. As long as revolving-door patients could be easily returned to these hospitals—by families, local agencies, or police authorities—deinstitutionalization was not a major political issue. State hospitals provided backup for the fledgling community mental health programs, which were able, in turn, to concentrate on the development of services for less disabled clients residing in the community.

In the second phase, a newer strategy of closing the front doors of state hospitals was instituted. Concurrently, the older policy was simultaneously transformed into a radical program of rapid census reductions. This period was marked by a leveling-off in the annual number of admissions and an emphasis on brief lengths of stay only for crisis-stabilization purposes, which combined to produce dramatic decreases in the size of the resident patient population. The real impacts of these policies, however, were felt in the local communities, which were unprepared for the influx of thousands of former patients. Deinstitutionalized patients encountered the hostility and rejection of the general public

---

32. Joseph Morrissey, "Deinstitutionalizing the Mentally Ill: Process, Outcomes, and New Directions," in *Deviance and Mental Illness,* ed. W. Gove (Beverly Hills, CA: Sage, 1982).

33. See, for example, Ellen Bassuk and Samuel Gerson, "Deinstitutionalization and Mental Health Services," *Scientific American,* 238:46-53 (1978); Franklyn Chu and Sherman Trotter, *The Madness Establishment* (New York: Grossman, 1974); and Charles Windle and Diana Scully, "Community Mental Health Centers and the Decreasing Use of State Mental Hospitals," *Community Mental Health Journal,* 12:239-43 (1976).

34. Bachrach, *Deinstitutionalization: An Analytical Review and Sociological Perspective.*

and the reluctance of community mental health and welfare agencies to assume responsibility for their care. Tens of thousands ended up in rooming houses, foster homes, nursing homes, run-down hotels, and on the streets. The transfer of patients from the "back wards to the back alleys"[35] led to widespread concerns that deinstitutionalization was a disaster and that the states had abdicated their responsibilities to the mentally ill.

Nationally, the demarcation point between these two phases can be located in the late 1960s.[36] From 1955, when the state hospital census reached its peak of 558,922 patients, to 1965, the total census reduction amounted to only 15 percent, or about 1.5 percent per year. Over the next 15 years, 1965-80, the total census reduction jumped to 71 percent. For the 8-year period 1969-76, the rate of reduction averaged over 10 percent per year. The admissions rate, which had been steadily rising since 1955, started a downward trend following 1970. The rate of both census and admission declines began to stabilize in the late 1970s, however, and there now is evidence from several states that state mental hospital use is again on the increase.

The factors that precipitated the shift from benign to radical phases of deinstitutionalization involved civil libertarian litigation over the state hospital commitment process, the Medicaid and Medicare amendments to the Social Security Act of 1965, and the intensive lobbying efforts of community mental health advocates. Civil libertarian lawyers concerned about the rights of the mentally ill initiated litigation and statutory reforms that tightened and narrowed the criteria for involuntary hospitalization.[37] As a consequence, there now are greater restrictions on both procedures and criteria for commitment. Moreover, the right of the mentally ill to refuse treatment has been confirmed by all levels of the judicial system. Further, the early patients'-rights litigation clearly implied that the states either had to phase out their mental hospitals or invest considerable sums of money in bringing them up to court-ordered standards.[38]

The fiscal crises that began to envelop the states during the early 1970s created pressures to meet this judicial challenge by resorting to the rapid phase-down of state institutions both by accelerating discharges and by diverting admissions of the nondangerous mentally ill. Moreover, similar to the state care acts of the late nineteenth and early twentieth centuries, the Medicaid and Medicare reimbursements allowed for buck passing from one governmental budget to another—in this case, from the state level to the federal. According to federal regulations, patients between the ages of 21 and 64 years—the majority

35. Uri Aviram and Steven Segal, "Exclusion of the Mentally Ill: Reflections on an Old Problem in a New Context," *Archives of General Psychiatry,* 29:126-31 (1973).

36. Morrissey, "Deinstitutionalizing the Mentally Ill."

37. For an informative and comprehensive review of recent law and mental health issues, see Saleem A. Shah, "Legal and Mental Health System Interactions: Major Developments and Research Needs," *International Journal of Law and Psychiatry,* 4:219-70 (1981).

38. See, for example, Jonas Robitscher, "Legal Standards and Their Implications Regarding Civil Commitment Procedures," in *Dangerous Behavior: A Problem in Law and Mental Health,* ed. C. J. Frederick, National Institute of Mental Health, Department of Health, Education, and Welfare pub. no. (ADM) 78-563 (Washington, DC: Government Printing Office, 1978).

of patients in most state hospitals—are ineligible for Medicaid while residing in state mental institutions; once discharged to the community, however, these patients are eligible for such benefits. Within a short period of time, these fiscal and legal incentives led to the discharge of hundreds of thousands of patients from the state mental hospitals. CMHCs were almost totally unprepared—or unwilling, or both—to shoulder the responsibility of this chronic population. As with the psychopathic hospitals of an earlier era, CMHC leadership considered the centers' mission and promise to be preventing chronicity, not dealing with the failures of previous approaches to mental health care.[39]

Supported largely by federal Medicaid, Supplemental Security Income, and Social Security Disability Insurance payments, thousands of former patients now live in nursing homes, board-and-care homes, adult homes, and other institutional settings in the community.[40] These mostly private, profit-making facilities serve the custodial and asylum functions that were once performed almost exclusively by state mental hospitals. The growth of what has been characterized as "social control entrepreneurialism"[41] has thereby perpetuated the segregation of the chronically mentally ill in a new ecological arrangement in the community. Some observers felt that the conditions in local communities were as bad as those in the institutions that proponents of deinstitutionalization were trying to replace. Others thought that current policies were creating the same pre-asylum conditions that led to the reformist efforts of Horace Mann and Dorothea Dix on behalf of the insane poor in the first half of the nineteenth century.

Some national data will serve to illustrate the magnitude of these shifts.[42] In 1974 approximately 85,000 nursing home residents had been transferred directly from mental hospitals. Approximately half of the 1.3 million nursing home residents in 1977 had a psychiatric diagnosis, mostly organic mental disorders including senility without psychosis. Thus, many nursing home residents in the early 1970s had conditions that would have led to state hospital admissions in prior decades. Moreover, it is estimated that between 800,000 and 1.5 million chronically mentally ill patients now live in private homes or a variety of community residences, including board-and-care homes. These data clearly indicate that rather than deinstitutionalization, a process of transinstitutionalization from the mental health to the social welfare system has occurred for many former patients. Indeed, the patient flow between state hospitals and nursing homes seems to represent the reversal of the flow from almshouses to state hospitals in the early part of this century.

39. See, for example, Chu and Trotter, *Madness Establishment;* Bassuk and Gerson, "Deinstitutionalization and Mental Health Services."
40. Leonard J. Schmidt et al., "The Mentally Ill in Nursing Homes: New Back Wards in the Community," *Archives of General Psychiatry,* 34:687-91 (1977); Steven Segal and Uri Aviram, *The Mentally Ill in Community-Based Sheltered Care* (New York: John Wiley, 1978); H. Richard Lamb, "The New Asylums in the Community," *Archives of General Psychiatry,* 36:129-34 (1979); William Shadish and Richard Bootzin, "Nursing Homes and Chronic Mental Patients," *Schizophrenia Bulletin,* 7:488-98 (1981).
41. Warren, "New Forms of Social Control."
42. Howard Goldman, Neal H. Adams, and Carl Taube, "Deinstitutionalization: The Data Demythologized," *Hospital and Community Psychiatry,* 34:129-34 (1981).

Criminal justice and the mentally ill

It is more difficult to discern the extent to which similar transinstitutionalization has occured between the mental health and criminal justice systems in the aftermath of the rapid mental hospital census reductions in the 1970s. Arguments and data have been presented to document what has been called the psychiatrization of criminal behavior as well as the criminalization of mental disorder, but due to a variety of methodological limitations in available studies, the direction and relative magnitude of the flows are difficult to substantiate.[43] A strong test of these competing propositions calls for longitudinal data on patient/inmate flows between the two systems spanning the years prior to and following the deinstitutionalization movement. Such data are simply not available, however. Moreover, even when segmental data are available, part of the difficulty in inferring transinstitutionalization resides in the fact that neither the mental health system nor the criminal justice system is unitary or homogeneous. Rather, they both are composed of multiple legal or administrative processing points as well as a diverse array of treatment or confinement settings. Events at one point or setting often do not have uniform or consistent reverberations thoughout the system. Thus, although presumptive evidence of transinstitutionalization may be obtained at one or another interface between the two systems, the extent to which it can be generalized beyond that point is debatable.

Nevertheless, there are indications in many jurisdictions that one result of the tightened civil commitment standards and procedures is the increased use of the criminal process for hospitalization and treatment of seriously mentally ill but nondangerous persons.[44] One example is the use of competency-to-stand-trial examinations and determinations to divert persons directly from the criminal justice system into mental health facilities. The work of Geller and Lister suggests that during the early 1970s alleged offenders—mostly charged with misdemeanors—were increasingly being committed to state mental hospitals in Massachusetts for pretrial evaluation of competency as a substitute for criminal detention and incarceration.[45] In a study at Worcester State Hospital, they found in 72 percent of the cases for which they could obtain deposition information that the charges were dropped by the prosecutor after the person was returned to the court from a pretrial

---

43. See, for example, Mary Melick, Henry Steadman, and Joseph Cocozza, "The Medicalization of Criminal Behavior among Mental Patients," *Journal of Health and Social Behavior,* 20:228-37 (1979); Linda Teplin, "Criminalizing Mental Disorder: The Comparative Arrest Rate of the Mentally Ill," *American Psychologist,* 39(7):794-803 (1984).

44. There is also evidence that the tightening of civil commitment criteria has led to increased involuntary hospitalization. See H. Richard Lamb, Alvin Sorkin, and Jack Zusman, "Legislating Social Control of the Mentally Ill in California," *American Journal of Psychiatry,* 138:334-39 (1981); Glenn Morris, "Conservatorship for the 'Gravely Disabled': California's Nondeclaration of Nonindependence," *San Diego Law Review,* 15:201-37 (1978). For a thoughtful analysis of the systemic interdependency between civil and criminal commitment laws, see David Wexler, "The Structure of Civil Commitment: Patterns, Pressures, and Interactions in Mental Health Legislation," *Law and Human Behavior,* 7(1):1-18 (1983).

45. Jeffry Geller and Eric Lister, "The Process of Criminal Commitment for Pretrial Psychiatric Examination: An Evaluation," *American Journal of Psychiatry,* 135:53-63 (1978).

commitment. Further, the use of this procedure grew steadily between 1966 and 1975 as the ratio of criminal to civil commitments at the hospital increased incrementally from 0.076 in 1966 to 0.821 n 1975. Similar data are reported by Dickey for Wisconsin in the years immediately following that state's 1976 civil commitment code revisions.[46]

Data recently reported by Teplin on 844 police-citizen encounters involving 1798 persons in a large midwestern city suggest that, for similar offenses, persons perceived to be mentally disordered by police officers had a significantly greater chance of being arrested than others.[47] While Teplin interprets these data as evidence of the criminalization of the mentally ill, they focus only on the initial entry point to the criminal justice system, and they are based on cross-sectional rather than longitudinal data. On the basis of this study then, it is difficult to infer how pervasive the criminalization of the mentally ill may be throughout the criminal justice system or to what extent it has been increasing over time.

The data reported by Steadman and his colleagues from a longitudinal study of mental hospitals and prisons in six states, however, do not support claims about criminalization in the form of an increased flow of state mental hospital patients into the prison system.[48] Indeed, the authors argue that their data provide greater evidence for medicalization in that more mental hospital patients in 1978 had a history of prior arrests than did their counterparts in 1968. They also suggest that criminalization may be more pronounced in local jails than in prisons, but no data were available on jails in their multistate study. Nonetheless, their observation is consistent with numerous case-study reports of the increasing presence of the mentally ill in local jails.[49] The local jail may well be the interface point that is most sensitive to changing modes of social control and to shifting boundaries between the two systems. Clearly, this is an area that warrants close and careful research attention.

Despite these shifting boundaries and blurred responsibilities, the state mental hospital endures as the institution of last resort in the U.S. mental health system. The continuing functions of state mental hospitals involve custody, social control, and treatment for many of the most disturbed and most troublesome patients. The scope and mix of these residual functions vary considerably from state to state, but only national data are available.

In 1980, there were approximately 138,000 resident patients in state mental hospitals and nearly 375,000 admissions —mostly revolving-door patients—dur-

---

46. William Dickey, "Incompetency and the Nondangerous Mentally Ill Client," *Criminal Law Bulletin*, 16:22-40 (1980).

47. Teplin, "Criminalizing Mental Disorder." For some contrasting data that suggest that police invoke the penal code for mentally disordered persons only as a last resort, see Jennifer C. Bonovitz and Jay S. Bonovitz, "Diversion of the Mentally Ill into the Criminal Justice System: The Police Intervention Perspective," *American Journal of Psychiatry*, 138(7):973-76 (1981).

48. Henry J. Steadman et al., "The impact of State Mental Hospital Deinstitutionalization on United States Prison Populations, 1968-1978," *Journal of Criminal Law and Criminology*, 75(2):474-90 (1984).

49. See, for example, Mark Abrahamson, "The Criminalization of Mentally Disordered Behavior: A Possible Side Effect of a New Mental Health Law," *Hospital and Community Psychiatry*, 23:101-5 (1972); Gary Whitmer, "From Hospitals to Jails: The Fate of California's Deinstitutionalized Mentally Ill," *American Journal of Orthopsychiatry*, 50:65-75 (1980).

ing that year.[50] Of the total admissions, 156,000, or 42 percent, were voluntary and 219,000, or 58 percent, were involuntary. The involuntary admissions, in turn, consisted of 190,600 civil and 27,993 criminal commitments. Between 1972 and 1980, there was a 7 percent decrease in the total number of annual admissions, a 21 percent decrease in voluntary admissions, and a 5 percent increase in involuntary commitments.

Of particular significance in the present context is the trend in criminal commitments relative to other categories.[51] Whereas the annual number of involuntary civil commitments remained almost constant, with a decrease of less than 1 percent over this time interval, involuntary criminal commitments in 1980 increased by 12,542, or 81 percent, over 1972. Clearly, although they are a relatively small part of the annual admissions caseload, criminally committed, or forensic, cases are the fastest growing segment of the state mental hospital patient population.[52]

FUTURE PROSPECTS

In the late 1970s, the community mental health movement entered a transitional phase. The change was occasioned by the political backlash to several years of rapid census decreases and a fuller realization that the abrupt closure of state hospitals was premature. In response to this new wave of criticism, the National Institute of Mental Health launched its Community Support Program, designed to stimulate the development of crisis-care services, psychosocial rehabilitation services, supportive living and working arrangements, medical and mental health care, and case management for the chronically mentally ill.[53] In a number of respects the program defines a new, fourth cycle of reform in the mental health field aimed specifically at meeting the needs of the chronically mentally ill in community settings.[54] Many states also developed community support services for this target population as well. The explosive growth of urban homelessness and the extent to which it can be attributed to mental health policies or general economic conditions, however, stands as a challenge to community support programs and as a major public policy issue in the aftermath of deinstitutionalization.

The prospects for the future with regard to the emergence of a coherent national mental health policy and the restructuring of the service delivery system remain clouded. Over the past 25 years, the U.S. mental health service system has expanded and become much more diversified with the rapid growth of general hospital psychiatric units, CMHCs, and psychiatric outpatient programs of various sorts. Yet, the state hospitals persist, albeit in reduced form,

50. Unpublished statistical data from the 1980 Sample Survey of State and County Mental Hospitals, Survey and Reports Branch, Division of Biometry and Epidemiology, National Institute of Mental Health, Rockville, MD.

51. Ibid.

52. For a more comprehensive profile of the volume and range of facilities serving mentally disordered offenders in the United States, see Henry J. Steadman et al., "Mentally Disordered Offenders: A National Survey of Patients and Facilities," *Law and Human Behavior,* 6(1):31-38 (1982).

53. Richard C. Tessler and Howard H. Goldman, *The Chronically Mentally Ill: Assessing Community Support Programs* (Cambridge, MA: Ballinger, 1982).

54. Howard H. Goldman and Joseph P. Morrissey, "The Alchemy of Mental Health Policy: Homelessness and the Fourth Cycle of Reform," *American Journal of Public Health,* 75(7):727-31 (1985).

and many alternative institutions have been created at the local level. Much of this organizational change has exacerbated boundary control issues both within the mental health system and in relation to the social welfare and criminal justice systems.

Clearly, if informed public policies are to be developed in this fluid arena, then further research needs to be directed at the law and mental health interface and the transactions between the mental health, criminal justice, and social welfare systems. The articles in this issue of *The Annals* exemplify the work that needs to be done in the future.

Civil Commitment of the Mentally Ill: An Overview

By MARK J. MILLS

ABSTRACT: This article discusses historical themes that led to the civil commitment reforms of the sixties and seventies. The changes in the substantive criteria for commitment are analyzed and critiqued. The author believes that the present criteria tend to focus so specifically on various external indicia of mental illness that they render commitment difficult for many seriously ill patients. An alternative commitment scheme is discussed.

Dr. Mills received his B.A. from the University of California, Berkeley (1967), his J.D. from Harvard Law School (1970), and his M.D. from Stanford University (1975). He has been on the faculties of Stanford and Harvard, and he served for two years as the commissioner of mental health for the commonwealth of Massachusetts. Presently, he is chief, Psychiatry Service, West Los Angeles Veterans Administration Medical Center, Brentwood Division; professor, Department of Psychiatry and Biobehavioral Sciences, University of California, Los Angeles (UCLA); and director, Program in Psychiatry and Law, Neuropsychiatric Hospital, UCLA.

FIFTEEN years ago, the first modern civil commitment statute was enacted, as part of the California code. That law, the Lanterman-Petris-Short Act (LPS), initiated three kinds of changes to civil commitment law, which will be discussed in this article. Within a decade, essentially every state had revised its commitment statutes to incorporate similar changes.[1]

Such nationwide consensus about legislative matters is rare, perhaps unprecedented. For this, if for no other reason, these changes would merit evaluation; however, there are other important reasons to examine them. First, about a decade ago, and before many jurisdictions had revised their statutes, psychiatrists had begun to question the value of the revisions.[2] Second, the public, particularly in the last five years, has increasingly attributed the well-publicized increase in urban homelessness to these changes.[3] Third, public-sector hospital administrators increasingly report that mental hospitals are being filled with patients who are dangerous, not so ill—for example, those with antisocial personality or conduct disorders—and often treatment refractory.[4] Last, there is a growing empirical literature that facilitates the examination of these statutory changes.[5]

As noted, the changes in civil commitment law were tripartite. First, legislators changed the substantive criteria for civil commitment from something like being "in need of treatment by reason of mental illness" to something like being "mentally ill, and as a result of that illness, dangerous to oneself or others." Thus, the first of these changes specifically added a largely new[6] requi-

---

1. Clifford D. Stromberg, "Developments Concerning the Legal Criteria for Civil Commitment: Who Are We Looking For?" in *Psychiatry 1982: Annual Review*, ed. L. Grinspoon (Washington, DC: American Psychiatric Association, 1982), pp. 334-50.

2. Franklin M. Arnhoff, "Social Consequences of the Policy toward Mental Illness," *Science*, 188:1277-81 (June 1975); Paul Chodoff, "The Case for Involuntary Hospitalization of the Mentally Ill," *American Journal of Psychiatry*, 133:496-501 (May 1976); John A. Talbott, "What Are the Problems of the Chronic Mental Patient: A Report of a Survey of Psychiatrists' Concerns," in *The Chronic Mental Patient: Problems, Solutions and Recommendations for a Public Policy*, ed. J. A. Talbott (Washington, DC: American Psychiatric Association, 1978); Darold A. Treffert, "Dying with Their Rights On," *American Journal of Psychiatry*, 130:1041-42 (Oct. 1973).

3. Richard C. Baron, "Changing Public Attitudes about the Mentally Ill in the Community," *Hospital and Community Psychiatry*, 32:173-78 (Mar. 1981); H. Richard Lamb, "The New Asylums in the Community," *Archives of General Psychiatry*, 36:129-34 (Mar. 1979); Richard F. Mollica, "From Asylum to Community: The Threatened Disintegration of Public Psychiatry," *New England Journal of Medicine*, 308:367-73 (Feb. 1983); Mark J. Mills, "The Problem of Public Psychiatry," *New England Journal of Medicine*, 309:113-14 (July 1983).

4. H. Richard Lamb, Alvin P. Sorkin, and Jack Zusman, "Legislating Social Control of the Mentally Ill in California," *American Journal of Psychiatry*, 138:334-39 (Mar. 1981).

5. Joseph D. Bloom, James H. Shore, and Joseph Treleaven, "Oregon's Civil Commitment Statute: Stone's 'Thank-you Theory'—A Judicial Survey," *Bulletin of the American Academy of Psychiatry and the Law*, 7(4):381-89 (1979); Francis P. LeBuffe, Stephen I. Granger, and Thomas N. Wise, "The Virginia Commitment Law: Clinical Characteristics of Patients Hospitalized Involuntarily by Court Order," ibid., pp. 411-21; Mark R. Munetz, Kenneth R. Kaufman, and Charles L. Rich, "Modernization of a Mental Health Act: I. Commitment Patterns," ibid., 8(1):83-93 (1980); idem, "Modernization of a Mental Health Act: II. Outcome Effects," *Journal of Clinical Psychiatry*, 42:333-37 (Sept. 1981); Marc A. Rubenstein, Howard V. Zonana, and Lansing E. Crane, "Civil Commitment Reform in Connecticut: A Perspective for Physicians," *Connecticut Medicine*, 41:709-17 (Nov. 1977).

6. Frank T. Lindman and Donald M. McIntyre, *The Mentally Disabled and the Law* (Chicago: University of Chicago Press, 1961).

site to commitment, that of dangerousness.[7] The rationale for this change came from the civil libertarian perspective that people had a right to be different, that it was difficult to distinguish between difference—deviance—and illness, and that even the presence of significant illness did not necessarily entitle the state to abridge liberty.[8] It was anticipated by the advocates for these changes that the purview of civil commitment would be substantially narrowed by the addition of the dangerousness criterion.

Second, legislators changed the period of civil commitment from an indeterminate period—with the law's wording something like "so long as treatment shall be deemed necessary by the treating physician"—to a relatively brief, determinate period. In California, the initial period of commitment was shortened to 72 hours, which could be followed by up to two 14-day periods. In certain circumstances, California law provides for long-term commitment for those who are mentally ill and repetitively assaultive, or those who are incapable of providing themselves with food, clothing, and shelter. For the former group, the law provides the rarely initiated, 180-day post-certification commitment, and for the latter one, there are conservatorships that may last up to a year and are renewable.

The rationale for this second change was, so the advocates argued, that civil commitment constituted a massive intrusion into liberty and that thus it needed to be sharply delimited.[9] Further, the reformers believed that the burden of perpetuating a commitment should be explicitly on the state to make certain that all ambiguities were resolved in favor of the liberty of the person committed. Again, the proponents believed that such a change would markedly shorten the committed person's duration of hospitalization. Some hoped that if the duration were truncated, more resources would be available to the patient during hospitalization.[10]

Third, initially legislators and later the courts enshrouded commitment with a panoply of due-process procedures designed to safeguard rights of those civilly committed. In the California statute, people committed were entitled to a hearing within 5 days of initiation of a 14-day certification; further, they had the right to be represented by counsel and to have a jury trial; finally, they had the right to avoid continued commitment unless the state demonstrated by proof "beyond a reasonable doubt" that the patient fit the relevant criteria. The apparent rationale for this increase in due-process protection was that in commitment hearings

7. Stephen Rachlin, "The Influence of Law on Deinstitutionalization," in *New Directions for Mental Health Services,* ed. L. Bachrach (San Francisco: Jossey-Bass, 1983), pp. 41-54.

8. Stephen J. Morse, "A Preference for Liberty: The Case against Involuntary Commitment of the Mentally Disordered," *California Law Review,* 70:54-106 (1982).

9. Alexander D. Brooks, "Defining the Dangerousness of the Mentally Ill: Involuntary Civil Commitment," in *Mentally Abnormal Offenders,* ed. M. Craft and A. Craft (London: Balliere Tindall, 1984), pp. 280-307.

10. Morton Birnbaum, "The Right to Treatment," *American Bar Association Journal,* 46: 499-505 (May 1960).

11. With respect to legislators, see Stromberg, "Developments Concerning the Legal Criteria for Civil Commitment"; with respect to the courts, see *Lessard* v. *Schmidt,* 349 F. Supp. 1078 (E.D. Wisc. 1972; three-judge court), vacated and remanded on other grounds 414 U.S. 473, 94 Sup. Ct. 713 (1974), order on remand 379 F. Supp. 1376 (E.D. Wisc. 1974), vacated and remanded on other grounds 421 U.S. 957, 95 Sup. Ct. 1943 (1975), order reinstated on remand 413 F. Supp. 1318 (E.D. Wisc. 1976).

the social momentum favored the state. With these procedures in place, the reformers believed that unwarranted civil commitment would be curtailed.[12]

One could have anticipated that such broad-gauged reform would address most of the then-extant social concerns. However, what appears to have not been anticipated, even given the sweeping nature of the mandated changes, was that such changes would create new problems for the public, the mentally ill, the advocates, and the treating professionals. This article examines the three changes in civil commitment law. It details some consequences of the new laws and considers some alternative models to the present statutory framework.

HISTORY

Although the history of civil commitment is beyond the scope of this article, having a sense of the social themes that influenced legislators during the late sixties is useful. One of the difficulties in presenting a history is that there is often no single best appellation for a particular theme. Thus, for example, the Supreme Court's decision in *Brown* v. *Board of Education* in 1954 had at least two evident consequences: it legitimated a period of rights scrutinization, and it engendered a period of legal activism.[13] Both of these themes contributed to the civil commitment reforms of the late sixties and early seventies. During that period, first attorneys and later legislators acted as though many of the then-evident social ills could be rectified by legal means. A more concrete aspect of legal activism was legislative activism. The Great Society legislation is most representative of this latter theme, although the Community Mental Health Center Act of 1963 is the most obvious mental health manifestation of this theme. The *Zeitgeist* was one of enormous optimism regarding social reform.

Unrelated to themes of legal reform were considerations that questioned the value of traditional medical and psychiatric approaches to mental illness. Several examples are illustrative. Starting in the fifties, Eysenck developed data that seriously questioned the value of traditional psychotherapy. In the early sixties, Goffman claimed that psychiatric hospitalization was counterproductive because patients became "institutionalized," losing previously acquired social skills. Later, Szasz and Laing questioned either the existence of mental illness or the desirability of endeavoring to treat it.[14]

Such seemingly substantial critiques might of themselves have engendered commitment reform. However, contemporaneous with these new perceptions of mental illness were more general changes in the social value ascribed to being a physician. For the first time, physicians began to be sued much more frequently for malpractice or for the failure to obtain informed consent. And whereas psychoanalysis had been criti-

---

12. Alan A. Stone, "Psychiatric Abuse and Legal Reform: Two Ways to Make a Bad Situation Worse," *International Journal of Law and Psychiatry*, 5(1):9-28 (1982).
13. Mark J. Mills, James C. Gracey, and Bonnie D. Cummins, "Legal Issues in Mental Health Administration," *International Journal of Law and Psychiatry*, 6(1):39-55 (1983).
14. Hans J. Eysenck, "The Effects of Psychotherapy," *International Journal of Psychiatry*, 1:97-178 (Jan. 1965); Erving Goffman, *Asylums: Essays on the Social Situation of Mental Patients and Other Inmates* (New York: Doubleday, 1961); Thomas S. Szasz, *The Myth of Mental Illness* (New York: Harper & Row, 1961); Ronald D. Laing, *The Divided Self* (London: Tavistock, 1960).

cized on theoretical, empirical, and conceptual grounds,[15] it began to be criticized on ideological grounds. It was considered elitist because it was protracted and expensive; also, it was sexist because it tended to reinforce traditional beliefs about the role of women in society.

Different again from the loss of faith in medical values was the curiously concurrent theme of faith in medical technology. By the sixties, all the prototype compounds that constitute the present psychiatric pharmacopoeia had been synthesized.[16] Even in their earlier, slightly less effective incarnations, these compounds were believed to portend a new era in the treatment of the chronically mentally ill. Many psychiatrists predicted that the virtual cure for mental illness was close at hand. More importantly, by the late sixties, the number of state hospital beds devoted to psychiatric illness had diminished markedly, reinforcing the oft-articulated misperception that these agents held the potential to cure. Although not directly relevant, it is intriguing to observe that the discovery of each of the parent compounds was serendipitous: while attempting to synthesize one kind of compound—for example, a more potent general anesthetic agent—a new kind of compound—such as an antipsychotic—was discovered.

The last of these themes is difficult to differentiate from those described earlier, as it embodies pieces of each of them. It is the ideology of deinstitutionalization. By the late sixties, deinstitutionalization constituted a sociopolitical force unto itself.[17] It tended to support the major changes in civil commitment by suggesting vis-à-vis hospitalization that which Mies van der Rohe had suggested about design: that less is more.

SUBSTANTIVE CRITERIA

Although each of the three aspects of commitment reform is important, the alteration of the substantive criteria for commitment constitutes the most fundamental change.[18] Further, it is this element of present-day civil commitment that garners the greatest criticism from psychiatrists.[19] For more than a decade, psychiatrists have been noting the failure of the new civil commitment criteria: that as presently constituted they fre-

---

15. Harry Guntrip, *Psychoanalytic Theory, Therapy and the Self* (New York: Basic Books, 1971).

16. Phillip A. Berger, "The Medical Treatment of Mental Illness," *Science*, 200:974-81 (May 1978).

17. Leona L. Bachrach, "Is the Least Restrictive Alternative Always Best? Sociological and Semantic Implications," *Hospital and Community Psychiatry*, 31:97-103 (Feb. 1980); David L. Bazelon, "Institutionalization, Deinstitutionalization and the Adversary Process," *Columbia Law Review*, 75:897-912 (June 1975); Jonathan F. Borus, "Deinstitutionalization of the Chronically Mentally Ill," *New England Journal of Medicine*, 305:339-42 (Aug. 1981).

18. A. Louis McGarry, "Conclusions and Some Recommendations," in *Civil Commitments and Social Policy: An Evaluation of the Massachusetts Mental Health Reform Act of 1970*, A. L. McGarry et al., Department of Health and Human Services pub. no. (ADM) 81-1011 (Washington, DC: Government Printing Office, 1981), pp. 137-46.

19. A. Beigel, K. Hegland, and D. Wexler, "Implementing a New Commitment Law in the Community: Practical Problems for Professionals," in *Law and the Mental Health Professions: Friction at the Interface*, ed. W. E. Barton and C. J. Sanborn (New York: International Universities Press, 1978), pp. 273-95; Robert L. Sadoff, "Indications for Involuntary Hospitalization: Dangerousness or Mental Illness?" in ibid., pp. 297-309; Alan A. Stone, "Recent Mental Health Litigation: A Critical Perspective," *American Journal of Psychiatry*, 134:273-79 (Mar. 1977).

quently fail in their most important task, that of ensuring that those in our society who are too ill to seek treatment on their own have access to evaluation and treatment nonetheless.[20] To appreciate why this is the case requires a more detailed consideration of how two major requisites for commitment—mental illness and dangerousness—are conventionally defined and applied. Consideration is also given to some other grounds for commitment.

The present discussion does not focus on civil commitment for what under California law is termed grave disability, namely, the incapacity as a result of a mental illness to provide oneself with food, clothing, or shelter. Although commitments for grave disability constitute the majority of commitments—approximately 85 percent[21]—some states do not allow for commitment unless the patient is dangerous. More importantly, the essence of the civil commitment reforms of the sixties and seventies was to limit the availability of commitment and to require specifically some more objective test of disability than illness. Civil libertarians have argued that violent behavior is the most narrow and most specific basis for commitment.[22] Thus, for analytic purposes, a statute that requires dangerousness for civil commitment best illustrates the thrust of the civil commitment reform. This is true even though many states provide for civil commitment on grounds other than dangerousness.

Illness

The essential, historically validated requirement for civil commitment is serious mental illness. Perhaps because legislators as a group have relatively little formal training in the understanding of mental illness, there has been remarkably little consideration given to the kind and degree of illness that should be required before one is committed. When LPS was drafted, mental illness in California was defined as anything that was described in the second edition of the *Diagnostic and Statistical Manual of Mental Disorders (DSM-II)*.[23]

A priori, this might appear to be a sensible approach. Who better than the professionals involved would know the purview of their competence? Such a response fails to appreciate that defining mental illness for the purpose of establishing a standardized nomenclature is different from defining mental illness for the purpose of hospitalizing people against their will. Completeness, reliability, and validity are the essential attributes for a professional lexicon. On the other hand, given a desire to limit civil commitment, legislators might well have strived to restrict the kinds of illnesses that could give rise to commitment. Ironically, included in the early LPS definition of mental illness, which incorporated *DSM-II* by reference, was the entry "no psychiatric disorder." Obviously, the legislators did not intend such a broad definition of commitable illness.

---

20. Treffert, "Dying with Their Rights On."

21. John Monahan, Mary Ruggiero, and Herbert Friedlender, "The Stone-Roth Model of Civil Commitment and the California Dangerousness Standard: An Operational Comparison," *Archives of General Psychiatry*, 39:1267-71 (Nov. 1982); Lee C. Rubin and Mark J. Mills, "Behavioral Precipitants to Civil Commitment," *American Journal of Psychiatry*, 140:603-6 (May 1983).

22. "Mental Illness: A Suspect Classification?" *Yale Law Journal*, 83:1237-70 (1974).

23. American Psychiatric Association, *Diagnostic and Statistical Manual of Mental Disorders*, 2nd ed. (Washington, DC: American Psychiatric Association, 1968).

More telling, if not so dramatic, was the fact that *DSM-II*, as well as the third edition of the manual thereafter,[24] details the myriad organic conditions that can lead to psychosis. What remains uncomfortably vague, both at the level of legislative draftmanship and at the level of judicial interpretation, is the degree to which civil commitment is intended to deal with organic conditions. Again, a priori, there is no intrinsic reason why commitment should not include all disorders, irrespective of etiology, that lead to substantial behavioral impairment. Still, it is the degree of vagueness about what precisely constitutes a mental illness for the purpose of commitment that gives psychiatrists, jurists, and civil libertarians understandable concern. From the policy perspective, this is one of many important issues concerning civil commitment that awaits thoughtful elucidation.

As one surveys state commitment laws, this vagueness is widely evident.[25] Depending upon where one happens to be, one can be committed not only for mental illness, as the term is generally employed by psychiatrists, but also for mental retardation, developmental disability, epilepsy, alcoholism, and addiction to narcotics. Relatively few states have adopted the logical approach of defining mental illness, for the purposes of commitment, as any significant or substantial mental condition irrespective of cause.

In the abstract, this vagueness may not be problematic. However, given the perception that civil commitment was, at least historically, too readily available, it is important to define the purview of commitment in as workably narrow a fashion as possible. Failure to do so invites various problems and their associated reforms; and even well-intentioned reform can have unexpected consequences. As noted previously, the addition of the word "substantial" as a modifier to "mental illness" would suitably delimit the definition, though it would leave unresolved the question of etiology.

The recent trend of including the developmental disabilities, epilepsy, and the various addictions within the definitional purview of mental illness, for the purposes of commitment, is also troublesome. Here, too, these conditions could better be defined, for the purposes of civil commitment, as needing to be substantial.

Dangerousness

With a more limited definition of mental illness, the second requisite of commitment, that of dangerousness, could be relaxed. It is this criterion that has caused psychiatrists the greatest concern.[26] Similarly, it is this element of commitment that the advocates of reform believe to be essential if commitment is not to become a psychiatirc instrumentality. They believe that commitment, as a social instrument with substantial power, should be defined by legal, not mental health, forces. Thus, the essential questions regarding the dangerousness criterion for civil commitment involve such things as the manner in which dangerousness is defined legally

24. Ibid., 3rd ed. (1980).
25. There is no federal civil commitment statute although some commentators believe that there should be, so that those who become committed far from home can be legally transported home during treatment.

26. Loren H. Roth, "Mental Health Commitment: The State of the Debate, 1980," *Hospital and Community Psychiatry,* 31:385-96 (June 1980).

for this particular purpose, the degree of seriousness and likelihood of occurrence to be considered, and associated procedures.

Although the reformers had hoped that dangerousness would be a less elusive criterion than mental illness, in practice it has sometimes been more so. While there are consensually validated—professional—standards defining mental illness, such standards are not present with regard to dangerousness and so the concept remains overly elastic and unclear.[27] Yet, the fundamental questions are easy to articulate:

1. How broadly or narrowly should dangerousness be defined? Is a threat of physical violence to another sufficient, or does there have to be an attempt, or an "overt" act as required in some jurisdictions?
2. How recent does the act need to be?
3. How certain does a prediction of violence need to be?
4. Does dangerousness imply a sliding scale, equating the threat of a more violent act with an attempt at a less violent one?

Because of the very difficult nature of these questions, the guidelines provided by the courts have been only moderately useful; further, their requirements vary substantially across jurisdictions.[28]

What appears to have been underappreciated, at the time the dangerousness criterion was coupled to commitment, was the fact that most mentally ill people, like most non-mentally-ill people, are not dangerous.[29] Thus, if the overarching rationale for commitment is that some mentally ill individuals, by virtue of their mental illness, do not appreciate their need for evaluation and treatment, then the coupling of dangerousness to commitment as a way of limiting the scope of commitment was arbitrary. From the perspective of need for evaluation and treatment, in contrast to the perspective of protecting society, there is no fundamental difference between the rare violent mentally ill individual and the much less rare nonviolent mentally ill individual.

Further, even with the best intentions, the creation of such a distinction as a way of delimiting commitment means that many mentally ill are deprived the benefits of commitment. From the perspective of need for treatment, the dangerousness criterion arbitrarily segregates the mentally ill into two classes—violent and nonviolent—that have little to do with degree of clinical impairment. If one believes that evaluation and treatment ought to be provided on humanitarian grounds, then depriving an individual of treat-

---

27. On the nature of dangerousness as a criterion, see Saleem A. Shah, "Dangerousness and Civil Commitment of the Mentally Ill: Some Public Policy Considerations," *American Journal of Psychiatry,* 132:501-5 (May 1975); on the standards defining mental illness, see American Psychiatric Association, *Diagnostic and Statistical Manual,* 3rd ed.; on the lack of standards of defining dangerousness, see John Monahan, *The Clinical Prediction of Violent Behavior,* National Institute of Mental Health, Department of Health and Human Services pub. no. (ADM) 81:921 (Washington, DC: Government Printing Office, 1981).

28. Robert M. Wettstein, "The Prediction of Violent Behavior and the Duty to Protect Third Parties," *Behavioral Sciences and the Law,* 2:291-317 (Summer 1984); Saleem A. Shah, "Dangerousness: Some Definitional, Conceptual, and Public Policy Issues," in *Perspectives in Law and Psychology,* ed. B. D. Sales (New York: Plenum, 1977), 1:91-119; Stromberg, "Developments Concerning the Legal Criteria for Civil Commitment."

29. Monahan, *Clinical Prediction of Violent Behavior.*

ment, even involuntray treatment, because he or she has never been violent is deeply ironic.

At least two recent studies in the empirical literature validate this perspective. Both Monahan, Ruggiero, and Friedlender[30] and Rubin and Mills[31] found, in different states—California and Massachusetts—with different commitment criteria, that approximately 85 percent of those committed had done little that could be construed as violent. The most logical interpretation is that, in endeavoring to hospitalize those mentally ill who need evaluation or treatment and who are too ill to seek hospitalization on their own, psychiatrists routinely find that those who require commitment are, in fact, not dangerous.[32]

Furthermore, these data underestimate, probably even considerably, the percentage of nondangerous persons in the total population of the seriously mentally ill. As dangerousness was made a requisite for commitment, the police and many mental health professionals refuse to detain an individual unless there is prima facie evidence of dangerousness. Often, that dangerousness is the unintentional kind represented by the danger posed by allowing a serious illness to remain untreated for a protracted period. Seen in this light, the data from the two studies strongly support the notion that most seriously mentally ill people are not dangerous. This, in turn, bolsters the belief that the inclusion of dangerousness as the sine qua non of commitment is unwarranted.

Still, it is important not to overstate the argument. Dangerousness is a reasonable criterion for civil commitment, if commitment is also available for comparably ill nondangerous individuals. Further, because of the threat to society that dangerous individuals pose, it may be reasonable to impose a longer period of evaluation and treatment on those individuals judged potentially violent once they are perceived as sufficiently ill to warrant civil intervention.

Grave disability

A number of states allow for the civil commitment of nondangerous mentally ill persons by providing for those who are gravely disabled.[33] As noted earlier, the California law requires that nondangerous mentally ill individuals lack the capacity to provide themselves with food, clothing, or shelter in order to be considered gravely disabled. A similar end is reached in the Massachusetts law, albeit via a different statutory vehicle, by providing for the commitment of individuals who pose a "very substantial risk of physical impairment or injury" to themselves by virtue of their inability to care for themselves. However, the availability of public welfare and publicly supported shelters for the undomiciled works at very substantial cross-purposes to definitions such as California's, but arguably not the Massachusetts one. So long as food, clothing, and shelter are provided, then even very seriously mentally ill people do not generally meet the commitment criteria. This problem reveals the inequity that has arisen from civil commitment reform. Civil commit-

30. Monahan, Ruggiero, and Friedlender, "Stone-Roth Model."

31. Rubin and Mills, "Behavioral Precipitants to Civil Commitment."

32. Mills, Gracey, and Cummins, "Legal Issues in Mental Health Administration."

33. Samuel J. Brakel and Ronald S. Rock, *The Mentally Disabled and the Law*, revised ed. (Chicago: University of Chicago Press, 1971); "Developments in the Law: Civil Commitment of the Mentally Ill," *Harvard Law Review*, 87:1190-1406 (1974).

ment continues to be readily available for those, almost irrespective of the degree of their illness, who are violent or who threaten violence; yet, it has become much more difficult to commit those whose illness is not manifested by violence.

This pattern is not coincidental. Legislators intended to protect society by endeavoring to ensure that dangerous persons receive rapid attention by appropriate professionals; however, there is no medical speciality in, nor specific medical treatment for, dangerousness. The new laws virtually ensure, in the context of moderately successful public welfare programs, that individuals must be profoundly ill before they can be committed. As Gruenberg has suggested, delaying treatment makes treatment less certain;[34] in effect, treatment delayed may be treatment denied. This is an important and untoward consequence of civil commitment reform that appears not to have been anticipated.

A model statute

Lest these comments appear overly abstract, it might be helpful to consider a civil commitment model that addresses some of the issues previously raised. First, the range of illnesses considered for commitment under this model would need to be defined. That definition must reflect the specific public policy and legal purposes that are to be served. Hence, the more demanding definition of "substantial illness, irrespective of etiology" provides a helpful beginning.[35]

Next, given the reasonable desire to protect society from dangerous individuals, including those with serious mental illnesses, it may make sense to retain the present dangerousness criteria: that is, commitment would be available when the person is seriously mentally ill and a danger to self or to others. Civil commitment for dangerous persons who are only slightly mentally ill raises the issue of preventive detention: commitment must be linked directly to mental illness, otherwise such concerns are not groundless. Dangerousness, then, in such a statute, would merit a tighter definition than presently available. Although a full discussion of such a definition is beyond the scope of this article, such a definition could be linked to an overt act of violence, as it already is in some jurisdictions.[36]

What about commitment for nondangerous mentally ill persons? If one excludes dangerousness as the essential standard for civil commitment, one has to develop additional criteria for commitment that are both fair and practical. Several important commentators, including Stone and Roth, have done that.[37] In essence, they link commitment to serious mental illness, incapacity to consent to treatment, treatability, and the likelihood of the patient's appreciation of the care given. From the perspective of fairness, Stone and Roth have done an admirable job in articulating the normative calculus for commitment.[38] Yet,

34. E. Gruenberg, "The Social Breakdown Syndrome—Some Origins," *American Journal of Psychiatry*, 123:1481-89 (Dec. 1967).

35. The Massachusetts civil commitment laws provide an example of a detailed and useful definition; see Mass. Gen. Laws chap. 123 (1983).

36. Stromberg, "Developments Concerning the Legal Criteria for Civil Commitment."

37. Alan A. Stone, *Mental Health and Law: A System in Transition*, National Institute of Mental Health, Department of Health, Education, and Welfare pub. no. (ADM) 75-176 (Washington, DC: Government Printing Office, 1975); Loren H. Roth, "A Commitment Law for Patients, Doctors and Lawyers," *American Journal of Psychiatry*, 136:1121-27 (Sept. 1979).

38. Sometimes the separate but similar criteria

they appear to have overlooked the necessity of fashioning criteria that are workable in the context of emergency evaluation. Some of the concerns raised by the Stone-Roth criteria cannot realistically be determined in the emergency room. Until a therapeutic trial has been undertaken, for example, one cannot say whether for a given patient treatment is genuinely available. This determination can only be made retrospectively. For this reason, more practicable, if less ideal, commitment criteria are needed.

In addition to the presence of a serious mental illness, the most straightforward criterion—and hence of the greatest utility in emergency evaluation—would be a single additional one that addresses the patient's competence. As observed earlier, the fundamental premise underpinning commitment is that some mentally ill people are too ill to appreciate adequately the necessity of having their illness evaluated and—potentially—treated.[39] Given this, the gap in the patient's competence that occasions commitment should be related to the patient's failure to appreciate the necessity for a psychiatric evaluation. Thus, with respect to commitment, the emergency-room evaluation should be focused on whether the patient has lost, by virtue if his or her mental illness, the capacity to assent meaningfully to an in-hospital psychiatric evaluation. If the patient has lost that capacity, then the patient, even if not dangerous, should be committed for evaluation. However, such a commitment scheme only makes sense in the context of carefully observed procedural guarantees.

PROCEDURAL GUARANTEES

Nearly as important as the changes in the substantive criteria for commitment were those changes in procedural due process occasioned by the new commitment laws. Earlier, in the introduction, I divided the changes in the commitment laws into three parts; although such a division is useful to underscore that in the new laws the duration of commitment changed from indeterminate to determinate, it is also true that limiting the duration of commitment constituted a procedural reform. In fact, another way to conceptualize the commitment reforms of the late sixties and early seventies is to consider them bipartite: substantive and procedural.

Under the new laws, the limitations on the duration of commitment, the guaranteed access to a judge and jury, and the requirement of clear and convincing proof were each aspects of procedural reform. These reforms have been referred to by some as the "criminalization" of civil commitment, an expression that underscores the observation that similar reforms had occurred, somewhat earlier, in the criminal law.

As the term "criminalization" implies, however, some have critiqued the procedural reforms claiming that they were too procrustean to deal adequately with the complexities of clinical reality. Such criticisms largely are warranted only insofar as the duration of commitment is concerned. Although some of the specifications—for example, the

---

of Stone and Roth are collapsed into one set, the so-called Stone-Roth criteria. They include the following: the person suffers from a severe mental illness, and without treatment the prognosis is for major distress; treatment is available; the illness impairs the person's ability to understand information about the illness; and the risk-benefit ratio is such that a reasonable person would consent to a therapeutic trial.

39. Michael A. Peszke, *Involuntary Treatment of the Mentally Ill* (Springfield, IL: Charles C Thomas, 1975).

requirement that the psychiatrist appear in court to testify about the patient's illness—may be cumbersome to the clinician, the other procedural guarantees intrude relatively little into clinical practice.

The initial period of commitment in the 50 states varies from 48 hours to 14 days.[40] Although the variation is wide, the fact that the initial period is so brief suggests that the reforming legislators conceived of the initial commitment as a trial period, designed to allow the clinician to assess the patient and to allow the patient to consider the desirability of continuing the hospitalization. In most state-supported facilities, however, 48 hours is not sufficient time for the initial laboratory results to be returned to the clinician; thus, it appears too short a period to accomplish the intended result.

It is at the next level of commitment that the statutory duration of detainment is clinically problematic. A number of states, such as California, limit that period to 14 days. This period is adequate for assessing the effect on patients of neuroleptics, antipsychotic medications that act within hours. However, thymoleptics—medications designed to combat disorders of mood—with the exception of lithium, typically take three weeks to achieve their clinical effect. Even then, their effect is only achieved once the effective dose has been determined, a process that frequently consumes at least a week. Thus in many states the period of secondary commitment is too brief; patients with affective disorders are not adequately considered in the statutory time frames.

This criticism aside, the procedural reforms to commitment have an underappreciated advantage for clinicians: because of their presence, modifications in the substantive criteria for commitment, as presented previously, can be reconsidered. If advocates and legislators are going to countenance a broadening of the substantive criteria, they will need to be convinced that commitment will not return to the open-ended process that it was. The historically accepted procedural reforms forestall that possibility by circumscribing the duration of commitment and by ensuring rapid judicial review.

CONCLUSION

In this overview, the essential criticism of the new commitment laws is that they tend to overemphasize dangerousness. They do this to the point that many seriously mentally ill, nondangerous individuals cannot be evaluated as inpatients. This is problematic because the complexity of assessing, diagnosing, and treating serious mental illness often renders inpatient evaluation necessary. Under the new laws, by the time the patient's illness is sufficiently evident for the patient to be committed, the likelihood that the illness will respond to treatment is relatively remote.

The vehicle used to illustrate these concerns has been the elaboration of broadened civil commitment criteria to better address the nondangerous mentally ill. Various criteria have been considered, such as the treatability of the illness, the belief in the likelihood that the patient will eventually appreciate the need for involuntary hospitalization, and the belief that the illness, if untreated, will cause major distress. These criteria have been rejected because of their relative inapplicability in emergency settings.[41] Instead, the dual cri-

40. "Developments in the Law."

41. American Psychiatric Association, "Guidelines for Legislation on the Psychiatric Hospitalization of Adults," *American Journal of Psy-*

teria of serious mental illness and the incapacity to consent meaningfully to inpatient evaluation have been proposed.

These criteria are reasonable because of the procedural guarantees that have developed in civil commitment law over the last decade and a half. Were these broader criteria to be adopted, however, additional procedural safeguards might be needed to guarantee that nondangerous individuals would not be repetitively committed. The problem would become that of what to do with the chronically mentally ill person who falls repeatedly within the definitional purview of a broadened commitment statute. Many of these persons, even when clinically improved, would not wish multiple interventions on their behalf. Such wishes need to be protected.

An approach to this protection would be to allow for the commitment of nondangerous individuals a fixed number of times. Such a mechanism could provide for an initial evaluation and treatment of nearly all seriously mentally ill individuals. Yet, it would limit an individual's exposure to repeated commitments. A statute could, for example, provide for no more than one evaluation every five years; alternatively, it could provide for a limited number of such evaluations during an individual's lifetime.

The public has become increasingly aware of urban homelessness; some estimates have the mentally ill accounting for 90 percent of the urban homeless population.[42] This parallels a growing professional awareness that many characterologically disordered, dangerous, but largely treatment-unresponsive patients populate state psychiatric facilities. Such perceptions appear to have led some legislatures to reconsider civil commitment again. To the extent that such reconsiderations have occurred, they have tended to move in the direction described earlier, that of broadening the criteria for commitment.

In the best-studied state, Washington, civil commitment criteria were broadened in 1979.[43] The data following these changes reveal that commitment practices varied widely depending on the locale of one's residence: in what county one resided, or whether the county was urban or rural.[44] However, the effects on the availability of services to the nondangerous, seriously mentally ill were difficult to evaluate. Until the evidence supporting the desirability of broadening commitment criteria is unambiguous, it would be prudent to modify existing commitment statutes gradually.

Present commitment laws link commitment to dangerousness. A propensity to violence may result from mental illness, occur concurrently with mental illness, or occur in spite of mental illness. In general, civil commitment statutes imply that in order to be a criterion for commitment, dangerousness should be related to the mental illness. Given the present state of the art, psychiatrists cannot reliably determine how, and to what extent, a given individual's propen-

---

chiatry, 140:672-79 (May 1983); Clifford D. Stromberg and Alan A. Stone, "A Model State Law on Civil Commitment of the Mentally Ill," *Harvard Journal on Legislation,* 20(2):275-396 (1983).

42. Ellen L. Bassuk, "The Homelessness Problem," *Scientific American,* 251:40-45 (July 1984).

43. Mary L. Durham and Glenn L. Pierce, "Legal Intervention in Civil Commitment: The Impact of Broadened Commitment Criteria," this issue of *The Annals* of the American Academy of Political and Social Science.

44. Mary L. Durham and Glenn Pierce, "Beyond Deinstitutionalization: A Commitment Law in Evolution," *Hospital and Community Psychiatry,* 33:216-19 (Mar. 1982).

sity to violence relates to his or her illness, or even whether it relates to it at all. Thus, insofar as commitment statutes employ dangerousness as a criterion, they should not require that mental illness underpin that dangerousness; concurrence should be enough.

In summary, civil commitment reform has corrected most of the abuses of the past.[45] Unfortunately, many seriously mentally ill individuals remain unassessed and untreated. This absence is due in part to the concurrence of commitment criteria that emphasize dangerousness and a welfare system that, by providing food, clothing, and shelter, renders many of the nondangerous commitment criteria partially inoperative.

45. Stone, "Psychiatric Abuse and Legal Reform."

Legal Intervention in Civil Commitment: The Impact of Broadened Commitment Criteria

By MARY L. DURHAM and GLENN L. PIERCE

ABSTRACT: Recent legal changes in Washington State have broadened the grave-disability criterion for civil commitment of the mentally ill. Analysis of data from state mental hospitals and from records of commitment authorities in Washington's two largest counties revealed that, while there was an increase in the number of involuntary hospitalizations immediately before and after the changes in law, there was a virtual disappearance of voluntary patients in state hospitals. Moreover, expansion of the definition of "grave disability" resulted in a move toward a *parens patriae*-dominated civil commitment system. Analysis of the empirical consequences of the legal changes on commitment decisions is presented, along with the response of mental health officials and the public.

Mary L. Durham, Ph.D., is associate director, Center for Health Studies at Group Health Cooperative of Puget Sound and an associate professor of health services, School of Public Health and Community Medicine, University of Washington, Seattle. Her research interests are in mental health law, especially as it relates to the control of deviant behavior, and long-term care of the chronically ill.

Glenn L. Pierce, M.S., is associate director, Center for Applied Social Research, Northeastern University, Boston. He has conducted research in the area of criminal justice and mental health, with special emphasis on policy evaluation. He expects to receive his Ph.D. in sociology in June 1986.

NOTE: This research was supported in part by funds from the Center for Studies of Antisocial and Violent Behavior, National Institute of Mental Health, grant number RO1MH36220.

DESPITE the push for reform to tighten involuntary civil commitment laws, considerable concern has been expressed by members of lay and professional communities that commitment criteria that emerged during the 1970s were unnecessarily restrictive. Stromberg and Stone claim that legal reforms supporting deinstitutionalization led to a second generation of problems associated with the plight of seriously mentally ill persons who were no longer eligible for involuntary hospitalization.[1]

Throughout the United States, psychiatrists have reported horror stories related to their inability under restrictive commitment laws to secure treatment for patients.[2] Newspapers have reported stories of psychiatric ghettos in large cities where former patients live in squalor and isolation.[3] Psychiatric journals have published numerous articles suggesting that highly restrictive civil commitment legislation has had the effect of decreasing human dignity[4] and shifting the mentally ill into jails and prisons.[5] Clearly, considerable tension has been generated between the state's right to protect the civil rights of the mentally ill and its responsibility to protect the community from harm.

In 1979, after six years of working under very narrow civil libertarian criteria for commitment, Washington State revised its commitment statute to broaden the scope of persons who might be involuntarily confined. Several other states, including Texas, North Carolina, and Alaska, have now followed Washington's example and have moved further away from reliance on the dangerousness-to-self-or-others criterion toward increased use of grave disability as the major criterion for commitment.

The research reported here is an empirical analysis of a legal intervention in civil commitment in Washington State. Substantive criteria for commitment were changed in 1979 to make easier the involuntary hospitalization of mentally ill persons who were in need of care and treatment but who did not meet the stringent requirements of dangerousness to self or others. Our research was designed to assess the effects of the legal change on commitment decisions, as well as the impact on the allocation of scarce mental health service resources.

Our research is based on the assumption that the mental health system is bound by constraints placed upon it by finite resources. Broadening the criteria for admission to Washington State mental facilities led to a substantial increase in the number of people who were involuntarily detained. However, expansion of mental health resources lagged behind the service demand caused by the increased flexibility to detain patients

---

1. Clifford D. Stromberg and Alan A. Stone, "A Model State Law on Civil Commitment of the Mentally Ill," *Harvard Journal of Legislation,* 20:275-396 (1983)

2. *Project Release v. Prevost,* 463 F. Supp. 1033 (1978).

3. "Mental Patients and the Community," *New York Times,* 18 Nov. 1979; ibid., 19 Nov. 1979; ibid., 20 Nov. 1979.

4. Willard Gaylin, *Caring* (New York: Knopf, 1976); Loren H. Roth, "A Commitment Law for Patients, Doctors, and Lawyers," *American Journal of Psychiatry,* 136:1121-27 (1979).

5. J. C. Bonovitz and E. B. Guy, "Impact of Restrictive Civil Commitment Procedures on a Prison Psychiatric Service," *American Journal of Psychiatry,* 136:1045-48 (1979); J. C. Bonovitz and J. S. Bonovitz, "Diversion of the Mentally Ill into the Criminal Justice System: The Police Intervention Perspective," *American Journal of Psychiatry,* 138:973-76 (1981); Walter Dickey, "Incompetency and the Nondangerous Mentally Ill Client," *Criminal Law Bulletin,* 16:22-40 (Jan.-Feb. 1980).

involuntarily. There was a marked acceleration in the demand for involuntary services but a relatively inelastic supply of resources to meet that demand.

Our data yielded information regarding many aspects of the civil commitment process. Our comments will be limited to changes in detention practices that appear to be associated with the broadened commitment criteria. On the basis of our findings, we believe that substantive changes that broaden commitment authority, and the anticipation of these changes, can bring about modifications in commitment decisions made by mental health professionals.

CIVIL COMMITMENT IN WASHINGTON STATE

The state's authority to involuntarily hospitalize the mentally ill rests upon two different, sometimes competing, legal doctrines: *parens patriae* and police power. Under its *parens patriae* power, the state is empowered to act on behalf of persons who are believed to be incapable of taking care of themselves. The state's police power stems from its inherent authority to prevent harm to the community. Civil commitment statutes typically invoke both of these bases for the state's coercive interventions, although there are periodic shifts in emphasis from one to the other rationale.

Narrow commitment criteria

Washington State entered the modern era of commitment laws in 1973 with the Involuntary Treatment Act (ITA73) that was hailed by many observers as a civil libertarian model for commitment.[6]

6. See, for example, D. A. Treffert and R. W. Krajeck, "In Search of a Sane Commitment Statute," *Psychiatric Annals*, 6:56-57,61,63-65,69-70,72-73 (June 1976).

Prior to 1973, Washington State's commitment law was much like provisions in other states, allowing hospitalization of a "mentally ill" person if he was "found to be suffering from psychosis or other disease impairing his mental health, and the symptoms of such disease were of suicidal, homicidal or incendiary nature, or of such nature which would render such person dangerous to his own or the lives or property of others."[7]

ITA73 authorized commitment of an individual who, "as a result of a mental disorder presents a likelihood of serious harm to others or himself or is gravely disabled."[8] "Likelihood of serious harm" was specified as behavior that threatened or attempted harm to self or others. A person was dangerous to self if he or she threatened or attempted self-inflicted physical harm or suicide. Danger to others was evidenced by behavior that caused harm or substantial risk of harm in the past or that placed others in reasonable fear of sustaining harm, although the statute did not specify what acts constitute evidence of dangerousness or harm.

In ITA73 "grave disability" was a "condition in which a person, as a result of mental disorder, is in danger of serious physical harm resulting from a failure to provide for his essential human needs."[9] Commitment was not to be authorized if the patients could live outside of an institution on their own or through the support of family or friends. As a result of this, families were often frustrated in their attempts to commit a family member who needed inpatient care. If the family continued to provide essential human needs of food, clothing,

7. Rev. Code of Wash. §71.23.010 (1970).
8. Ibid., (1974).
9. Ibid., §71.23.100 (1974).

and shelter, the mentally ill person could not be involuntarily hospitalized as gravely disabled.

ITA73 provided procedural safeguards that would end indefinite commitment and shorten the length of involuntary hospital stays. The statute set forth conditions under which a 72-hour evaluation period might be authorized and followed, where appropriate, by nonrenewable commitments of 14 days and 90 days and renewable commitments of 180 days.

Any 14-day detention had to be preceded by a probable-cause hearing at the end of the 72-hour hold. Detention for 90 and 180 days required evidence that physical harm to self or others had been inflicted or attempted, either as the reason for custody or during the 72-hour period of evaluation and treatment. After the 14-day detention, the patient could be confined for another 90 days if threatening behavior was exhibited. To be held beyond 90 days, however, required a petition to the court and a hearing. Successive 180-day commitments could be made by the court, but no order could be authorized for a period exceeding 180 days.

Another notable revision in ITA73 was the removal of property destruction as the dangerous behavior for which a person might be involuntarily detained. Several commentators claim that omission of the property-destruction provision was more a result of oversight than of a logical or philosophically based revision.[10]

ITA73 established a county-based involuntary commitment network in the state of Washington. Prior to 1973, any licensed practicing physician could decide if a person should be involuntarily detained. As a result of ITA73, involuntary commitment offices were established in each county throughout the state, with some smaller counties sharing a common resource. Counties designated mental health professionals to investigate and evaluate the appropriateness of all complaints of mental disorder that came from private citizens or health care providers. The county-designated mental health professional must be a psychiatrist, licensed clinical psychologist, psychiatric nurse, social worker, or some other designated individual with special training and/or experience in mental health.[11] The "mental health professional, after investigation and evaluation of the specific facts alleged, and of the reliability and credibility of the person or persons, if any, providing information to initiate detention, may summon such person to appear at an evaluation and treatment facility for not more than a seventy-two hour evaluation and treatment period."[12]

After passage of ITA73, yearly attempts were made to revise and expand civil commitment admission and retention eligibility. Psychiatrists resented the fact that authority for initial commitment had been placed into the hands of the county mental health professional a non-medically trained person located at the countywide Office of Involuntary Commitment.

Restrictive criteria for involuntary commitment often meant that families were unable to commit a family member to a mental institution. In 1978, Washington Advocates for the Mentally Ill was formed by a group of frustrated family members after what appears to have been a key event leading to the 1979

---

10. Personal communication with the authors from several state officials, Jan.-Feb. 1980.

11. Rev. Code of Wash. §72.23.010.7 (1974).
12. Ibid., §72.23.010.20 (1974).

revision of ITA73, the MacFarlane murder case.

A number of crimes committed by alleged former mental patients had received considerable attention from the media. In 1978, a wealthy Seattle couple was murderered by their 23-year-old next-door neighbor who, only hours before, had been denied voluntary admission to Western State Hospital. MacFarlane's trial put into public view the long plight of his family to secure mental health services for him. Other families also related stories of their inability to get help for family members due to restrictive civil commitment legislation.

Although the MacFarlane case itself did not directly address the issue of grave disability, it publicized the limitations on involuntary treatment for persons believed to be gravely disabled or dangerous. Washington Advocates for the Mentally Ill began to lobby for changes in ITA73 that would broaden the scope of grave disability to include individuals whose condition was deteriorating in the community. They argued, along with other professional and private groups, that many mentally ill people were falling through the cracks of the involuntary commitment system.

BROADENED COMMITMENT CRITERIA

After considerable debate of a number of proposed revisions of the law, a revised Involuntary Treatment Act went into effect in Washington on 1 September 1979. The revised law was intended to provide continuity, not a departure from the earlier statute.

Four revisions reflect the legislative intent to broaden commitment criteria:

—expanded definition of "gravely disabled";

—expanded definition of "likelihood of serious harm" to include destruction of property;

—provisions for easier revocation of conditional release; and

—allowing testimony by a spouse against the person for whom detention is sought.

Gravely disabled

Changes in the definition of "gravely disabled" allowed mental health professionals to commit people who could not function independently in the community or who manifested severe deterioration in routine functioning because of mental impairment.

The Involuntary Treatment Act of 1979 (ITA79) revised the definition of "grave disability" to mean "a condition in which a person, as a result of a mental disorder (a) is in danger of serious physical harm resulting from a failure to provide for his essential human needs *of health or safety, or (b) manifests severe deterioration in routine functioning evidenced by repeated and escalating loss of cognitive or volitional control over his or her actions and is not receiving such care as is essential for his or her health and safety.*"[13] Thus, families who had been able to maintain the patient's physical safety could now plead that the person's essential health and safety needs could not be provided outside a hospital.

Another provision added in 1979 was designed to address the notion of decompensation. Patients who were discharged into the community were often able to function adequately for a short period—60 to 90 days—but then rapidly

---

13. Ibid., §71.05.020 (1979); italics added, to indicate additions made by the 1979 amendments.

deteriorated after they stopped taking their prescribed medication. ITA79 provided for commitment when there was evidence of repeated and escalating loss of cognitive or volitional control of actions. Family groups had lobbied hard for the inclusion of this provision in the 1979 bill. They claimed that this clause would enhance their ability to obtain involuntary hospitalization services for the mentally ill during the period of decline often following release from a mental health facility and before the patient's condition hit bottom.

Property damage

The provision for harm to property that was removed from ITA73 was reintroduced in the 1979 amendments. ITA79 specified that, " 'likelihood of serious harm' means either (a) a substantial risk that physical harm will be inflicted by an individual upon his own person, as evidenced by threats or attempts to commit suicide or inflict physical harm on one's self; (b) a substantial risk that physical harm will be inflicted by an individual upon another, as evidenced by behavior which has caused such harm or which places another person or persons in reasonable threat of sustaining such harm; or, (c) *a substantial risk that physical harm will be inflicted by an individual upon the property of others, as evidenced by behavior which has caused substantial loss or damage to the property of others.*"[14]

The inclusion of destruction of property in the 1979 revision was an important development. This type of police authority was a provision in early mental health legislation and is still a feature

14. Ibid.; italics added, to indicate additions made by the 1979 amendments.

of many state commitment statutes. Property damage, or "substantial risk" of its occurrence, may relate to tampering with any object that belongs to another and is of some value. This provision gives a great deal of discretion to mental health professionals for detaining troublesome mentally ill persons.

Conditional release

Under ITA73, if a person was given a conditional release from a mental hospital and then violated the conditions of the release, mental health professionals had few options for returning the individual to the hospital. Because the 1973 law stated that violation of the conditional release had to be accompanied by actions dangerous to self or others, grave disability was not a sufficient reason for rescinding a conditional release. With the 1979 revisions, violation of any condition of release was, in itself, sufficient reason for rescinding a release. The law provided that if the terms of the conditional release were violated the person must return to the institution, where a hearing would then take place.

Testimony by the spouse

Prior to 1973, a spouse could not testify in courtroom proceedings against the person whose detention was being sought. According to county mental health professionals, some counties—King, Pierce, and others—had actually permitted spouse testimony during the period from 1973 to 1979. However, because of the variations in legal interpretation from one county to the next, the right of spouses to testify was formalized by statute to ease the ability to commit in some counties.

Fallout from the legislative change

There was clear intent in Washington's 1979 commitment law to broaden the substantive criteria for involuntary hospitalization. This amounted to a mandated increase in the likelihood of commitment to public mental health facilities for certain types of behaviors by mentally ill persons that would not have led to commitment prior to the statutory revision.

The increase in the volume of patients that occurred following the passage of ITA79 could not be absorbed by existing state hospital resources. Both staffing and bed space in state mental hospitals were insufficient. Western State Hospital (WSH) was particularly hard hit by the increased demand for admissions. Although WSH was able to respond to a 180 percent increase in involuntary admissions by opening a large inpatient ward, the new ward was soon filled to capacity. With the demand for beds far exceeding the ability to admit new patients, officials at WSH imposed a limited admissions policy that set admissions at 90 percent of WSH bed capacity.

This cap on admissions to WSH meant that the county-designated mental health professionals throughout western Washington were hampered in their ability to refer patients to the hospital from local evaluation and treatment facilities. As a result, psychiatric patients who would have been admitted to local evaluation and treatment facilities were detained in hospitals, nursing homes, or other locations until a bed could be found in an evaluation and treatment unit. The situation became so acute that the Pierce County mental health professional obtained a temporary restraining order that forced WSH to admit—without regard for the availability of bed space—patients who had been involuntarily detained under state law.

In an attempt to shorten the length of stay at state facilities, state mental health officials established a policy that required special approval from the Division of Mental Health to reimburse local providers for detentions in excess of 14 days beyond the probable-cause hearing. Such a provision meant that state hospitals would be the location of virtually all 90- and 180-day commitments.

The following section presents the changes that occurred in conjunction with the implementation of ITA79.

METHODS

The revision of Washington's civil commitment law presented an opportunity to study the direct as well as the indirect—and unanticipated—impact of a legislative revision. By choosing a study period that included two years prior to the legal change and two years following the change, we were able to compare pre-ITA79 behavior with post-ITA79 behavior.

Washington's statutory change was also an opportunity to compare consequences of broadened civil commitment provisions with earlier studies that had analyzed the effects of changes that narrowed commitment authority in other states, namely California, Wisconsin, North Carolina, Arizona, Nebraska, Washington, and Massachusetts.[15]

15. For California, see Teknekron, Inc., "Improving California's Mental Health System: Policy Making and Management in the Invisible System" (Report, Permanent Subcommittee on Mental Health and Developmental Disabilities, California Assembly, 1978); Carol A.B. Warren, "Involuntary Commitment for Mental Disorder:

The research reported here draws on two data sources. First, we obtained from Washington State's Department of Social and Health Services a copy of the computerized data base of persons served by state mental hospitals, including each patient's demographic characteristics, diagnosis, admission status—voluntary or involuntary—and prior admission history. Second, we gathered a large volume of data from individual case records of a randomly selected group of 3570 persons who were referred to the Offices of Involuntary Commitment in King and Pierce counties—where Seattle and Tacoma are located, respectively—from September 1977 through August 1981. This data base contained information on a total of 8100 referrals to the civil commitment system, including 3900 commitments. These data included persons who were seen by county-designated mental health professionals but who were not committed, as well as those who were committed under state law for 72 hours or 14, 90, or 180 days.

The decision to study two counties was based on the rationale that commitment decisions are strongly influenced by the availability of resources at the disposal of community authorities. When inpatient mental health resources are unavailable in a community, authorities will find some way to control deviant behavior—for example, through outpatient commitment or arrest for petty crimes such as defrauding an innkeeper or vagrancy. Pierce County was chosen because it is the site of the state mental hospital for western Washington; King County was selected because it is a major urban center and handles a major portion of all Involuntary Treatment Act activity in the state.

RESULTS

The examination of state mental hospital data and individual case record data from two counties revealed (1) a reinstitutionalization of the civil commitment system and (2) a shift toward a *parens patriae*-dominated system for such commitment.

Reinstitutionalization of the mentally ill

It is clear from examination of the Department of Social and Health Services' computerized data file on state mental hospital admissions and discharges that involuntary admissions began to increase in the year prior to the implementation of ITA79 (see Table 1),

---

The Application of California's Lanterman-Petris-Short Act," *Law and Society Review*, 11:629-49 (Spring 1977); for Wisconsin, see Dickey, "Incompetency and the Nondangerous Mentally Ill Client"; for North Carolina, see Virginia A. Hiday, "Reformed Commitment Procedures: An Empirical Study in the Courtroom," *Law and Society Review*, 11:651-66 (Spring 1977); R. D. Miller and P. B. Fiddleman, "Involuntary Civil Commitment in North Carolina: The Results of the 1979 Statutory Changes," *North Carolina Law Review*, 60:985-1026 (1982); for Arizona, see David B. Wexler, *Criminal Commitments and Dangerous Mental Patients*, National Institute of Mental Health, Department of Health, Education, and Welfare pub. no. (ADM) 76-331 (Washington, DC: Government Printing Office, 1976); for Nebraska, see James W. Luckey and John J. Berman, "Effects of a New Commitment Law on Involuntary Admissions and Service Utilization Patterns," *Law and Human Behavior*, 3(3):149-61 (1979); for Washington, see L. S. Sata and E. E. Goldberg, "A Study of Involuntary Patients in Seattle," *Hospital and Community Psychiatry*, 28:834-37 (1977); for Massachusetts, see A. Louis McGarry et al., *Civil Commitment and Social Policy*, National Institute of Mental Health, Department of Health and Human Services pub. no. (ADM) 81-1011 (Washington, DC: Government Printing Office, 1981).

TABLE 1
ADMISSION TO STATE MENTAL HOSPITALS IN WASHINGTON,
JANUARY 1977 THROUGH AUGUST 1980

Year	Month	Involuntary admissions		Voluntary admissions		Total[†]
		Number	Percentage of total	Number	Percentage of total	
1977	1-4	268	23.4	580	50.6	1,147
	5-8	270	21.0	652	50.7	1,287
	9-12	325	25.5	634	49.7	1,276
1978	1-4	333	26.6	613	49.0	1,251
	5-8	404	31.6	563	44.1	1,277
	9-12	396	31.2	581	45.8	1,268
1979	1-4	486	36.2	586	43.6	1,344
	5-8	591	42.4	518	37.1	1,395
	9-12*	858	54.3	442	28.0	1,579
1980	1-4	872	55.2	441	27.9	1,580
	5-8	1,129	62.1	382	21.0	1,819

SOURCE: From *American Journal of Psychiatry*, vol. 142, pp. 104-7 (1985). Copyright 1985, the American Psychiatric Association. Reprinted by permission. Data are from the computerized data file of the Department of Social and Health Services, State of Washington.
*The Involuntary Treatment Act of 1979 went into effect on 1 Sept. 1979.
†Total admissions include involuntary, voluntary, and legal offender admissions.

with additional growth occurring after the legal change. The increase that occurred prior to the law's effective date, 1 September 1979, has been referred to as an "anticipation effect" and is described elsewhere in greater detail.[16] In the four months that followed ITA79's implementation, involuntary hospital admissions increased by 45.2 percent and voluntary admissions declined by 14.7 percent. By the time ITA79 had been in effect for a full year, the absolute number of voluntary admissions had fallen from 37.1 percent to only 21.0 percent of total admissions.

Although there had been a substantial increase in the number of criminal commitments—mentally ill defendants, offenders, and sexual psychopaths—between 1974 and 1979, the absolute number of such admissions leveled off after ITA79 went into effect. Proportionate to the increase in civil commitments, the relative number of criminal commitments decreased from 24.2 percent of mental hospital admissions in 1974 to 15.8 percent in 1980.

These data indicate that the enactment of ITA79 led to a shift toward involuntary admissions and a dramatic decline in voluntary treatment. Moreover, the sharp increase in involuntary detentions that followed ITA79 was not due to a revolving door of rapid admission, discharge, and readmission. The proportion of involuntary admissions that were readmitted in the year immediately following the implementation of ITA79 was less than 7 percent, indicating that the observed increase in civil commitments to state hospitals that followed ITA79 was not due to the accelerated readmission of previously committed patients.[17]

16. Glenn L. Pierce, Mary L. Durham, and William H. Fisher, "The Impact of Public Policy and Publicity on Admissions to State Mental Hospitals," *Journal of Health Politics, Policy and Law* (in press).

17. Glenn L. Pierce, Mary L. Durham, and William H. Fisher, "The Impact of Broadened Civil Commitment Standards on Admission to

Our data also indicate that some of the increase in involuntary admissions that followed the implementation of ITA79 was due to former voluntary patients who were readmitted on an involuntary basis. In the year following 1 September 1979, the probability of involuntary hospitalization increased for patients admitted for the first time, from 47.3 to 63.2 percent, and for patients previously admitted on a voluntary basis, from 25.1 to 41.7 percent. These changes were not due to changes in the sociodemographic and diagnostic characteristics of the population.[18]

Shift toward a parens patriae system

While most states have shifted toward statutory schemes that favor commitment based on police power, Washington State enacted legislation that expanded its *parens patriae* authority.[19] The 1979 commitment statute expanded the definition of "grave disability" to include individuals who, because of mental impairment, cannot function independently in the community or who manifest severe deterioration in routine functioning.

Along with the increase in the number of involuntary commitments the use of grave disability as a commitment criterion began to increase dramatically. Although grave disability held a slim lead as the primary commitment criterion prior to 1979, by 1981 three out of every four commitments involved this criterion. At the same time, detentions based on dangerousness to self fell to 29.7 percent of commitments and those based on dangerousness to others fell to 25.7 percent.[20]

Change in clientele. The increased use of grave disability as a commitment authority was due to an influx of newly committed patients as well as a continuous flow of prior patients who were committed as gravely disabled (see Table 2).[21] The absolute number of newly committed patients far exceeded the absolute number of recommitments although the ratio of new to old patients remained constant in the year immediately preceding and following ITA79. However, by 1981 there was a drop in the number of first-time commitments and a concurrent increase in the number of recommitments. It appears that the gravely disabled patients who were detained under ITA79 began a continuing relationship with commitment authorities. By 1981, 80 percent of the increase in commitments on the basis of grave disability was due to recommitments.

Police power. The increased use of grave disability as the criterion for commitments was accompanied by a tendency to replace the use of police power with *parens patriae* authority. Examination of the commitment history of a group of 747 patients who had been committed both before and after implementation of ITA79 revealed that 34.6 percent had been committed solely as dangerous to self or others prior to 1979,

---

State Mental Hospitals," *American Journal of Psychiatry*, 142:104-7 (1985).

18. Ibid.
19. The analysis in this section employed the individual case records from King and Pierce counties.

20. Mary L. Durham and John Q. La Fond, "The Empirical Consequences and Policy Implications of Broadening the Statutory Criteria for Civil Commitment," *Yale Law and Policy Review* (in press).
21. A new patient is defined as an individual who has not been committed in Washington State before; an old patient is an individual with a prior commitment history in the state.

TABLE 2
COMMITMENTS FOR NEW AND OLD PATIENTS BY AUTHORITY, 1977-81

	September 1977 to August 1978		September 1978 to August 1979		September 1979 to August 1980		September 1980 to August 1981	
	Number	Percentage*	Number	Percentage*	Number	Percentage*	Number	Percentage*
New patients								
Grave disability	443	47.0	578	51.4	878	59.2	901	67.0
Danger to self	429	45.5	369	32.8	536	36.2	462	34.3
Danger to others	378	40.1	441	39.2	511	34.5	410	30.5
Danger to property	5	0.5	—	0.0	41	2.8	39	2.9
Total new patients, number and as percentage of total commitments	943	66.5%	1125	62.3%	1482	62.3%	1345	57.3%
Old patients								
Grave disability	257	54.0	376	55.3	642	71.6	747	74.5
Danger to self	138	29.0	210	30.9	166	18.5	208	20.7
Danger to others	210	44.1	294	43.2	363	40.5	386	38.5
Danger to property	—	0.0	2	0.3	41	4.6	42	4.2
Total old patients, number and as percentage of total commitments	476	33.5%	680	37.7%	897	37.7%	1003	42.7%
Total commitments	1419	100.0%	1805	100.0%	2379	100.0%	2348	100.0%

SOURCE: Mary L. Durham, "The Empirical Consequences and Policy Implications of Broadening the Statutory Criteria for Civil Commitment," *Yale Law and Policy Review* 3:395-446 (1985). Reprinted by permission. Data are from individual case records from King and Pierce counties.

NOTE: Counts of cases are duplicated where more than one authority was cited as a basis for commitment; except for total commitments, percentages will therefore not sum to 100.

*Percentage is the result of dividing the number of new—or old—patients in an authority type by the total number of new—or old—patients.

but were committed as gravely disabled following revision of the law.[22]

While there is considerable overlap in the type of behavior most often associated with each type of commitment authority, patterns do emerge (see Table 3). Bizarre behavior—disruptive behavior that is troublesome and annoying to the community—which occurs frequently in all categories of authority, is most often mentioned in conjunction with other types of behavior. The category of grave disability known as "health and safety" suggests passive neglect on the patient's part. Passive neglect is also suggested by cognitive and volitional impairment, but such impairment appears to represent more active, threatening behavior. Not surprisingly, danger to oneself reflects an affirmative act of self-destruction such as suicidal behavior and drug or alcohol abuse.

Analysis of trends from 1977 to 1981 indicates that there has been a shift in the primary authority used to commit individuals who perform violent acts. In 1977, danger to others was used to commit 79.4 percent of patients who had engaged in violent behavior, compared to 32.5 percent of cases where grave disability was used. By 1981, grave disability was being used more often to commit patients who had performed violent acts—in 65.1 percent of cases—than police-power authority—namely, dangerousness to others, used in 60.7 percent of the cases. Inasmuch as commitment officials can use multiple types of authority as a basis for detention—for example, grave disability and dangerousness—we can also observe a greater tendency to use dual commitment authorities following the implementation of ITA79.

22. Durham and La Fond, "Empirical Consequences and Policy Implications."

These findings suggest that the *parens patriae*-dominated system in Washington State has resulted from an ongoing trend toward reclassification of former patients under *parens patriae* authority and from greater use of that designation for new patients. In addition, there has been a definite shift in the reliance by county-designated mental health professionals on grave disability to commit those engaged in violent behavior.

SUMMARY AND CONCLUSION

It is not surprising that the 1979 revision of the commitment law brought about a dramatic increase in the number of involuntary hospitalizations in the state. The growing number of detentions conformed to legislative intent to broaden commitment authority. Our findings suggest that the revised law did not result in the detention of new types of patients in terms of factors such as age, sex, diagnosis, and so forth; rather, it made the process by which their hospitalization occurred involuntary. Patients whose previous hospitalizations were on a voluntary basis were likely to return as involuntary patients following the enactment of ITA79. The growing number of mentally ill persons who were committed involuntarily for the first time following ITA79 returned as readmissions in later years, thus establishing an ongoing relationship with the involuntary system.

As new and returning patients entered the involuntary system, an increasing number was committed as gravely disabled rather than as dangerous to self or others. Within one year after ITA79 was implemented, grave disability had outstripped dangerousness as the most frequently used commitment authority. While part of the

TABLE 3
TYPES OF BEHAVIOR ASSOCIATED WITH COMMITMENT AUTHORITY (Percentage)

			Characteristic Behavior						
	Bizarre behavior*	Health- and safety- related behavior†	Cognitive and volitional behavior‡	Violence§	Threatened violence‖	Active emotional upset#	Passive emotional upset**	Sucidal ideation††	Suicide Attempt‡‡
Gravely disabled									
Health and safety reasons	61.3	54.2	53.8						
Cognitive and volitional reasons	67.0	43.4	50.8			32.5			
Danger to others	62.0		33.0	68.3	42.3				
Danger to self	36.1						46.8	37.3	33.2

SOURCE: Durham, "The Empirical Consequences and Policy Implications of Broadening the Statutory Criteria for Civil Commitment," *Yale Law and Policy Review* 3:395-446 (1985). Reprinted by permission.

NOTE: Reasons for detention are recorded by the county-designated mental health professional in the mental health record. Because numerous behaviors, or reasons, may have been recorded for a single client, the sums of these percentages across rows or columns exceed 100.
*Includes active hallucinations, delusions, paranoia, obsessions, incoherent speech, and poor impulse control not stated as harmful or hazardous but disruptive or disturbing to others.
†Includes neglecting self, not eating, losing weight, having no money, wandering, not being responsible for self, environment, or children, being incontinent, not washing, and being unable to sleep.
‡Includes being confused, disoriented, or dazed; memory loss is a characteristic; "decompensation" is mentioned in the data file.
§An explicit act of violence toward others that did or could have done harm.
‖Threat of violence to others, such as verbal threats, gestures, or harassment.
#Includes agitation, running away, and verbal abuse.
**Includes depression, despondence, not speaking, so-called nervous breakdown, so-called emotional upheaval, being withdrawn or catatonic, crying, shaking, and regression.
††Sucidal ideas are mentioned as reason for referral.
‡‡Unsuccessful, explicit suicide attempt by any active means.

increased frequency of commitments for grave disability was due to the use of grave disability as the basis for admission of new patients, it appears that part of the increased use of this criterion resulted from reclassification of patients who in prior years had been committed solely on grounds of dangerousness to self or others. By the final year of the study, grave disability was more likely to be used than dangerousness as the detention authority for patients who exhibited violent behavior.

In broadening the involuntary civil commitment statutes in 1979, the Washington legislature made decisions that directly and indirectly influenced the allocation of mental health resources for mentally ill persons. Civil commitment became focused almost exclusively on involuntary patients, and the number of voluntary admissions to the state mental hospital system was reduced drastically. While private hospitals might have provided services for some involuntary and voluntary patients, it appears unlikely that they did so. Private mental health facilities in King County, Washington's largest county, showed little change in the number of involuntary hospitalizations. As most involuntary patients are indigent,[23] their ability to pay for mental health services through private sources is severely limited. It appears that without resources to pay for mental health services, people must be involuntarily hospitalized or manage on their own—sometimes with the support of family or community agencies established for a somewhat different purpose.

The lesson to be learned from Washington State's experience with civil commitment is that changes in the law that broaden commitment authority can indeed lead to a variety of changes in behavior—or, at the very least, laws will be passed that reflect changing patterns of behavior. Perhaps more important is that legislators must look beyond the specific intent of a law to estimate the impact of a statutory change on other aspects of a very complex human services system.

23. Legislative Budget Committee, "Joint Study of the Washington State Involuntary Treatment Act" (Office of Program Research, Washington House of Representatives, 1983).

Indexing Civil Commitment in Psychiatric Emergency Rooms

By STEVEN P. SEGAL, MARGARET A. WATSON, and L. SCOTT NELSON

ABSTRACT: A reliable prototype index, Three Ratings of Involuntary Admissibility (TRIAD), was developed to reflect the way psychiatric emergency room clinicians apply legal criteria for involuntary commitment. The interrater reliability coefficients—Pearson's r—of the TRIAD system for rating patients are 0.94, danger-to-self score; 0.89, danger-to-others score; 0.77, grave-disability score; and 0.89, total-admissibility score. TRIAD scores accounted for 82 percent of 89 disposition decisions in two metropolitan county hospital psychiatric emergency rooms. Study results indicate that (1) psychiatric emergency room clinicians shared constructs of danger to self, danger to others, and grave disability; (2) these constructs are reliably applied in actual cases; (3) TRIAD is a valid reflection of these constructs; and (4) case disposition is predictable from the severity of the patient's status with regard to these criteria.

Steven P. Segal, Ph.D., is professor and director of the Mental Health and Social Welfare Research Group of the School of Social Welfare, University of California, Berkeley, and principal investigator at the Institute for Scientific Analysis.

Margaret A. Watson, D.S.W., is project director, Institute for Scientific Analysis; assistant clinical professor of psychiatry, University of California, San Francisco; and visiting lecturer in social welfare, University of California, Berkeley.

L. Scott Nelson, D.S.W., is a research specialist in the Mental Health and Social Welfare Research Group, School of Social Welfare, University of California, Berkeley, and the Institute for Scientific Analysis. At the Mental Research Institute, Palo Alto, he serves as a director of the Family Stress and Coping Project. He also maintains a private clinical practice in El Cerrito.

NOTE: This research was supported by NCHSR grant number HS04564, NIMH grant number MH37310, and the University of California, Berkeley, Campus Committee on Research.

CIVIL commitment of the mentally ill poses a major dilemma for mental health professionals throughout the nation. Given persistent ambiguities in commitment statutes and the difficulty inherent in predicting behavior, clinicians must make commitment decisions that may, on the one hand, violate individual rights or, on the other, result in the neglect of community safety or of individuals who need care and treatment. While it is generally agreed that commitment is necessary in some cases, there is widespread concern that the commitment process is irrational, arbitrary, and discriminatory.[1] Further, these laws and practices have been seriously questioned by the courts.[2]

Most efforts to prevent improper use of commitment have focused on procedural safeguards to ensure the protections of due process.[3] Due process implies the existence of a standard that is consistently applied in all cases. To a large extent legislatures and courts have left the substantive interpretation of commitment criteria to professional discretion.[4] They have assumed that, despite lack of evidence for accuracy in predicting behavior, there are professional standards that can be consistently applied. In view of this assumption, it is surprising to find that of the several studies that have examined clinical reasons for admission decisions,[5] none has attempted to describe the clinical application of legal or statutory criteria.

According to Schwitzgebel, most states specify two or three criteria for involuntary commitment.[6] Criteria of danger to self or others, or likelihood of serious harm to self or others, are usually combined with a criterion similar to California's grave-disability standard.[7] While state statutes vary in the degree of restrictiveness implied by their wording, "the trend has been to narrow the population of those who may be committed."[8] As the California statute was a harbinger of this trend when first implemented in 1969, information about its application by clinicians may be presumed to be relevant to most other states as well.

Criteria for civil commitment in California were established by the Lanterman-Petris-Short Act (LPS),[9] but the law provides very little in the way of definitions for these standards.[10] The commitment process begins with a 72-

---

1. Bruce J. Ennis and Thomas R. Litwack, "Psychiatry and the Presumption of Expertise: Flipping Coins in the Courtroom," *California Law Review*, 62:693-752 (1974).

2. See, for example, *Lessard v. Schmidt*, 349 F. Supp. 1078 (E.D. Wisc. 1972), vacated and remanded, 94 Sup. Ct. 713 (1974); *O'Connor v. Donaldson*, 422 U.S. 563 (1975).

3. Paul R. Friedman and Jane B. Yohalem, "The Rights of the Chronic Mental Patient," in *The Chronic Mental Patient*, ed. John A. Talbott (Washington, DC: American Psychiatric Association, 1978).

4. Paul S. Appelbaum and Robert M. Hamm, "Decision to Seek Commitment," *Archives of General Psychiatry*, 39:447-51 (1982).

5. See, for example, Richard H. Allen et al., "A Multi-Tiered Screening System for the Least Restrictive Setting," *American Journal of Psychiatry*, 137:968-71 (1980); Arthur T. Meyerson et al., "Influence of Experience on Major Clinical Decisions: Training Implications," *Archives of General Psychiatry*, 36:423-27 (1979).

6. R. Kirkland Schwitzgebel, "Survey of Civil Commitment Statutes," in *Civil Commitment and Social Policy*, A. L. McGarry et al. (Washington, DC: Government Printing Office, 1981).

7. "Welfare and Institutions Code," in *West's Annotated California Codes* (St. Paul, MN: West, 1980), chap. 2, §5150.

8. Paul D. Lipsitt, "Emergency Admission of Civil Involuntary Patients to Mental Hospitals Following Statutory Modification," in *Civil Commitment and Social Policy*, McGarry et al.

9. "Welfare and Institutions Code" §5000-5401.

10. See, for example, ibid., §5008, 5150.

hour emergency detention for observation and treatment. While a variety of mental health and law enforcement officials are authorized to begin this process, the critical decision about hospitalization is made by personnel in the psychiatric emergency rooms of general hospitals. No data have been compiled to indicate how these clinicians apply legal commitment criteria.

According to LPS, emergency involuntary hospitalization requires that the person be suffering from a mental disorder, as a result of which he or she is dangerous to self or to others or gravely disabled. Thus, the law requires that two separate assessments—as to mental disorder and as to danger or disability—be made with little statutory guidance. In failing to provide clear definitions and criteria for the commitment standard the legislature evidently intended that these determinations be guided by clinical judgment.

The criteria that have been the focus of greatest concern are those of dangerousness and grave disability. Schwitzgebel and Swenson have noted an uncertainty among clinicians about how key provisions of the involuntary commitment law should be interpreted, and they have raised the possibility of a corresponding inconsistency in its application. But their findings do not belie the existence of a body of relevant clinical opinion, nor do they tell us in what particular ways and to what extent applications of the commitment law are in fact inconsistent.[11]

While a number of studies over two decades are widely cited to suggest that admission decisions are significantly and inappropriately influenced by social characteristics of the patient or the emergency room setting, many of the findings are contradictory, and studies report a role for social factors that is secondary to that of the "severity of illness."[12] This is usually a global concept that includes violent or suicidal activity or an inability to care for oneself. Moreover, most previous studies of determinants of admission decisions are seriously flawed. The conclusions of these studies are valid only to the extent that all significant variables that influence the admission decision were included in the analysis. Yet studies purportedly demonstrating the sociodemographic or environmental determinants of admission decisions have not specifically considered the influence of legal commitment criteria as they are clinically construed and applied.[13] Indeed, only two studies included as an independent variable a clinical assessment of the patient with regard to a legal criterion for commitment.[14] The results of these two studies are striking and suggest that admission decisions may be explained in terms relevant to the legal criteria. However, these studies refer to only two subgroups of patients who may pose a danger to themselves or others, and they do not address the grave-disability criterion. No study to our knowledge has

11. R. Kirkland Schwitzgebel and Edwin W. Swensen, *Evaluation of Involuntary Care and Treatment under the Lanterman-Petris-Short Act* (Sacramento: State of California, Department of Mental Health, 1981).

12. Appelbaum and Hamm, "Decision to Seek Commitment."

13. See, for example, Allen et al., "A Multi-Tiered Screening System"; Meyerson et al., "Influence of Experience on Major Clinical Decisions."

14. Charles H. Browning, Robert L. Tyson, and Sheldon I. Miller, "A Study of Psychiatric Emergencies: Part II. Suicide," *Psychiatry in Medicine,* 1:359-66 (1970); Larry Kirstein et al., "Utilization Review of Treatment for Suicide Attempts," *American Journal of Psychiatry,* 132:22-27 (1975).

used an independent rating by an observer other than the evaluating clinician of the patients' status on any of the legal criteria.

In short, it is too soon to conclude that mental health professionals are unable to achieve substantial agreement and consistency in applying involuntary admission criteria. Further research is warranted to establish (1) the extent to which there is already agreement among clinicians as to the meaning of the criteria and (2) the extent to which there is consistency in their application. Note that the question being addressed here is not the predictive validity of emergency psychiatric assessments but, rather, the prior question of whether clinicians respond to similar cases with similar judgments.

In this article we report the preliminary results of efforts to develop a tool to describe clinical application of legal commitment criteria in psychiatric emergency rooms.

METHOD

In an attempt to reflect the way clinicians in psychiatric emergency rooms interpret and apply the legal criteria of danger to self, danger to others, and grave disability, we developed a prototype index, Three Ratings of Involuntary Admissibility (TRIAD). The instrument was developed through an iterative process resulting in the identification and ranking of patterns of behavior and circumstance more and less likely to lead to a determination that a patient is involuntarily admissible by LPS standards.

Rationale

A conceptual distinction was made between the assessment of dangerousness and grave disability per se and other clinical assessments—such as diagnosis and response to treatment—that the emergency room clinicians must make from the same information base. Noting that emergency room clinicians often ask themselves, "Is this person holdable?" we hypothesized that the term "holdable" represents a shared construct that we labeled "involuntary admissibility." The question "Is this person holdable?" is the equivalent of the question "To what extent does this person meet the clinician's idea or understanding of the legal criteria for involuntary admissibility?" The construct of involuntary admissibility includes the constructs danger to self, danger to others, and grave disability.

The disposition of a given case will also be influenced by the clinical assessment of legal standards not reflected in TRIAD—for example, the presence or absence of mental disorder—and in addition may be influenced by intervening factors that are not derived from legal standards of admissibility. The study of the influence of such legally extraneous factors as available bed space should proceed from a clear understanding of how much variance in decisions is already explained by application of the legal criteria. Hence, TRIAD represents an attempt to answer a logically prior question.

Development of TRIAD began with a review of clinical texts and articles on emergency psychiatric assessment and a survey of the literature on the prediction of violent behavior, including suicide. Indicators of dangerousness and grave disability were listed, and an effort was made to anticipate the process by which clinicians might combine information relevant to these indicators to arrive at a judgment in any particular case. Our reasoning in the design of TRIAD was as follows. The inference that a person may be a danger to himself or herself or others, or gravely disabled, may be suggested to a clinician by a limited number of current behaviors, such as a suicidal threat or ruminations, an angry outburst, or refusal to eat. These behaviors are of greater concern when they appear as part of a particular constellation of behaviors and circumstances, as when a suicide threat follows the death of a spouse, than when they appear as part of a different constellation of behaviors and circumstances, such as when a suicide threat occurs during a domestic dispute that has since been resolved. The clinician's assessment is therefore a clustering process.[15]

We reasoned that other investigations had failed to reveal regularities in the decision-making process because they had merely sought statistical correlations between assorted variables in the clinical or social picture and an isolated presenting behavior, such as suicidal threat. It seemed to us that in order to understand and predict admission decisions it was necessary first to describe each presenting behavior in its clinically relevant dimensions and then assign a value to it as a cluster or pattern vis-à-vis other presenting problems— clusters or patterns—that are superficially similar but clinically different.

Suicidal threats, for example, have different clinical values depending on whether they are accompanied by a specific plan, are in the context of recent losses or other ominous changes in the patient's life, and/or whether the patient responds to crisis-intervention efforts with a broadened perspective and a more hopeful outlook.[16] A number of other dimensions are also relevant to the evaluation of suicide threats, and each of these can be operationalized. Finally, these dimensions combine to form coherent patterns or clusters that can be ranked in terms of the likelihood that the clinician will find them to provide grounds for admission. A number of other patterns, made up of different presenting behaviors and related dimensions, may carry roughly the same weight in assessment of danger to self as the suicide-threat cluster described earlier. Others will carry slightly more weight and still others much less.

We theorized that through professional training and experience clinicians are sensitized to clusters or patterns of behavior and circumstance that are associated with danger to self, danger to others, and grave disability and, moreover, that they internalize certain clinical criteria or scales by which they weigh or rank these patterns, some of which are of equivalent rank. Thus, clinicians will react to some patterns as unambiguously dangerous or not dangerous, and they will consistently respond to these patterns with decisions that a person is admissible or not admissible under involuntary hospitalization criteria.

We predicted, therefore, that admission decisions will be highly consistent among clinicians in cases involving unambiguous patterns thought to be associated with dangerousness and grave disability. Other patterns will be experienced as more ambiguous, and

15. Roy R. Grinker, "Diagnosis and Schizophrenia," in *Schizophrenic Reactions,* ed. Robert Cancro (New York: Brunner/Mazel, 1970).

16. Arthur T. Meyerson, Robert A. Glick, and Ari Kiev, "Suicide," in *Psychiatric Emergencies,* Robert A. Glick et al. (New York: Grune & Stratton, 1976); Andrew E. Slaby, Julian Lieb, and Laurence R. Tancredi, *Handbook of Psychiatric Emergencies* (New York: Medical Examination, 1975).

this ambiguity will lead to greater variation in the outcome of the decision-making process. This hypothesis is supported by the findings of Meyerson and his colleagues that clinician experience affected admission decisions in the middle range of illness severity but, at the extremes of illness severity, experienced and inexperienced clinicians admitted patients at the same rate.[17]

Expecting that many patients would present complaints or behaviors related to more than one of the legal criteria, we further hypothesized that an ambiguous presentation on any one criterion would be more likely to lead to a decision that the person was admissible if it was accompanied by at least a low-level presentation on another criterion. For example, a person who presented some moderate threat to the safety of others would more likely be judged admissible if he also seemed to present a moderate or mild potential for harming himself. Thus, we expected that in these cases a total score across scales would also predict the clinician's judgment.

Observations

Using successive drafts of TRIAD, we observed evaluation interviews in Psychiatric Emergency Services (PES) of San Francisco General Hospital and Highland General Hospital, Oakland. These are the major emergency evaluation units for the two largest San Francisco Bay Area counties. Eighty-nine patients were chosen on the basis of their availability at a time when an observer was free to follow a new case. Observation was refused in only four cases. Observers, who were psychiatric social workers experienced in assessment of acutely disturbed persons, followed a patient and the assigned clinician for as long as the patient remained in the PES, usually for a period of several hours. TRIAD was scored by the observer when a dispositional decision had been reached by the evaluating clinician. The clinician handling the case was not involved in the scoring process.

Each case observation was followed by debriefing of the evaluating clinician in order to elicit any pertinent considerations not yet reflected by the instrument. Items and patterns were then edited or added, and patterns were reranked to incorporate the new information. The resiliency of the index was tested in additional interviews with clinicians and in two psychiatric emergency staff case conferences in which we asked clinicians to present unusual cases they thought would stump the instrument. Continued observation of more than 50 cases failed to yield new items or patterns. A 44-page manual was developed to instruct raters on the use of each item.

Interrater reliability of the sixth draft of TRIAD was tested in joint observation of the last 30 of the 89 cases. Clinicians observed in this phase of the study were given very little information about our purpose and no information about the instrument. Pairs of observers were permitted to sit in while staff clinicians evaluated patients.

In addition to TRIAD itself, the TRIAD Context Form was also developed to gather data on variables other than dangerousness and grave disability that have been found by other researchers to influence hospital admissions.[18]

---

17. Meyerson et al., "Influence of Experience on Major Clinical Decisions."

18. See, for example, Ronald J. Diamond, "The Role of the Hospital in Treating the Chronically Disabled," in *Community Support*

RESULTS

The result of our literature review, observation of actual cases, and debriefing of clinicians was the development of an easily scored instrument, TRIAD, consisting of three scales organized as checklists. The three checklists consist of a total of 88 numbered items that can be combined to yield 156 patterns of behavior and circumstance relevant to the clinical prediction of violence and suicide and the assessment of grave disability. On each of the scales, a number of patterns are assigned to the highest score, a number are assigned to the next highest score, and so on.

No pattern combines more than nine items, and most involve two, three, or four items. For example, "threatened to harm another" is one item that, by itself, would receive a score of 2—a moderate level—on the danger-to-others scale. However, such a threat may yield a score of 4—the highest score—if it occurs in combination with three other items. The first additional item has to do with provocation or lack thereof. The others involve indications of having a concrete plan and/or weapon, and/or being in a volatile or unpredictable or enraged state—operationalized by six sub-items—and/or having a history of assault. According to our hypothesis, if such a presenting picture is accompanied by a mental disorder, the evaluating clinician will determine that the patient is clearly admissible by LPS standards. In order to prevent hospitalization, the clinician may attempt to bring about some change in the picture through crisis intervention or medication in the emergency room, but if these efforts fail, admission will follow. If the efforts succeed, the danger-to-others score will be lower than it would otherwise have been. Other patterns seem equally clear, but some are more ambiguous and yield intermediate scores.

TRIAD is scored at the time of disposition by finding the standard pattern represented by the items checked during the evaluation that are applicable at that time and that yield the highest scores.

Interrater reliability

Three pairs of observers rated 10 cases each and achieved interrater reliability coefficients—Pearson's r—of 0.94 for the danger-to-self score; 0.89 for the danger-to-others score; 0.77 for the grave-disability score; and 0.89 for the total admissibility score. These results demonstrated that it is possible to use this instrument reliably to rate actual cases in the psychiatric emergency room.

Patient characteristics

Of the patients observed, 62 percent were white, 69 percent were male, 65 percent were between 26 and 44 years of age, 87 percent were born in the United States, and 94 percent were fluent in English. A sizable portion—47 percent—had never been married; 63 percent had 10 to 12 years of education; 70 percent were out of the job market as a result of disability, and 54 percent were receiving Supplemental Security Income due to this unemployment. Most—74 percent—were brought to the psychiatric emergency room by police officers. The

---

Systems for the Long-Term Patient, ed. Leonard I. Stein (San Francisco: Jossey-Bass, 1979); Werner M. Mendel and Samuel Rapport, "Determinants of the Decision for Psychiatric Hospitalization," *Archives of General Psychiatry,* 20:321-28 (1969).

officers had placed most of the patients— 64 percent—on involuntary holds on grounds of danger to self, for 63 percent; danger to others, 53 percent; and/or grave disability, 37 percent. Patients were more likely to receive a diagnosis of psychosis than of nonpsychotic disorder. About two-thirds of the patients were given diagnoses of schizophrenia, major affective disorder, brief reactive psychosis, or dementia, delirium, or hallucinosis. The remaining patients—34 percent—were given nonpsychotic diagnoses or had no Axis I diagnosis of mental disorder.[19]

Examination of available data on the populations of patients seen in these two emergency rooms indicates that, although the subjects were not chosen at random, there appears to have been no systematic bias in selecting the study sample.

Psychiatrists evaluated 55 percent of the cases; 18 percent were evaluated by nurses, 18 percent by social workers, and 8 percent by other professionals, paraprofessionals, or unlicensed professionals in training. The evaluators' clinical experience ranged from 2 to 23 years, and the emergency psychiatric experience of the clinicians ranged from less than six months to 13 years. Of the patients observed, 93 percent were examined by clinicans with 2 years or more of PES experience.

The number of patients evaluated in the emergency service on the day of our observations ranged from 14 to 32, and in most cases was 20 to 26. Average occupancy rates for the inpatient wards at the two hospitals during the study period were 94 percent and 91 percent.

19. The diagnoses refer to various categories in American Psychiatric Association, *Diagnostic and Statistical Manual of Mental Disorders,* 3rd ed. (Washington, DC: American Psychiatric Association, 1980).

Severity of presenting problems

The major independent variable was the overall severity of the patient's clinical presentation on the three legal criteria measured by TRIAD. Severity is the degree to which the patient's presentation on any one criterion or across criteria corresponds to the hypothesized construct of involuntary admissibility. Severity scores take into account individual TRIAD scale scores—namely, scores on the danger-to-self scale (DSS), the danger-to-others scale (DOS), and the grave-disability scale (GDS)—and also the sum of all TRIAD scale scores, the total score.

Our observations led us to believe that if the patient does not present a strong picture of admissibility on any one criterion, the overall picture—moderate or low-level presentation on more than one criterion—becomes most relevant to the disposition. In our analysis, therefore, we attended not only to the patient's presentation on individual criteria, but also to the overall presentation.

The severity score is a summary of the TRIAD assessment. The highest severity level, 4, is made up of the highest scores. Of the patients in our sample, 62, or 70 percent, scored at the highest severity level. The next highest level of severity—reflected by a total score of three with a score of two on one scale, namely DSS, DOS, or GDS— involved only 2 patients, or 2.2 percent. The 9 patients—10.1 percent—who scored at severity level 2 rated only a moderate score on danger to self or others or grave disability. The lowest level of severity, reflected by DSS, DOS, and GDS scores of zero or one, was scored by 16 patients, or 18 percent. (See Table 1.)

The authors predicted that patients scoring at level 4 of severity would be judged by clinicians to be definitely admissible; those at levels 3 and 2 presented a more ambiguous basis for decision; and those at level 1 would not be viewed as admissible under LPS criteria.

Disposition

Disposition was consistent with TRIAD severity scores in 82 percent of the cases (gamma = 0.82); and agreement was roughly equivalent for both hospitals. After the initial evaluation, which often extended over several hours, 58 patients, or 65 percent, were retained—that is, admitted to an inpatient ward, assigned to a PES holding bed for up to 24 hours, or transferred to another facility for further evaluation or admission.

As expected, the most and least severe presentations were most predictive of disposition; 84 percent and 81 percent of the predictions, respectively, were correct. The high scorers who were retained and the low scorers who were released are the true positives and true negatives, respectively. The false negatives are patients who scored low on TRIAD but were retained by the clinicians; in Table 1, these are the 3 level-1 patients retained involuntarily. The false positives are the high scorers who were released by the clinicians; in Table 1, these are the 10 level-4 patients who were released. At severity level 1, there were 13 patients, or 81 percent, who were released and 3, or 19 percent, who were retained.

Severity levels 2 and 3 represent the hypothesized ambiguous range on TRIAD. Severity level 2 also turned out to be quite discriminating, with 78 percent of that level's patients—7 cases—released and 22 percent—two patients—retained. At severity level 2 the picture presented by the patients was ambiguous, but at this level of severity clinicians were inclined to let the patient go. The least predictive score configuration represents the situation in which the patient presented only a moderate degree of concern on any one criterion but raised one other issue at a low level, providing an overall configuration severity score of three. With only two cases at this level, level 3, the figures of 50 percent released and 50 percent admitted are inconclusive. However, the difference between severity levels 2 and 3 does suggest that the index is capable of representing salient dimensions of the decision-making process at a fine level. Future observations will be necessary to test our hypothesis that severity level 3 represents more ambiguous situations that provide wider latitude for clinical discretion.

Most of the 89 patients—69.7 percent—scored at the highest level of severity. Table 2 describes the disposition of patients at severity level 4 according to whether their high score resulted from danger to self—8 percent of the total sample; danger to others—35 percent; grave disabililty—38 percent; or a combination—2 percent of the total sample. Twelve patients—13 percent—scored at the highest level on two scales.

Of the patients whose scores on the scales measuring danger to others and grave disability put them into the highest severity level, 87 percent and 97 percent, respectively, were retained. Of the seven patients who attained the highest severity level by reason of a high danger-to-self score, five, or 71 percent,

TABLE 1
DISPOSITION OF CASE BY SEVERITY LEVEL (N = 89)

Severity Level	Released		Retained Voluntarily		Retained Involuntarily		Total	
	Number	Percentage	Number	Percentage	Number	Percentage	Number	Percentage
Level 1 DSS, DOS, GDS* = 0 or 1; total = 3 or less	13	81	0	0	3	19	16	100
Level 2 DSS, DOS, GDS* = 2; total = 2	7	78	0	0	2	22	9	100
Level 3 DSS, DOS, GDS* = 2; total = 3	1	50	0	0	1	50	2	100
Level 4 DSS, DOS, GDS* = 3 or 4; total = 4 or more	10	16	4	7	48	77	62	100
Total	31		4		54		89	

SOURCE: From Steven P. Segal, Margaret A. Watson, and L. Scott Nelson, "Applications of Involuntary Admission Criteria in Psychiatric Emergency Rooms," *Social Work*, vol. 30, no. 2 (March-April 1985), p. 163. Copyright 1985, National Association of Social Workers, Inc. Reprinted with permission.

*DDS = danger-to-self scale score; DOS = danger-to-others scale score; GDS = grave-disability scale score.

TABLE 2
DISPOSITION OF CASES AT SEVERITY LEVEL 4
BY SCALE OR TOTAL SCORE

Score Qualifying Case for Severity Level 4	Released		Retained Voluntarily		Retained Involuntarily		Total	
	Number	Percentage	Number	Percentage	Number	Percentage	Number	Percentage
Danger to self = 3 or 4	5	71	0	0	2	29	7	100
Danger to others = 3 or 4	4	13	2	6	25	81	31	100
Grave disability = 3	1	3	2	6	31	91	34	100
Total score = 4 or more but no scale score = 3 or 4	0	0	0	0	2	100	2	100
Total	10		4		60		74	

SOURCE: From Segal, Watson, and Nelson, "Applications of Involuntary Admission Critieria," *Social Work*, vol. 30, no. 2 (March-April 1985), p. 163. Copyright 1985, National Association of Social Workers, Inc. Reprinted with permission.
NOTE: N = 62; 12 cases scored at the highest level on two scales.

were released, contrary to our expectation, and two, 29 percent, were retained.

Diagnosis

Disposition must, according to the LPS statute, be influenced by clinical considerations in addition to dangerousness and grave disability. The presence or absence of a mental disorder and the severity of the disorder were major criteria of concern. To the extent that the presence or absence of psychosis captured those concerns, we were able to report their influence on disposition.

To facilitate analysis, Axis-I diagnoses[20] were categorized as psychotic, such as major functional and organic mental disorders, and nonpsychotic, such as anxiety, adjustment, psychosexual, impulse-control, substance-use disorders, and conditions not attributable to a mental disorder. While the presence of psychosis was moderately related to severity of presentation on TRIAD (gamma = 0.53), it was strongly related to disposition (gamma = 0.79), although not as strongly as TRIAD severity was (gamma = 0.82). Thus, it appears that severity of dangerousness and grave disability, on the one hand, and presence or absence of psychosis, on the other, make partially independent contributions to the explanation of disposition. Not surprisingly, the relationship between disposition and TRIAD severity was stronger for nonpsychotic patients (gamma = 0.89) than for psychotic patients (gamma = 0.74). Presence or absence of psychosis is helpful in explaining dispositions that differ from those predicted by the TRIAD score.

20. Ibid.

Discrepant cases

It appears that the best explanation for the discrepancy between TRIAD scores and disposition in the 10 false positive cases was the clinician's judgment in each case that admission was not clinically indicated. Process notes and clinician comments lead us to believe that clinicians did not doubt that these patients met the legal criteria; rather, they seemed to have decided on clinical grounds against hospitalizing these patients despite presentations on the legal criteria that would have justified holding them. Severity of mental disorder, insofar as it is reflected by the diagnosis, the availability of treatment alternatives, and the judgment that patients would not benefit from hospital care appear to have been the critical factors involved, although at least one release appears to have been influenced by nonclinical considerations.

The 10 high-scoring patients who were released—the false positives—were more likely to have nonpsychotic than psychotic diagnoses: six cases and four cases, respectively. Of the 4 patients diagnosed as psychotic, 2 had come to the hospital voluntarily and were thought by staff to be attempting to appear dangerous to self and others in order to obtain admission. The third false positive, a patient with senile dementia who was found disoriented in the street, was released voluntarily to a board-and-care home because hospitalization would have been of no value to him. The fourth and rather unique case in our experience involved the release of a patient with both a high TRIAD score and a psychotic diagnosis. This was a controversial case among PES staff. The disposition appeared to have been motivated by concerns that were substantially unrelated to the patient's situation, but that cannot be further described without risking a breach of confidentiality.

At lower levels of severity, also, the variance in disposition seems to be partially explained by severity of mental disorder. The six patients who were retained involuntarily despite lower severity levels—severity levels of 3, 2, or 1—were more likely to have psychotic diagnoses—83 percent—and were more often referred by medical or mental health professionals—50 percent—than the sample as a whole—22 percent. However, the small number of cases renders these differences inconclusive.

COMMENT

The results of this preliminary study strongly suggest that clinicians in the San Francisco Bay Area urban psychiatric emergency rooms employed shared constructs of danger to self, danger to others, and grave disability, and that these constructs can be reliably applied in actual cases. At least in observed cases, most involuntary admissions were predictable from the severity of the patients' status with respect to these criteria. Further, it appeared that these shared constructs can be operationalized to provide a behavioral description of how a patient comes to be seen as admissible under one or more of the involuntary admission standards.

The study provides a test of TRIAD as an instrument that can describe the process and content of these clinicians' judgments about whether a patient meets legal standards for involuntary admission. In this instance, the concurrent measure was disposition. By this criterion, the construct validity of the scales of danger to others and grave disability was supported. Also supported was the validity of the total TRIAD score as a measure of the construct of "involuntary admissibility."

However, the validity of the danger-to-self scale has yet to be demonstrated. Because so few patients received high scores on danger to self, the results are less convincing than those for the other two scales. Although the scale included some items to capture the basis for clinicians' suspicions of being manipulated, we were apparently not successful in capturing it sufficiently. On the other hand, this scale may hold up better in settings with more inpatient resources and a less transient, more economically advantaged population with less apparent secondary gain from clinically unnecessary hospitalization.

While disposition proved to be a useful concurrent measure of the construct validity of TRIAD, it has some obvious limitations. Factors beyond the clinicians' assessment of the patients' dangerousness and disability appropriately influence disposition. Other legal criteria include the willingness of the patient to accept treatment, the presence of mental disorder, and the availability of less restrictive alternatives. Clinical considerations include the severity of symptoms and the likelihood that the patient will benefit from hospitalization.

These additional clinical and legal considerations overlap in the area of symptom severity. Not surprisingly, disposition was related almost as strongly to the presence or absence of psychosis as to severity of the patient's presentation on the key legal criteria. The important point here, however, is that patients were rarely admitted unless they presented, in addition to psychosis, behavior strongly suggestive of danger to self, danger to others, or grave disability. Both psychotic and nonpsychotic patients who did not present such behavior were, with rare exceptions, released.

Judging by TRIAD scores, clinicians in our study tended to err, if indeed they did err, in the direction of releasing patients rather than treating them in the hospital. In doing so, they were apparently considering the severity of mental disorder, the availability of alternatives, and the likelihood that the patient would benefit from hospitalization.

If additional research on TRIAD establishes that it continues to reflect the way clinicians interpret the legal criteria, the discussion of emergency involuntary commitment criteria and procedures should be greatly facilitated. TRIAD could provide a very useful description of the state of patients considered involuntarily admissible as well as assurance that it is possible to apply the legal criteria consistently and equitably.

How Did *Tarasoff* Affect Clinical Practice?

By WILLIAM J. BOWERS, DANIEL J. GIVELBER
and CAROLYN L. BLITCH

ABSTRACT: The *Tarasoff* decisions of the California Supreme Court in 1974 and 1976 held that psychotherapists could be held liable for failing to protect the victims of their potentially violent patients. Our survey of psychiatrists, psychologists, and social workers in eight metropolitan areas showed that Californians were more likely to have heard of the case, to believe it required warning the likely victim, and actually to issue warnings in such cases than were psychotherapists from other jurisdictions. Therapists were more willing to take steps to protect victims in 1980 than in 1975, but willingness to warn increased more among Californians than among those in other states. We conclude that although *Tarasoff* has influenced therapists' attitudes and behavior more in California than elsewhere, the case has also affected psychotherapeutic practice nationally.

Dr. Bowers is director of the Center for Applied Social Research at Northeastern University, Boston, Massachusetts. He received his Ph.D. in sociology from Columbia University.

Professor Givelber is dean of the Law School at Northeastern University. He is a graduate of Harvard Law School.

Carolyn Blitch is senior research associate at the Center for Applied Social Research. She holds a master's degree in sociology from Northeastern University.

IN 1974 the California Supreme Court held in *Tarasoff* v. *Regents of the University of California* that when a psychotherapist reasonably believes that one of his or her patients presents a credible threat of physical danger to another identifiable person, the therapist has a legal obligation to warn the potential victim.[1] Should the therapist fail to discharge this obligation and the patient attacks the victim, then the therapist could be liable to the victim for money damages.

The 1974 *Tarasoff* decision was rendered in the face of a fervent argument by psychiatric associations that the proposed obligation contradicted the physicians' ethical mandate to center attention on the welfare of their patients and imperiled the therapeutic process itself by compromising confidentiality,[2] and, moreover, that it subjected therapists to potential liability for failing to predict what they claimed they could not—future violence. These arguments apparently moved the California Supreme Court to take the relatively unusual step of reconsidering the decision imposing a duty to warn on psychotherapists. Eighteen months later the court was evidently moved enough by the reargument to change the duty from warning the likely victim to one of exercising reasonable care for the protection of the victim.

The discharge of this duty may require the therapist to take one or more of various steps, depending on the nature of the case. Thus it may call for him to warn the intended victim or others likely to apprise the victim of the danger, to notify the police, or to take whatever other steps are reasonably necessary under the circumstances.[3]

In the court's view, the matter was clear: "The protective privilege ends where the public peril begins."[4] But if the psychiatric arguments are sound, the public peril may increase with the demise of the confidentiality said to be necessary for the effectiveness of psychotherapy, particularly psychotherapy with potentially violent persons.[5]

DETERRENCE THEORY,
TORT LAW, AND
THE *TARASOFF* RULING

Classic deterence theory holds that the perceived threat of legal sanctions, especially their certainty, severity, and celerity, will inhibit unlawful behavior, particularly when the perceived cost of the potential punishment outweighs the expected benefits of committing or continuing in the prohibited conduct.[6] While most deterrence studies have concentrated on the impact of criminal law, the same deterrence logic applies to the operation of tort law. In the tort system, those who injure others through substandard behavior are, in effect, punished under the law when a court orders

1. *Tarasoff* v. *Regents of the University of California*, 529 P.2d 553, 118 Cal. R. 129 (1974).

2. Brief for the American Psychiatric Association, Area VI of the Assembly of the American Psychiatric Association, Northern California Psychiatric Society, California State Psychological Association, San Francisco Psychoanalytic Institute and Society, California Society for Clinical Social Work, National Association of Social Workers, Golden Gate Chapter, and California Hospital Association as Amicus Curiae in Support of Petition for Rehearing of *Tarasoff* v. *Regents of the University of California* (1975).

3. *Tarasoff* v. *Regents of the University of California*, 551 P.2d 334, 131 Cal. R. 14 (1976).

4. Ibid., p. 347.

5. Alan A. Stone, "The *Tarasoff* Decisions: Suing Psychotherapists to Safeguard Society," *Harvard Law Review*, 90:358-78 (1976); Howard Gurevitz, "*Tarasoff*: Protective Privilege vs. Public Peril," *American Journal of Psychiatry*, 134:289-92 (1977).

6. Franklin Zimring and Gordon Hawkins, *Deterrence* (Chicago: University of Chicago Press, 1973).

them to pay damages to the persons they have injured.[7] Thus, persons who wish to avoid the possibility of being sued and held liable—or being sued even if not held liable—can be expected to regulate their behavior to conform with legally sanctioned standards of conduct.

Unlike the criminal law, the tort system is judicially administered and privately enforced. What actions or inactions are tortious is normally not the result of legislation but of standards of responsibility developed and applied by the courts. Whether violations of such standards will come to court does not depend on police or prosecutors but on the injured victims. Court-enforced standards of responsibility do not generally forbid or require specific actions but impose general duties and obligations that may be fulfilled in various ways. Moreover, the courts may change the law to include or exclude duties or parties to whom it applies, in accordance with evolving standards of responsibility as the courts define them. Thus, a person may be punished via the payment of damages for an action that is not specifically prohibited by statute or identified as tortious in a previous tort ruling.

It has been argued that the deterrent efficacy of criminal law is weak because it is generally applied to outsiders, for example, career criminals who have little stake in mainstream society. By contrast, tort law is usually applied to educated affluent persons in society's mainstream and often to the organizations in which they work, quite specifically because their financial resources are sufficient to make the private enforcement of a tort remedy worth pursuing. Because organizations as well as individuals can be sued and held liable, tort law may capitalize on the desires of both to avoid liability as an added impetus for compliance.

Of course, professionals who might be sued typically purchase malpractice insurance to offset the financial risk—though not the stigma or increased premiums that may result from being sued, even if not found liable. Yet malpractice insurance among the members of a profession tends also to spread and equalize the cost of noncompliance within the professional community; hence the professional community will have a stake in compliance among its constituent members.

A further implication of private enforcement is that when a court in one jurisdiction applies a broader tort standard, it is not only new law for that jurisdiction, but it may also be grounds for a lawsuit in other jurisdictions. Injured parties in another state can seek to have the newly articulated standard established as law in their own jurisdiction by bringing a suit on these grounds. Thus, while both criminal and tort law are jurisdictionally specific, the private enforcement and after-the-fact determination of liability in the tort system mean that persons and organizations may be sued on grounds that have succeeded in other jurisdictions and thus suffer the stigma and psychic distress of a lawsuit even if not found liable because the new standard is not adopted where they reside.

While these features of the tort system suggest why therapists might be responsive to *Tarasoff*, there are features of this ruling that also cut the other way. In the typical case, a suing patient claims that the provided treatment fell below the standard that a competent

---

7. William B. Schwartz and Neil K. Komesar, "Doctors, Damages, and Deterrence," *New England Journal of Medicine,* 298:1282-89 (1978).

physician would normally observe. Through the testimony of experts, the profession itself supplies the standard of care; courts simply enforce it. In *Tarasoff*, however, the court did not pretend that it was simply enforcing the customary professional standard when it held that psychotherapists had an obligation to warn or otherwise protect potential victims. Rather, the court itself articulated a new standard of professional practice based on its own view of wise social policy and announced that psychotherapists ignored it at their peril. Thus, as the professional associations argued, *Tarasoff* may require psychotherapists to contravene normal, competent clinical practice in order to avoid liability—to follow a course of conduct that a court, rather than psychotherapists, believes feasible and necessary.

In this article we examine *Tarasoff*'s impact on psychotherapeutic practice. We first explore what therapists know about the *Tarasoff* decision, what they understand it to mean, and whether they consider themselves bound by its prescriptions. We then turn to the effect of *Tarasoff* on their self-reported behavior and changes in their behavior over time. As we show, the decision has influenced therapists' beliefs and behavior. Finally, we consider why such influence occurred.

METHODOLOGY

Our analysis is based on a 1980 survey of psychiatrists, psychologists, and social workers in the eight largest metropolitan areas in the United States, as of the 1970 census. Psychotherapists were selected from the biographical directories of the American Psychiatric Association, the American Psychological Association, and the National Association of Social Workers. Questionnaires were mailed to 1000 members of each professional group stratified according to experience, type of practice, and location. The 1722 respondents —471 psychiatrists, 599 psychologists, and 652 social workers—were equally distributed among the eight urban areas—Boston, Chicago, Detroit, Washington, D.C., Los Angeles, New York, Philadelphia, and San Francisco. At the time of the survey, the *Tarasoff* ruling was the law in San Francisco and Los Angeles, but not elsewhere.[8]

In the survey instrument, we asked therapists two kinds of questions designed to reveal the possible impact of *Tarasoff*. One kind concerned their perceptions and beliefs about the *Tarasoff* decision itself: their knowledge of the case, their understanding of what it required, and their beliefs about whether and for what reasons it may apply to them. The other questions concerned their behavior when confronted with a *Tarasoff*-relevant situation: the steps they actually took in the "most recent case" in which they treated someone who might harm another person, and the steps they have become more willing to employ with potentially dangerous clients since the *Tarasoff* decision was handed down. Our purpose was to learn whether the behavior of therapists had come to incorporate the *Tarasoff* obligation, at least as they understood it.

FINDINGS

The analysis that follows examines, first, perceptions and beliefs therapists hold about *Tarasoff* and, second, the

---

8. For further details of sampling design and for selected portions of the questionnaire, see Daniel Givelber, William Bowers and Carolyn Blitch, "*Tarasoff*, Myth and Reality: An Empirical Investigation of Private Law in Action," *Wisconsin Law Review*, 2:443-97 (1984).

TABLE 1
KNOWLEDGE OF THE *TARASOFF* CASE

| | Percentage for Each Profession and Location | | | | | |
| | Psychiatrist | | Psychologist | | Social worker | |
	California	Other states	California	Other states	California	Other states
Heard of the *Tarasoff* case	96	87	86	56	76	32
Heard of a case like it	1	7	8	18	13	24
Never heard of *Tarasoff* or a case like it	3	6	6	26	11	44
(N of respondents)	(113)	(341)	(146)	(432)	(163)	(472)

SOURCE: Reprinted with permission of the *Wisconsin Law Review* from William J. Bowers, Daniel J. Givelber, and Carolyn L. Blitch, "*Tarasoff*, Myth and Reality: An Empirical Study of Private Law in Action," *Wisconsin Law Review* (1984), p. 443. Copyright 1984, University of Wisconsin.
NOTE: Alternative response categories add to 100 percent.

actions they have taken in *Tarasoff*-relevant cases.

Perceptions and beliefs about Tarasoff

At the very end of the questionnaire, after respondents had answered questions about themselves, their professional practice, and the kinds of patients or clients who might harm others, we turned specifically to the *Tarasoff* decision. We asked whether they had heard of the case, when they first learned of it, what their sources of information were, when the ruling applies, what it requires therapists to do, whether—including the reasons why—they feel bound by it, and what, if any, reservations they have about the *Tarasoff* decision or the principle embodied in it. In this section, we examine whether they had heard of the case, what they thought it required, and whether they believed it applied to them.

As indicated in Table 1, there is an astonishing degree of familiarity with *Tarasoff* by name among psychiatrists in both California and other jurisdictions and among Californians in all three professions. Although when the questionnaire was prepared there was no other "case like" *Tarasoff*, we presented therapists this option in order to see whether people were aware of the decision even if they could not remember the name. Those least apt to say they knew the case by name—social workers and psychologists outside of California—were the ones most apt to say they knew of a case like *Tarasoff*. In all professions and locations, a majority of our respondents had heard of *Tarasoff* or a case like it.

Requirements of Tarasoff. Awareness is only the beginning, however. One may know of a judicial decision without understanding what it requires. Indeed, there were two *Tarasoff* decisions: one, in 1974, that required warning, followed in 1976 by one that substituted exercise of reasonable care for warning and cited warning as an example of reasonable care. To see how psychotherapists interpreted this legally complicated development, we asked our respondents who had heard of *Tarasoff* or a case like it, "What does the case require therapists

TABLE 2
PERCEIVED REQUIREMENTS OF *TARASOFF*

	Percentage for Each Profession and Location					
	Psychiatrist		Psychologist		Social worker	
	California	Other states	California	Other states	California	Other states
Warn potential victim	92	84	91	76	94	72
Call the police	25	33	41	26	43	29
Notify superiors or administrators if in an institutional setting	17	37	36	44	50	53
Warn family or guardian of potential victim	21	33	42	41	39	38
Use reasonable care to protect victim	30	33	31	43	38	40
Deal with potential violence in continued therapy	13	20	21	30	30	33
Seek professional consultation	6	14	11	17	22	24
Seek emergency involuntary commitment	10	20	8	11	13	15
Other or nothing	2	3	2	2	2	3
Unsure	—	13	1	18	13	27
(N of respondents)	(109)	(318)	(138)	(315)	(145)	(253)

SOURCE: Reprinted with permission of the *Wisconsin Law Review* from William J. Bowers, Daniel J. Givelber, and Carolyn L. Blitch, "*Tarasoff*, Myth and Reality: An Empirical Study of Private Law in Action," *Wisconsin Law Review* (1984), p. 443. Copyright 1984, University of Wisconsin.

NOTE: Multiple responses, adding to more than 100 percent; only respondents who are familiar with *Tarasoff* or a case like it are included.

to do?" and listed 11 possibilities including "nothing," "unsure," and "other." Among those aware of *Tarasoff* or a case like it, Table 2 shows the percentage by profession and location saying that a given response was required.

Tarasoff was widely, if wrongly, understood to require a therapist to "warn the potential victim." Of 10 Californians in each professional group, 9 believed that warning was required by *Tarasoff*, and 7 or 8 of 10 non-Californians in each group held this belief. California psychologists and social workers were also more likely than their counterparts elsewhere to say that the decision requires calling the police, though California psychiatrists were not. Regardless of location, social workers said that they were required to notify the appropriate supervisor or administrator in an institutional setting, and psychologists said that the decision required warning the family or guardian of a potential victim.

On the other hand, Californians were less likely in each professional group to say that *Tarasoff* required other steps such as seeking emergency involuntary commitment, dealing with the potential for violence in continued therapy, and seeking professional consultation. Indeed, Californians were less likely than their counterparts in other states to recognize that *Tarasoff* required them to use "reasonable care"—the language of the decision itself—to protect potential victims.

Combinations of Tarasoff *requirements.* Most therapists cited more than one *Tarasoff* requirement—usually warning the victim and one or more other steps. To show what combinations of requirements they thought *Tarasoff* imposed, we have tabulated the major patterns of responses to the question about what the ruling requires in Table 3. The response patterns fall into three successively more inclusive groupings—namely, warning the potential victim as the only requirement; warning the victim and notifying other persons; and warning the victim, notifying others, and taking other steps not limited to notificaiton or warning. There was also a residual category of combinations that do not fall into one of these three groupings.

California psychiatrists tended to take the narrow view that warning the potential victim was the only requirement of *Tarasoff;* more than a third of them adopted this position, a view also more common among psychologists and social workers in California than elsewhere. When California psychiatrists mentioned something in addition to warning the victim it tended to be a single additional step within a broader group of options, chiefly, calling the police. Almost half of the California psychiatrists said that *Tarasoff* required either warning only or warning plus calling the police; the figure exceeds half when we include notifying the family or guardian of the potential victim along with the victim.

By contrast, California psychologists took a somewhat broader view of the *Tarasoff* requirements. They were the group most likely to give responses that included warning the victim and notifying others, but not including steps beyond notification. Moreover, within this category of responses, they were likely to say that several or all forms of notification, in addition to warning the potential victim, were required by *Tarasoff.*

As a further contrast, California social workers appeared to take an even broader view of the *Tarasoff* requirement. They were the most likely to say that in addition to warning the victim and notifying others, the *Tarasoff* ruling also required steps that did not explicitly involve notification. From the specific combinations of responses within this broader category, moreover, it is clear that California social workers were more likely than others to include the requirement of "reasonable care" among these other steps—perhaps because they explicitly recognized this as the language of the *Tarasoff* decision or possibly because it was a broad commonsense statement of the *Tarasoff* principle of responsibility for protecting potential victims.

Among the combinations of requirements that do not fall within one of these successively more inclusive groupings, there were two notable patterns. First, non-Californians were overrepresented chiefly because they were less likely than Californians to cite warning the potential victim as a *Tarasoff* requirement. Second, California psychiatrists were more likely than others to cite reasonable care in these residual combinations as a *Tarasoff* requirement. Strictly speaking, reasonable care alone is the *Tarasoff* requirement, but this specific option was cited by only 26 respondents. Reasonable care and warning the potential victim, with 56 respondents, might be regarded as the best stand-in as it includes the legal requirement and a judicially articulated example of how it may be exercised.

TABLE 3
PATTERNS OF PERCEIVED *TARASOFF* REQUIREMENTS

	Psychiatrist		Psychologist		Social worker	
	California	Other states	California	Other states	California	Other states
Warn potential victim only	36	27	21	13	21	8
Warn victim and notify others	23	20	33	21	21	24
Warn victim and notify police	12	7	8	4	9	6
Warn victim and notify family	6	4	7	4	–	8
Warn victim and notify all others	5	9	18	13	12	10
Warn victim, notify others, and take other actions	22	37	32	37	48	42
Warn victim, notify others, take other clinical actions	6	13	12	13	15	18
Warn victim, notify others, and use reasonable care	5	11	8	10	13	8
Warn victim, notify others, use reasonable care, and take other clinical actions	11	13	12	14	20	16
Residual patterns	19	16	14	29	10	26
Warn victim and use reasonable care	8	3	4	6	1	4
Use reasonable care only	5	2	3	3	1	2
All others	6	11	7	20	8	20
(N of respondents)	(109)	(318)	(138)	(315)	(145)	(253)

NOTE: Major headings sum to 100 percent; minor headings sum to major headings.

Among Californians, then, the common theme was warning; the differences are in what goes with it. California psychiatrists tended to take the single-minded view that nothing goes with it, that *Tarasoff* required warning alone; California psychologists tended to extend the scope of requirements one step to include other notifications as well as warning; and California social workers tended to extend the scope another step to include actions beyond warning or other notifications, chiefly including reasonable care. The most consistent differences between Californians and others in each profession came with respect to the place of warning the potential victim (as reflected in the top and bottom rows of Table 3). Californians in each profession more often saw warning alone as the requirement; non-Californians more often mentioned requirements that did not include warning at all (bottom row).

Obligation to Tarasoff. One may know of a judicial decision and understand rightly or wrongly what it requires but not feel legally or ethically obligated to abide by the decision or to embrace the principle embodied in it. This is especially likely, as here, when a judicial decision is widely known by those living and working outside of the jurisdiction promulgating it. To learn whether and for what reasons therapists felt bound or obligated by the *Tarasoff* principle, we asked our respondents to indicate whether "the principle of responsibility on the part of a therapist for the physical well-being of another person threatened by his patient/client applies to you," for any of the six reasons listed in Table 4.

The table shows that the vast majority of therapists across the country who were aware of *Tarasoff* or a case like it acknowledged that the principle of responsibility for others threatened by their clients or patients applied to them, though for different reasons in different locations. Roughly 9 out of 10 Californians recognized that the decision applied as law where they practiced—in California—and more than 8 out of 10 non-Californians correctly understood that the *Tarasoff* decision or one like it was not the law of their state.

But there is more to be said about perceived legal obligation. Approximately half of the non-Californians said they considered themselves legally obligated by *Tarasoff* or a case like it because it "applies to their profession" (line 3, Table 4). Strictly speaking, this is not true. The formal source of legal authority is the state as governmental unit. *Tarasoff* applied legally only in California. Nor were many of the non-Californians referring to some other law, administrative regulation, or license provision applicable to their profession in the state where they practiced (line 4, Table 4). Perhaps they were acknowledging the reality that once an influential state court attaches a particular responsibility to a professional group, the law elsewhere may be viewed as in flux until such time as the courts of other states make definitive rulings on the same point.

What about ethical obligation to the *Tarasoff* principle? Clearly, most therapists felt obligated to protect endangered persons as a matter of personal and professional ethics, quite apart from the law. With the exception of California psychiatrists, at least 6 out of 10 respondents believed that their professional ethics required them to protect threatened victims, and, even including California psychiatrists, at least 3 out of 4 felt that their personal ethics imposed such a responsibility. Thus, the following picture emerged. Californians were more apt to believe that they were legally, rather than ethically, obligated by the *Tarasoff* principle; for non-Californians the reverse was true. This is not due to differences in ethical beliefs—which were relatively constant by profession and location—but to the wide differences in legal beliefs by location, differences that accorded with legal reality except insofar as therapists outside of California held that *Tarasoff* or a case like it applied legally to their profession.

We now know that, as of 1980, most therapists across the country and virtually all of them in California had heard of *Tarasoff* or a case like it. Most who knew of it believed that it required warning a potential victim and many believed it also required notifying other parties including family, friends, police, and other authorities. Finally, most therapists felt ethically obligated to the

TABLE 4
REASONS THE *TARASOFF* PRINCIPLE MAY APPLY TO THE RESPONDENT

| | Percentage for Each Location and Profession | | | | | |
| | Psychiatrist | | Psychologist | | Social worker | |
	California	Other states	California	Other states	California	Other states
Because the decision applies where respondent practices	94	18	90	17	84	19
Because a like ruling applies where respondent practices	49	17	56	18	55	27
Because the decision applies to the respondent's profession	77	48	93	53	83	50
Because other laws require it	13	7	43	14	31	18
Because professional ethics require it	48	60	77	69	72	71
Because personal ethics require it	75	78	85	82	81	83
No reason; principle does	—	4	—	2	—	2
N of respondents*	(77-111)	(257-323)	(95-138)	(260-321)	(50-145)	(208-266)

SOURCE: Reprinted with permission of the *Wisconsin Law Review* from William J. Bowers, Daniel J. Givelber, and Carolyn L. Blitch, "*Tarasoff*, Myth and Reality: An Empirical Study of Private Law in Action," *Wisconsin Law Review* (1984), p. 443. Copyright 1984, University of Wisconsin.

NOTE: Multiple responses, adding to more than 100 percent; only respondents who are familiar with *Tarasoff* or a case like it and answered yes or no to each specific reason are included.

*Number of respondents on which percentages are based for a given response varies with the range shown.

Tarasoff principle; virtually all Californians also felt legally bound, as did about half of the non-Californians, who said the *Tarasoff* decision or a ruling like it was legally binding on their profession.

The next step in our analysis is to examine the actual behavior of psychotherapists in *Tarasoff*-relevant situations.

Actions taken in
Tarasoff-*relevant situations*

What do therapists actually do when confronted with a patient or client who might, in their judgment, attack or harm another person? To answer this question we asked respondents about the most recent case in which they treated someone whom they believed "likely to physically attack or harm other people." Specifically, we asked, "What action or actions did you take in response to your judgment that the patient/client was potentially harmful to others?" and we listed some 15 alternative steps they might have taken. In Tables 5-8 we show their specific notification and hospitalization responses and the other actions they took, grouped under these headings: treatment, documentation, consultation, and decline/terminate/transfer treatment.

For purposes of this analysis, we disregard cases handled before the *Tarasoff* ruling and we distinguish between cases with and without an

TABLE 5
ACTIONS TAKEN IN LAST DANGEROUS CASE
WITH NO SPECIFIC VICTIM THREATENED

	Percentage for Each Profession and Location					
	Psychiatrist		Psychologist		Social worker	
	California	Other states	California	Other states	California	Other states
Warning potential victim	12	8	11	8	8	8
Notifying others						
Family/friends	31	30	17	24	26	34
Police	4	11	2	6	8	3
Other public authorities	8	9	13	9	14	15
Hospitalization						
Voluntary	25	26	21	22	28	24
Involuntary	29	29	2	12	22	14
Treatment	96	87	92	87	81	88
Documentation	67	68	60	53	60	64
Consultation	20	23	36	28	25	37
Decline/terminate/transfer	6	6	6	6	6	9
(N of respondents)	(49)	(140)	(47)	(156)	(72)	(176)

NOTE: Multiple responses, adding to more than 100 percent.

explicitly identified potential victim who was threatened. Of the 1236 "last dangerous cases" reported by therapists between 1975 and 1980, 479 had an identified victim and 757 did not. Inasmuch as the number of respondents providing information on each of these situations falls well below the numbers represented in Tables 1-4, the percentages in Tables 5-8 may be somewhat less stable than those in Tables 1-4.

Last dangerous case without a specific victim threatened. There is virtually no evidence of a *Tarasoff* effect in cases where a potentially dangerous patient had not identified a specific victim (Table 5). The perceived *Tarasoff* requirement of warning the possible victim was, of course, problematic in such cases; the data showed that this was an uncommon step that varied little by profession or location. It was slightly more common among psychiatrists and psychologists—though not social workers—in California than elsewhere, but not enough to be a statistically reliable difference. Likewise, the other disclosures to third parties—notifying family or friends of the patient, calling the police, and contacting other public authorities —were steps that varied only slightly and not consistently by location for each profession. Differences by location in documentation, consultation, and treatment alternatives were also slight, scattered, and inconsistent among the professions. In fact, only 2 of the 30 comparisons between Californians and others in Table 5 resulted in differences of 10 percent or more, despite the reduced sample sizes relative to earlier tabulations.

Last dangerous case with a specific victim threatened. When there was a named victim the picture changed dramatically. Warning this likely victim was a consistently more common practice among all categories of psychotherapists regardless of location, although the magnitude of the difference between Californians and non-Californians varied from 10 percentage points for psychiatrists to a high of 22 points for social workers and a low of 3 points for psychologists.

Among psychiatrists, warning the victim was the only notification that distinguished Californians from others by more than a very few percentage points. Thus, the strictly victim-warning interpretation of *Tarasoff*, held chiefly by California psychiatrists (as shown in Table 3) was also manifested in their self-reported behavior.

Among psychologists, it was notifying family or friends, or other public authorities, more than directly warning the potential victim that distinguished Californians from non-Californians. Thus, the group most likely to cite other notifications in addition to warning the potential victim as required by *Tarasoff*, in practice preferred these other notifications as alternatives to the one mandated in the first *Tarasoff* decision and suggested in the second.

California social workers appear in practice as well as principle to have adopted the broadest interpretation of *Tarasoff*. In practice they employed every notification option—contacting the patient's family or friends, calling the police, and alerting other public authorities, as well as warning the potential victim—more commonly than social workers elsewhere. They were also the most likely of any group in Table 6 to document the danger, seek consultation from other professionals, and decline or terminate treatment. Apparently, the *Tarasoff* ruling had had a broad impact on their behavior.

Notification combinations. Strictly speaking, the data in Table 6 do not tell us in what combinations therapists employed the steps they took, as their responses were tabulated separately for each type of action. For a clearer picture of the choices they made between warning the victim and other notifications, in Table 7 we have tabulated notification combinations in the last dangerous case with an identified victim. There we show those whose only notification was warning the likely victim, those who chose any other notification response except warning, and those who chose both warning and other notifications.

The pattern in this section of the table is remarkably clear. Among psychiatrists the only difference by location was in warning the victim only. Among psychologists, the only difference occurred in notifications other than warning. And among social workers the only difference was in warnings joined by other notifications. Note that the consistency in Table 7 lies in the greater use of some notification response among Californians as compared to non-Californians of each professional group.

Changes in willingness to act. Any impact of the *Tarasoff* decision must be reflected in changes that have occurred in therapists' behavior since the decision was handed down. We therefore asked therapists about their willingness to employ ten specific steps if faced with a potentially violent patient now—at the time of the survey in 1980—as compared to five years earlier. Respondents' judgments about changes in their willingness to employ these ten specific responses to such patients are shown in Table 8.

Willingness to warn potential victims of impending harm was the response that increased most between 1975 and

TABLE 6
ACTIONS TAKEN IN LAST DANGEROUS CASE
WITH A SPECIFIC VICTIM THREATENED

	Percentage for Each Profession and Location					
	Psychiatrist		Psychologist		Social worker	
	California	Other states	California	Other states	California	Other states
Warning potential victim	38	28	31	28	43	21
Notifying others						
Family/friends	43	47	50	37	63	38
Police	14	12	11	12	23	7
Other public authorities	16	12	14	5	29	16
Hospitlization						
Voluntary	19	36	33	28	40	34
Involuntary	35	33	14	12	20	21
Treatment	84	83	92	93	91	95
Documentation	65	77	58	71	86	66
Consultation	14	22	25	33	46	34
Decline/terminate/transfer	8	6	6	5	20	12
(N of respondents)	(37)	(94)	(36)	(86)	(35)	(122)

NOTE: Multiple responses, adding to more than 100 percent.

1980. Among Californians, three-quarters of the psychiatrists and two-thirds of the psychologists and social workers said they were more willing to warn at the time of the survey than they had been five years earlier. In this response, Californians led non-Californians in each profession, and psychiatrists led the other professional groups in each location. Note that California psychiatrists, who led the parade of increased willingness to warn, fell behind the other groups in increased willingness to hospitalize when faced with a potentially dangerous patient.

In addition, Californians in each professional group have increased their willingness to notify public authorities and the police more than non-Californians have. The increased willingness to make various notifications designed to protect a potential victim appear to be what the California Supreme Court meant by "reasonable care"; such actions were mentioned by the court as examples of reasonable care in the second *Tarasoff* decision. Moreover, these retrospective self-evaluations indicate that it is not only the willingness to warn the potential victim but also the willingness to notify other parties that distinguished Californians from others.

Note further that the willingness to notify third parties, especially endangered victims, also increased markedly outside of California over this period. More than half of the non-California psychiatrists and psychologists said they were more willing to warn potential victims in 1980 than they had been five years earlier. The data suggest that notification in general and warning an endangered victim in particular became more accepted practice over this period not only in California but elsewhere as well, if not as fully. Thus, the impact of

TABLE 7
PATTERNS OF NOTIFICATION IN LAST DANGEROUS
CASE WITH SPECIFIC VICTIM THREATENED

| | Percentage for Each Profession and Location | | | | | |
| | Psychiatrist | | Psychologist | | Social worker | |
	California	Other states	California	Other states	California	Other states
Warning potential victim only	14	3	11	9	9	7
Notifying others only	30	30	42	25	34	36
Warning potential victim and informing other	24	25	20	19	34	14
No notifying or warning action	32	42	27	47	23	43
(N of respondents)	(37)	(94)	(36)	(86)	(35)	(122)

NOTE: Mutually exclusive groupings of actions add to 100 percent.

Tarasoff, though concentrated where the decision applied as law, appears also to have been felt in jurisdictions where *Tarasoff* was not the law, but where it may increasingly have become a standard of professional practice.

This evidence that the ruling's major impact is not strictly contained within jurisdictional boundaries means that comparisons between Californians and non-Californians in their handling of potentially dangerous persons present a conservative picture of the overall impact of the *Tarasoff* decision. To the extent that therapists in both locations have been influenced by *Tarasoff,* comparisons of their behavior reflect only the differential effects of the ruling's overall impact. We must examine how therapists' awareness and interpretation of the *Tarasoff* decision and their commitment to the *Tarasoff* principle have affected the steps they are willing to take and have actually taken both inside and outside of California. The findings presented here are, therefore, a preliminary assessment of how the *Tarasoff* decision affected clinical practice in the first five years after it was handed down.

DISCUSSION

As professionals, health care providers are supposed to share and are expected to conform to a common set of standards and practices. The typical malpractice case amounts to an accusation that a particular professional has failed to perform with the same level of skill and knowledge possessed by other competent practitioners. In this way, tort law is thought to reinforce existing professional standards. But an atypical malpractice case like *Tarasoff* may actually serve to change professional norms and do so beyond the jurisdictional boundaries within which it is binding. Both inside and outside of California between 1975 and 1980 there was a substantial increase in the willingness to warn potential victims, and as of 1980 there was a widespread endorsement of the *Tarasoff* obligation to protect potential victims as a personal and professional norm. During this period, both the *Tarasoff* principle—protection of the potential victim—and the *Tarasoff*-specific intervention—warning—appear to have been adopted or

TABLE 8
CHANGE IN WILLINGNESS TO EMPLOY VARIOUS ACTIONS
WITH POTENTIALLY VIOLENT PATIENTS: 1975-80

	Percentage for Each Profession and Location					
	Psychiatrist		Psychologist		Social worker	
	California	Other states	California	Other states	California	Other states
More willing to warn potential victims	76	60	66	54	66	38
More willing to notify others						
More willing to notify police	49	38	50	37	46	27
More willing to notify other authorities	61	51	66	46	53	43
Hospitalization						
More willing to initiate voluntary hospitalization	29	36	47	45	44	44
More willing to initiate involuntary hospitalization	24	33	39	32	37	34
Documentation/consultation						
More willing to consult lawyers	34	39	26	30	30	28
More willing to consult administrators	29	41	30	28	33	36
More willing to take notes	34	38	40	37	39	36
Decline/terminate/treatment						
Less willing to treat	38	35	31	32	33	27
More willing to terminate	34	29	21	27	24	26
(N of respondents)*	(96-100)	(286-93)	(114-17)	(352-67)	(126-34)	(384-404)

NOTE: Multiple responses, adding to more than 100 percent.
*Number of respondents on which percentages are based for a given response varies within the range shown.

enhanced as values and practices of professional psychotherapists. Perhaps this is what our respondents were expressing when they told us that *Tarasoff* was legally binding upon them because it "applies to my profession." Of course, we cannot attribute all post-*Tarasoff* beliefs and actions to the impact of the decision. No doubt a certain threshold of readiness or receptivity must be present before professional standards of conduct will change.

Yet, the California Supreme Court did not write upon a blank slate when it decided *Tarasoff*. Despite litigation-inspired claims to the contrary, the ethical guidelines of the mental health professionals represented in our study have explicitly stated for years prior to *Tarasoff* that confidentiality may be compromised in the event that failure to do so would endanger the client or others.[9] *Tarasoff* put the force of tort sanction behind this ethical precept. At

9. See, for example, American Psychiatric Association, "Official Actions: The Principles of Medical Ethics with Annotations Especially Applicable to Psychiatry," *American Journal of Psychiatry*, 130:1058-64 (1973); American Psychological Association, "Ethical Standards of Psychologists," in *Biographical Directory of the American Psychological Association* (Washington, DC: American Psychological Association, 1973); National Association of Social Workers, "Code of Ethics," in *NASW Professional Social Workers' Directory* (Washington, DC: National Association of Social Workers, 1973).

the same time, it provided therapists with a legally required solution to the clinical and ethical dilemma of how to respond when the therapist is genuinely concerned about the patient's danger to others. Thus, the dilemma of dealing with potentially violent patients and the ethical guidelines of the mental health professions may have provided the threshold of readiness and receptivity necessary for the acceptance of the *Tarasoff* principle and its implications for practice—a climate in which the tort sanction will promote normative change.

What is more, the social organization of mental health training and practice may make these professionals as a group especially responsive to the law and promote the incorporation of legal changes into professional standards. Legal decisions like *Tarasoff* may immediately be incorporated into the training programs of professional schools. The institutional settings in which many psychotherapists work are likely to be sensitive to the law and may issue directives and regulations designed to ensure compliance. Indeed, differences among the respective professions in the organization of training and practice may account for their contrasting interpretations and actions where *Tarasoff* applies as law, and the national reach of the professionally organized communities may help explain why non-Californians have been affected by the *Tarasoff* decision, issues that we will explore in continuing analyses.

But whether they are right or wrong about what *Tarasoff* requires and upon whom it is legally binding, most professional psychotherapists, according to the data presented here, have come to accept the *Tarasoff* principle as an article of personal and professional ethics, to regard the *Tarasoff* decision as legally binding upon themselves, and in turn to have their behavior influenced by these ethical and legal beliefs. We suggest that the *Tarasoff* principle was more readily accepted because it was consistent with preexisting ethical guidelines of the professions and because it provided a legal solution to a fundamental dilemma of practice. We further suggest that it affected professional behavior not primarily because individual psychotherapists are especially law compliant, but because the socially organized professional communities have adopted the *Tarasoff* principle as the right way to do things—as an emergent professional standard.

Oregon's Psychiatric Security Review Board: A Comprehensive System for Managing Insanity Acquittees

By JEFFREY L. ROGERS, JOSEPH D. BLOOM, and SPERO M. MANSON

ABSTRACT: The insanity defense is a particularly controversial aspect of the interaction between law and mental health. During the past decade, many states have revised or abolished their insanity defenses. Oregon, however, chose in 1978 to retain its existing defense and create a new, unique system for the post-adjudication management of insanity acquittees. Oregon's legislature established the Psychiatric Security Review Board (PSRB), which is composed of five part-time members drawn from different disciplines, to conduct periodic hearings to determine the placement and supervision of defendants who successfully raise the insanity defense and remain mentally ill and dangerous. The PSRB has received national attention as a promising approach to managing mentally ill offenders. The authors first describe the structure and operation of the Oregon system. Then they summarize the empirical studies they have conducted of the PSRB in action.

Jeffrey L. Rogers received his J.D. from Yale Law School in 1973. Since then he has practiced trial law in Portland, Oregon, with an emphasis on forensic psychiatry. He is currently city attorney for Portland and clinical associate professor of psychiatry at Oregon Health Sciences University (OHSU).

Joseph D. Bloom received his M.D. from the Albert Einstein College of Medicine in 1962 and completed his psychiatric training at the Massachusetts Mental Health Center. He is currently professor and acting chairman of the Department of Psychiatry, OHSU.

Spero M. Manson received his Ph.D. in anthropology from the University of Minnesota in 1978. He is currently director of social research, Department of Psychiatry, OHSU.

IN 1978 the state of Oregon created a unique system designed to provide effective management of those persons found not guilty by reason of insanity. The legislature established the Psychiatric Security Review Board (PSRB),[1] a panel whose mandate is to ensure the appropriate care and control of individuals who have asserted successful insanity defenses and are considered to present substantial danger to others. The Oregon system has received national attention as a potentially viable response to the medical, moral, and legal concerns about management of this special population.

We begin this article by discussing concerns that led to the creation of the PSRB. Next, we describe the structure and functioning of Oregon's system. Finally, we discuss our initial analyses of the PSRB's performance during its first six years. Throughout, we note some of the ways in which this comprehensive system presents opportunities for adding to the knowledge about mentally ill offenders and their management.

OREGON'S RESPONSE TO THE INSANITY DEFENSE DEBATE

The insanity defense occupies a uniquely controversial place in the interaction between law and mental health. Compared with the total number of criminal prosecutions, the insanity defense is infrequently utilized and is rarely successful.[2] However, in spite of decades of debate and repeated attempts at reform, the insanity defense remains a focal point for discontent with the criminal justice system and with the mental health professionals involved in that system. Public opinion has consistently overestimated the degree to which the defense is used.[3] Many equate a successful insanity defense with beating the charge.

Most recently, the case of John Hinckley, Jr., focused national attention on the insanity defense. The intensity of the resulting debate rivaled that created in England by the McNaughton case in the 1840s. The Hinckley trial was a media event cast so as to emphasize all of the controversial aspects of insanity defense trials. Furthermore, the verdict was simply unbelievable to most people. In the post-verdict furor professionals and politicians intensified the search for insanity defense reforms. Debate began in the Congress and in many state legislatures on a multitude of proposed bills. The American Psychiatric Association, the American Bar Association, and the American Medical Association all issued position statements on the insanity defense.[4]

These developments were merely the continuation of growing dissatisfaction with insanity defense systems as they had evolved over the preceding decades. Changes in insanity defense systems

---

1. Ore. Rev. Stat. §161.295-.400 (1983).
2. Henry J. Steadman, "Insanity Acquittals in New York State, 1965-1978," *American Journal of Psychiatry*, 137:321-26 (1980).
3. Richard A. Pasewark and Mark Pantle, "Insanity Plea: Legislator's View," *American Journal of Psychiatry*, 136:222-23 (1979); Richard A. Pasewark and Deborah Seidenzahl, "Opinions Concerning the Insanity Plea and Criminality among Mental Patients," *Bulletin of the American Academy of Psychiatry and the Law*, 7:199-203 (1979).
4. American Psychiatric Association, "Statement on the Insanity Defense," reprinted in *American Journal of Psychiatry*, 140:681-88 (1983); American Bar Association, "Recommendations on the Insanity Defense," reprinted in *Mental Disability Law Reporter*, 7:136 (1983); "Committee Report: Insanity Defense in Criminal Trials and Limitation of Psychiatric Testimony," *JAMA*, 251(22):2967-81 (1984).

inevitably followed the legal reforms in involuntary civil commitment that occurred from the late 1960s through the 1970s.[5] The mental health bar argued that because a person who was found not guilty by reason of insanity had not been convicted of a crime, equal protection and due process required that the person be subject only to the rules governing civil commitments.[6] Many states began handling their insanity acquittees as if they had been civilly committed. This led to short hospitalizations for insanity acquittees, with little or no community monitoring, and in some instances it resulted in highly publicized cases of recidivism.[7]

The ascendance of dangerousness as a prerequisite to hospitalizing a person against his or her will was another trend in civil commitment that had a significant effect on the administration of post-insanity-defense procedures. Experts soon pointed out the limitations of scientific predictions of dangerousness.[8] The narrow construction of the dangerousness standard as applied in the insanity defense arena increased the obstacles to maintaining jurisdiction over acquittees for purposes of supervision and treatment. These developments punched holes in the existing procedures for handling persons found not guilty by reason of insanity.

Consequently, the search for new insanity defense systems was under way well before the Hinckley case.[9] Several models were developed in the late 1970s. Michigan was the first to pass a guilty-but-mentally-ill statute.[10] The guilty-but-mentally-ill verdict was designed to stand as a somewhat parallel verdict to the insanity defense but would carry with it a guilty verdict, a criminal sentence, and an attempt to provide treatment for the person's mental illness. Guilty-but-mentally-ill provisions have been adopted in a number of states. The available evidence suggests that it has not reduced the number of persons found not guilty by reason of insanity or provided enhanced treatment.[11] Taking a second approach, Montana and, more recently, Idaho and Utah have adopted

5. Alan A. Stone, *Mental Health and the Law: A System in Transition,* National Institute of Mental Health, Department of Health, Education, and Welfare pub. no. 76-176 (Washington, DC: Government Printing Office, 1975); *Baxstrom* v. *Herold,* 383 U.S. 107 (1966); *Lessard* v. *Schmidt,* 349 F. Supp. 1078 (E.D. Wis. 1972); *O'Connor* v. *Donaldson,* 422 U.S. 563 (1966).

6. *Bolton* v. *Harris,* 395 F.2d 642 (D.C. Cir. 1968).

7. Paul S. Appelbaum, "The Insanity Defense: New Calls for Reform," *Hospital and Community Psychiatry,* 33:13-14 (1982).

8. Saleem A. Shah, "Dangerousness: A Paradigm for Exploring Some Issues in Law and Psychology," *American Psychologist,* 33:224-38 (1978); idem, "Dangerousness: Conceptual Prediction and Public Policy Issues," in *Violence and Violent Individuals,* ed. J. R. Hays, T. K. Roberts, and K. S. Solway (New York: SP Medical and Scientific Books, 1981), pp. 151-78; John Monahan, *The Clinical Prediction of Violent Behavior,* National Institute of Mental Health, Department of Health and Human Services pub. no. (ADM) 81-921 (Washington, DC: Government Printing Office, 1981).

9. Grant Morris, "Acquittal by Reason of Insanity: Developments in the Law," in *Mentally Disordered Offenders: Perspectives from Law and Social Science,* ed. John Monahan and Henry J. Steadman (New York: Plenum Press, 1983).

10. Mich. Comp. Laws Ann. §768.36(1) *et seq.* (1975).

11. Michael Criss and D. Robert Racine, "Impact of Change in Legal Standard for Those Adjudicated not Guilty by Reason of Insanity," *Bulletin of the American Academy of Psychiatry and the Law,* 8(3):261-71 (1980); Lynn W. Blunt and Harley V. Stock, "Guilty but Mentally Ill: The Michigan Experience," mimeographed (Ann Arbor, MI: Center for Forensic Psychiatry, 1983); Gore A. Smith and James A. Hall, "Evaluating Michigan's Guilty but Mentally Ill Verdict: An Empirical Study," *Journal of Law Reform,* 16:77-113 (1982).

statutes intended to abolish their insanity defenses.[12] No empirical evidence has been reported on the effects of the changes in these states.

All four of these states took the same approach as that embodied in most of the post-Hinckley reform proposals. Guilty-but-mentally-ill verdicts, abolition of the special defense of insanity, restricting expert testimony on ultimate legal issues, eliminating the volitional test, and placing the burden of proof on the defendant are all intended, at least in part, to reduce the number of insanity acquittees. Although proponents of such changes advance various medical, moral, and legal arguments, their proposals share a common assumption: one major problem with insanity defenses is that there are too many of them. Implicit in these proposals is the premise that the insanity defense is bad public policy. Even if it is a moral and constitutional necessity, goes the unstated argument, it is at best a necessary evil whose availability should be strictly limited.

Why does the insanity defense periodically become the bête noire of criminal law? As noted, many concerns center on the insanity test itself and its availability at trial. A second major source of disrepute is the widespread belief that those found not guilty by reason of insanity are promptly released back into the community with no safeguards to protect future victims. Although some have noted the crucial importance of follow-up mechanisms,[13] relatively few of the insanity defense reforms have focused on this posttrial phase. A few states, such as Illinois and Maryland, have created community release programs or strengthened existing ones.[14]

In the mid-1970s Oregon was experiencing serious concerns about the insanity defense, particularly the public and professional perception that the system was becoming a revolving door that placed public safety in jeopardy. In addition, the forensic unit at the state mental hospital was overcrowded with insanity acquittees, and efforts to release patients were hampered by the lack of adequate community programs to supervise or treat dangerous mentally ill offenders. Following several years of study, Oregon decided not to change the insanity test or the trial procedures. Instead the legislature created a specialized and comprehensive statewide system for managing insanity acquittees.[15] The heart of that system is the PSRB, which began operation on 1 January 1978. The PSRB's only function is management of insanity acquittees who are considered to present a substantial danger to others.

The PSRB is unique in both its composition and its independence. It is a five-member part-time board, required by law to be composed of a lawyer, a psychiatrist, a psychologist, a parole or probation expert, and a lay citizen.

---

12. For the relevant statutes for Montana, Idaho, and Utah, see, respectively, Mont. Rev. Codes §45-2-101 (34), 46-14-102, 46-14-201 (1980); Idaho Code Ann. §18-207(a), added by S. 1396, 46th Idaho Legislature, 2d reg. sess. (1982); Utah Code Ann. §76-2-305(1) (1983).

13. American Psychiatric Association, "Statement on the Insanity Defense"; David B. Wexler, *Mental Health Law, Major Issues* (New York: Plenum Press, 1981), pp. 117-54.

14. For Illinois, see Robert M. Wettstein, "Experience in the Aftercare of Insanity Acquittees in Illinois" (Paper delivered at the Fourteenth Annual Meeting of the American Academy of Psychiatry and the Law, Portland, OR, 1983); for Maryland, see U.S., Congress, Senate, Committee on the Judiciary, Subcommittee on Criminal Law, *Treatment and Aftercare for Insanity Acquittees in Maryland,* Testimony by Stuart B. Silver, serial no. J-97-122 (Washington, DC: Government Printing Office, 1982), pp. 378-83.

15. Ore. Rev. Stat. §161.295-.400 (1983).

Board members are appointed by the governor to serve four-year terms. The PSRB is independent of the court system and of the Oregon Mental Health Division. Neither the psychiatrist nor the psychologist member can be an employee of the Mental Health Division. The attorney member cannot be a district attorney or public defender. The members receive per diem expenses for their meetings. The board has an attorney as executive director and two additional full-time staff members.

After an insanity verdict is rendered at trial, the judge may place the person under the jurisdiction of the PSRB, which then assumes sole authority to determine whether the person should be hospitalized in a secure state facility, released into the community with conditions, or discharged from PSRB jurisdiction. Unless discharged first, the person remains under the jurisdiction of the PSRB until the expiration of a period of time equal to the maximum sentence he or she could have received if found guilty. A key policy innovation is the statutory requirement that the PSRB retain jurisdiction over those individuals whose mental illness and resulting dangerousness is in remission.

A person affected by a mental disease or defect in a state of remission is considered to have a mental disease or defect requiring supervision when the disease may, with responsible medical probability, occasionally become active, and when active render the person a danger to others.[16]

This statutory section attempts to deal with medication-induced remission, which is a major loophole in most contemporary post-insanity-defense procedures.

In both name and practice the PSRB is primarily concerned with public security. The statutes direct the board to "have as its primary concern the protection of society."[17] To counterbalance this emphasis, the law provides substantial legal safeguards for individuals under PSRB jurisdiction. These include the rights to periodic hearings, presence at hearings, legal representation at all hearings, cross-examination, subpoena power, independent professional evaluation prior to hearings, and appeal of PSRB decisions to the Oregon appellate courts.

Another key aspect of Oregon's system is the conditional-release mechanism. When a defendant is hospitalized following a successful insanity defense, the PSRB conducts periodic hearings to determine, among other things, whether the person is suitable for conditional release into the community. If conditional release is deemed appropriate, the statutes nonetheless prohibit the PSRB from releasing an individual until there is a plan developed to provide adequate supervision and treatment for that individual in the community. To supply such services, the legislature has appropriated a total of several million dollars to the state Mental Health Division, which contracts with both public and private agencies to provide a range of mental health services for PSRB clients.

Oregon's new system has become a potential national model in the area of post-insanity-defense procedures. In December of 1982 the Board of Trustees of the American Psychiatric Association approved its position paper on the insanity defense, noted previously. In a section dealing with procedures following the successful plea of not guilty by reason of insanity, the American Psychiatric Association cited Oregon's system.[18] In addition, several states are

16. Ibid., §161.336(3) (1983).

17. Ibid., §161.336(10).
18. American Psychiatric Association, "Statement on the Insanity Defense," p. 687.

considering PSRB-type legislation and many others are observing Oregon's experiment with interest.

The PSRB is widely supported within Oregon by diverse professional groups. During legislative appraisals of the new system, testimony commending the PSRB was presented by the American Civil Liberties Union, district attorneys' association, defense lawyer associations, Oregon's Mental Health Division, public advocacy groups, and the judges' association. In light of such testimony, some legislators discussed adopting the PSRB approach for supervision of convicted mentally ill prisoners and parolees. In short, the PSRB has assumed an important place in deliberations regarding management of mentally ill offenders.

The Oregon system is not without critics. For example, although the legislature rejected his position, Oregon's attorney general has asserted that the PSRB is not cost effective in protecting the public. The research to date is insufficient to evaluate his assertion, although the studies to be discussed later in this article suggest the opposite.

THE PSRB IN OPERATION

To aid in understanding the strengths and weaknesses of the Oregon model we will now describe the current day-to-day functioning of Oregon's system.

Trial procedures

In Oregon, defendants prevail with an insanity defense if they prove by a preponderance of the evidence that they meet a modified American Law Institute test:

1. A person is guilty except for insanity if, as a result of mental disease or defect at the time of engaging in criminal conduct, the person lacks substantial capacity either to appreciate the criminality of the conduct or to conform the conduct to the requirements of law.

2. ... the terms "mental disease or defect" do not include an abnormality manifested only by repeated criminal or otherwise antisocial conduct, nor do they include any abnormality consisting solely of a personality disorder.[19]

Oregon has modified the American Law Institute test in two interesting ways. First, the 1983 legislature changed the name of the insanity defense verdict to "guilty except for insanity." This term, thought to be more descriptive and more palatable, did not change procedures in any way. The new name should not be confused with verdicts such as guilty but mentally ill, discussed earlier, which constitute findings of guilt and result in criminal sanctions. To the contrary, a finding in Oregon of guilty except for insanity is not a conviction, but a successful insanity defense resulting in the processes described in this article for managing insanity acquittees. Second, the 1983 legislature specifically excluded personality disorders from qualifying as a mental disease or defect. We discuss elsewhere the expected impact of these two innovative modifications of the traditional American Law Institute standard.[20]

In Oregon, as in most states, no reliable data have been compiled showing how many defendants file notice of insanity. Criminal prosecutions occur in each of Oregon's 36 counties and until recently not much data had been col-

19. Ore. Rev. Stat. §161.295 (1983).
20. Jeffrey L. Rogers, Joseph D. Bloom, and Spero M. Manson, "1983 Changes in Oregon's Insanity Defense System," mimeographed (Portland: Oregon Health Sciences University, 1984).

lected statewide about court proceedings. However, the 1983 legislature enacted a requirement that each district attorney submit to the state court administrator information concerning the assertion and trial verdicts of insanity defense cases.[21] The state court administrator noted that during the first 12 months of data compilation, January through December of 1984, Oregon district attorneys reported 114 cases in which insanity defense notice was filed during the year. Of those, 37, or 32 percent, ended in insanity verdicts; 15, or 13 percent, in guilty verdicts; 4, or 4 percent, in not-guilty verdicts; and the remaining 58, or 51 percent, were not concluded by year's end.

Post-adjudication determinations and dispositions

After an Oregon defendant prevails with an insanity defense, the trial judge must make several additional determinations. Based either on the evidence at trial or that presented in a separate hearing, if either the prosecution or defense requests a separate hearing, the judge must decide what crime or crimes the person would have been convicted of had the person been found guilty.[22] The maximum sentence possible for the crime or crimes in turn becomes the maximum length of jurisdiction if the judge places the individual under PSRB supervision. Oregon defendants successfully raise the insanity defense to a wide variety of both felonies and misdemeanors.

The judge must also determine whether there is a victim of the defendant's crime or crimes and whether the victim wishes to be notified of any PSRB hearing about that defendant and of any conditional release, discharge, or escape of the defendant.[23] If so, and if the defendant is placed under the PSRB, the PSRB must make reasonable efforts to notify the victim of its actions.[24] Preliminary indications are that in approximately one-third of the cases the judges find there is a victim who wishes notification.

The judge must then decide whether the preponderance of the evidence shows that (1) the person continues to be affected by a mental disease or defect, and (2) the person presents a substantial danger to others and therefore requires commitment to a state mental hospital or conditional release.[25] If the answer to either question is no, jurisdiction terminates and the defendant is discharged, a free person. This result parallels a not-guilty verdict—in effect it is the one situation in which insanity is a total defense in Oregon. However, this appears to be a relatively rare occurrence. Based on records covering two years in Oregon's largest county, we previously estimated that only 8 percent of insanity acquittees are discharged by judges after an insanity verdict.[26] The recent data from the state court administrator, mentioned earlier, show that in 1984, only 1 of the 37 persons in that sample reportedly found guilty except for insanity was discharged.

Thus, the vast majority of defendants successfully asserting the insanity defense in Oregon are not set free, but are subject to the PSRB management system, which includes the probability of confinement and close supervision

21. Ore. Rev. Stat. §161.403 (1983).
22. Ibid., §161.325(2).
23. Ibid., §161.325.
24. Ibid., §161.326.
25. Ibid., §161.327(1).
26. Jeffrey L. Rogers et al., "Women in Oregon's Insanity Defense System," *Journal of Psychiatry and Law*, pp. 515-32 (Winter 1983).

for an extended period of time. We have termed this result the insanity sentence, as it is far more analogous to the consequences of a conviction than of a not-guilty verdict.[27]

The judge makes one final decision: if the defendant can be

> adequately controlled with supervision and treatment if conditionally released and . . . necessary supervision and treatment are available, the court may order the person conditionally released, subject to those supervision orders of the court as are in the best interests of justice, the protection of society, and the welfare of the person.[28]

Once the person is placed on conditional release, the judge must notify the PSRB, which then assumes jurisdiction, and the judge's role terminates. If the judge determines the person is not suitable for conditional release, the person is committed to the state hospital and jurisdiction automatically transfers to the PSRB. During the first five years of PSRB operation, 1978-83, the judges opted for conditional release of 17 percent of all defendants placed under PSRB jurisdiction. Over the years, however, the percentage has been rising, from a low of 5 percent in 1978 to a high of 30 percent in 1983. The rise may reflect, at least in part, increasing judicial confidence in the conditional-release programs developed by the PSRB system.

The disposition of minor misdemeanants

The 1981 legislature, in an effort to avoid overburdening the PSRB with minor misdemeanants, carved out a small category of acquittees who, even though still mentally ill and dangerous, are not placed under the PSRB.[29] Those persons found guilty except for insanity of misdemeanors committed "during a criminal episode in the course of which the person did not cause physical injury or risk of physical injury to another" are referred for disposition under Oregon's civil commitment procedures.[30] For this group of persons the state's burden of proof is eased to preponderance of the evidence instead of the otherwise constitutionally required and statutorily prescribed standard for civil commitments of clear and convincing evidence. Additionally, unlike the usual 180-day renewable period for civil commitments, the insanity acquittees referred for civil commitment are subject to being committed for no longer than the maximum sentence they could have received if they had been found guilty of the crime or crimes charged.[31]

Until recently no statewide data were being compiled on the frequency with which this minor-misdemeanor diversion route was utilized. The state court administrator reports that during 1984 10 persons were reported to have been referred to civil commitment.

During PSRB's first five years of operation, 1978-83, the trial courts placed, on the average, 93 defendants per year under PSRB jurisdiction. The number per year dropped from a high of 116 in 1979 to a low of 81 in both 1982 and 1983. In addition, 152 persons who before 1978 were found not guilty by reason of mental disease were auto-

---

27. Jeffrey L. Rogers and Joseph D. Bloom, "The Insanity Sentence: Oregon's Psychiatric Security Review Board," *Behavioral Sciences and the Law,* 3(1):69-84 (1985).
28. Ore. Rev. Stat. §161.327 (1983).

29. Jeffrey L. Rogers, "Oregon Legislation Relating to the Insanity Defense and the Psychiatric Security Review Board," *Willamette Law Review,* 18(1):23-48.
30. Ore. Rev. Stat. §161.368 (1983).
31. Ibid., §161.328.

matically transferred to PSRB jurisdiction, effective 1 January 1978.

Periodic review hearings

Oregon statutes require the PSRB to conduct periodic review hearings for each individual under its jurisdiction. The individual, the hospital, and the community monitoring agencies may request additional reviews. Each hearing is conducted like a mini-trial, with relaxed rules of evidence allowing the members of the PSRB to consider the trial proceedings, information submitted by any interested party, and the person's entire psychiatric and criminal history.

The PSRB generally conducts approximately five hearings during half a day each week, most often at the Oregon State Hospital in Salem. During the days preceding the hearings, PSRB staff compiles and provides to each board member documents concerning each case to be reviewed. These documents, which sometimes consist of several hundred pages, are also provided to the patient and the patient's attorney, who in over 90 percent of the cases is appointed by the board because the patient is indigent. The records are also provided to the attorney general and the district attorney so they may decide whether to have an attorney represent the state at the hearing. Although the board has urged that an attorney for the state be required to appear, financial and personnel limitations have prevented routine appearances. The board also may receive written reports from a private psychiatrist or psychologist appointed by the board to examine the patient.

The hearings themselves are conducted with at least three board members present, including the psychiatrist or psychologist. Usually the board hears testimony from one or more state hospital psychiatrists or other staff members and from community treatment program staff if the hearing concerns a person seeking conditional release or a person already conditionally released. The patient is present at the hearing and can subpoena and cross-examine witnesses. All hearings are recorded, and the transcript, along with documents introduced into evidence, constitutes the record if the patient exercises his or her right to appeal the board's decision to the appellate courts. The burden of proof on all issues is by a preponderance of the evidence. The state bears the burden of persuasion in all hearings except those held specially to consider a patient's application for change of status. In the latter type of hearing patients must prove their suitability for release or discharge. The board must provide a written decision within 15 days of the hearing.

The conditional-release mechanism

One of the most notable features of the PSRB system is the conditional-release mechanism. Using funds appropriated by the legislature specifically for this purpose, the PSRB and the Mental Health Division have assisted counties to develop programs tailored for insanity acquittees. At the PSRB's request, the community programs conduct a thorough evaluation of each patient the PSRB is contemplating releasing. In cooperation with the PSRB, the program staff then designs a treatment plan tailored to the needs of each individual. This plan usually provides for case management, monitored medication, day treatment, living arrangements, and social assistance, as well as other specific conditions imposed by the PSRB such as prohibition of driving or possession of weapons. The board designates a particular person, usually the case manager, to monitor the person's progress and to make reports to the board monthly or at any time if "the person has violated the terms of the conditional release or [if] the mental health of the individual has changed."[32] In addition, the PSRB staff has close working relationships with the staff of the community programs, and they talk with each other frequently about those under supervision.

Thus, even though Oregon is large geographically—approximately 400 miles by 300 miles—and has a relatively large number of insanity acquittees, the PSRB staff knows at all times the location, program, and progress of each person on conditional release.

The community program staffs usually report by telephone any problem requiring prompt PSRB action. Upon receiving such a report about one of its clients, the board or its chairperson may immediately issue a written order of revocation that is a sufficient warrant for the police to take the person into custody. The person may not be jailed but must be transported to the state hospital. The entire process from report to rehospitalization may be accomplished in a matter of hours. The board must then hold a hearing within 20 days to decide if the person should remain committed to the hospital, be returned to conditional release, or be discharged. More than half of the persons placed on release have their release revoked within one year, but only a few because of new criminal charges. Most revocations occur because the person has violated conditions of release such as taking medication or refraining from alcohol use, or because the person's mental health has deteriorated.

Persons may be discharged either while in the hospital or on conditional release. Discharge is a termination of supervision and jurisdiction; it should not be confused with release from the hospital. A person is automatically discharged after having been under the PSRB's jurisdiction for a period of time equal to the maximum sentence he or she could have received if convicted. In addition, at any hearing, the board must discharge a person found to be no longer affected by mental disease or defect or no longer presenting a substantial danger to others. Thus, both the criteria —mental disease or defect and dangerousness—must be met to retain jurisdiction. If the board concludes that either one, or both, no longer exists, then the person is discharged.

EMPIRICAL STUDIES

An advantage of Oregon's insanity defense system is its centralization of records and decision making, which creates an excellent opportunity for research regarding this group of mentally ill offenders and their management. Oregon has a centralized, statewide body of data including information not only about hospitalized insanity acquittees, but about those on conditional release. The PSRB has detailed records on the hospital and community courses of over 700 insanity acquittees through 1983.

In 1981 we entered into a formal agreement with the PSRB to conduct research and evaluation studies on various aspects of the PSRB system.

32. Ibid., §161.336(5).

Using a computerized data base constructed from PSRB files we have initiated a series of studies that have provided insights into the operation and effectiveness of the PSRB in managing insanity acquittees.

Our first study described the functioning of the PSRB and some basic characteristics of 440 persons who had been committed to the PSRB during its initial three years of operation.[33] Of the persons in the study, 91 percent were male, 9 percent female. Their ages ranged from 17 to 74 with a mean of 30.8 years. They had succeeded with insanity defenses for a wide variety of crimes; 19 percent had committed only misdemeanors, but 47 percent had committed crimes of serious violence. Most were affected by a major mental illness. The state hospital staff assigned primary diagnoses to committed insanity acquittees as follows: 67 percent psychotic, 20 percent personality disorders, 6 percent organic brain syndromes, 5 percent mental retardation, 2 percent miscellaneous. Among the 440 acquittees, psychoses were distributed as follows: 61 percent had schizophrenic disorders, 5 percent affective disorders, and 1 percent paranoid disorders.

Even in this initial study the importance of the PSRB conditional-release policies became apparent. In the first three years of PSRB functioning, 165 persons had been on conditional release. During that time 16 of these persons were charged with new crimes, only 6 of which were felonies. Although it was much too soon to draw conclusions about PSRB effectiveness, this recidivism rate appeared favorable. During the study period the PSRB revoked the conditional release of 66 of the 165 persons on release. As most of the revocations were as a result of deterioration in mental health status or other reasons not related to new crimes, it seemed probable that close supervision, allowing for prompt revocation, accounted in part for the apparent low rate of new criminal charges.

Inasmuch as the centralized and closely monitored conditional-release mechanism was so unusual in terms of the national insanity defense literature, we designed our next study to examine PSRB decisions on conditional release in more detail.[34] Groups of acquittees were developed to allow for comparison of those who remained hospitalized during the study period with those placed on conditional release during the same period of time. Our analyses showed that a significantly higher percentage of women were conditionally released. Other variables, such as age, diagnosis, and the crime that led to PSRB jurisdiction, did not vary significantly between the released and not-released groups. However, for those conditionally released, the more serious the original crime, the longer the period of hospitalization prior to release. The results indicated that the PSRB allows or denies conditional release without clear bias in relation to diagnosis or type of crime, but understandably is slower to release persons charged with serious crimes.

Another aspect of this study was an analysis of factors correlated with success or failure of conditional release. No

33. Jeffrey L. Rogers and Joseph D. Bloom, "Characteristics of Persons Committed to Oregon's Psychiatric Security Review Board," *Bulletin of the American Academy of Psychiatry and the Law,* 10(3):155-64 (1982).

34. Joseph D. Bloom, Jeffrey L. Rogers, and Spero M. Manson, "After Oregon's Insanity Defense: A Comparison of Conditional Release and Hospitalization," *International Journal of Law and Psychiatry,* 5:391-402 (1982).

significant relationships were found between conditional-release performance and sex, crime type, seriousness of the crime, or diagnosis. However, those on conditional release whose release was later revoked were significantly younger than those who remained successfully on conditional release. Furthermore, persons who failed on conditional release were likely to be psychotic and male; 87 percent of the failed group was psychotic and 90 percent was male. The results concerning those whose release was revoked reflect findings in the emerging literature on the chronically mentally ill that suggest that there is a subgroup of younger chronically psychotic men who are very difficult to manage in either the mental health or criminal justice systems.[35]

We next explored in detail the characteristics of women under PSRB supervision compared to men.[36] Although women and men did not differ significantly in mean seriousness of the crime leading to PSRB jursidiction, there were significant differences in the distributions of the seriousness of the various crimes by sex. A greater percentage of the crimes committed by women were misdemeanors. At the opposite end of the seriousness spectrum, homicide or attempted homicide was the most frequent type of felony for women, compared to car theft for men. Whereas women clustered at either end of the seriousness scale, men were more evenly distributed along this dimension. Women also were underrepresented in crimes that take place between strangers. For example, they committed no robberies or burglaries. As noted previously, women were placed on conditional release by both the judges and the PSRB significantly more frequently than men were. Similarly, a higher percentage of women than men were discharged during our study period.

In our fourth study we looked back to the trial process that led to PSRB jurisdiction. We examined the surprising finding that over 85 percent of successful insanity defenses in Oregon had not been contested by the prosecution.[37] Prosecutors were more likely to contest cases involving those defendants later diagnosed by the state hospital staff as displaying only personality disorder. Not surprisingly, there was a higher frequency of disagreement about diagnosis among multiple experts examining defendants who had been involved in contested cases as compared with those involved in uncontested cases. Even among the contested cases, however, there was diagnostic agreement on about two-thirds of the defendants, with the trial contest presumably centering on whether the mental disease or defect led to lack of legal responsibility. Jury trials occurred in only 4 percent of successful insanity defense cases.

A fifth study focused on the persons discharged by PSRB during its first three years of operation.[38] We searched

35. Leona L. Bachrach, "Young Adult Chronic Patients: An Analytical Review of the Literature," *Hospital and Community Psychiatry,* 33:189-97 (1982); John L. Sheets, James A. Prevost, and Jacqueline Reihman, "Young Adult Chronic Patients: Three Hypothesized Subgroups," ibid., pp. 197-203; Joseph D. Bloom et al., "The Young Adult Chronic Patient and the Legal System: A Systems Analysis," in *Effective Aftercare for the 1980's: New Directions for Mental Health Services,* ed. D. L. Cutler (San Francisco: Jossey-Bass, 1983), pp. 37-50.
36. Rogers et al., "Women in Oregon's Insanity Defense System."

37. Jeffrey L. Rogers, Joseph D. Bloom, and Spero M. Manson, "Insanity Defenses, Contested or Conceded?" *American Journal of Psychiatry,* 141(7):885-88 (1984).
38. Joseph D. Bloom, Jeffrey L. Rogers, and Spero M. Manson, "Lifetime Police Contacts of

three computerized police data systems and compiled information on all the contacts with police that had been recorded during the lifetimes of 123 discharged persons. Before being placed under the post-insanity-defense system, these persons had an average of 7 police contacts, including arrests for criminal charges, juvenile arrests, contacts for public drunkenness, and police holds for mental illness under the Oregon civil commitment system. During court jurisdiction—before 1978—and PSRB jurisdiction—after 1978—following insanity acquittal, the subjects had an average of 0.6 police contacts per person. When presented as yearly rates we found that the mean rate of arrest per person was 0.9 before, 0.3 during, and 0.6 after PSRB jurisdiction. Following discharge they averaged 1.4 contacts per person. At each stage, the contacts consisted primarily of arrests, with misdemeanors slightly outnumbering felonies.

Individuals discharged by PSRB because they were considered no longer dangerous were compared to those who were discharged automatically because their jurisdictional time had expired. There was no significant difference between these two groups in the number of subsequent arrests. Interestingly, those persons who had at least one recorded police hold for mental illness at some time in their life had a significantly higher number of arrests than did those who had no such holds. Similarly, those who had at least one police encounter as a juvenile and those who had at least one drunkenness contact had higher numbers of adult arrests for criminal charges than did those without such contacts.

The sixth study reviewed the first five years of PSRB operation.[39] The paper that resulted was very useful in the legislative debate from which the PSRB emerged virtually unchanged. The paper summarized salient findings from earlier research and added analyses of data from other sources.

We reported that the census of insanity acquittees at the Oregon State Hospital, after climbing rapidly since the early 1970s, peaked in 1979. During the following year it declined by about 20 percent to a level where it has remained since. This drop in the number of hospitalized acquittees apparently resulted from a combination of factors including decrease in the number of persons placed under the jurisdiction of the PSRB, the increased use of conditional release by judges as an alternative to hospitalization, and conditional release or discharge by the PSRB of a large number of acquittees who were initially hospitalized.

By the end of 1982 the PSRB had discharged approximately half of those who had been placed under its jurisdiction. The most frequent reasons for discharge were: no longer presenting a substantial danger, which occurred 46 percent of the time; expiration of maximum jurisdiction, 33 percent; and no longer being affected by mental disease or defect, 13 percent. The remainder were discharged for miscellaneous reasons, including natural death and suicide.

Discharged Psychiatric Security Review Board Clients," *International Journal of Law and Psychiatry* (in press).

39. Jeffrey L. Rogers, Joseph D. Bloom, and Spero M. Manson, "Oregon's New Insanity Defense System: A Review of the First Five Years—1978-1982," *Bulletin of the American*

Also during those first five years, 295 people, who constituted 47 percent of those under PSRB jurisdiction, were conditionally released at least once. While they were conditionally released, 18 of those 295, or 6 percent, were charged with new felonies, 21, or 7 percent, with new misdemeanors. Interestingly, 14 of the total of 39 persons charged with new crimes were found guilty of the new charges; these findings of guilt indicate that in Oregon a previous insanity acquittal is no guarantee of a subsequent insanity acquittal. The most recent PSRB data show that in 1983 there were 15 people who were charged with new crimes while on conditional release; however, only 2 of these people were charged with felonies.

The issue of recidivism is of paramount concern to policymakers and lay citizens in Oregon and elsewhere. Many of them assert, or imply, that recidivism would be reduced and community security increased by narrowing or eliminating the insanity defense, but restricting the insanity defense will inevitably shift mentally ill offenders to other systems such as prison and parole. There is a vital need to determine whether such a result would actually enhance public safety. Virtually no research has been done on the comparative effectiveness of the insanity defense system and the correctional system in treating and managing seriously mentally ill offenders. Oregon's comprehensive approach to managing insanity acquittees provides an opportunity for detailed comparison of these models and other evaluations, based on data, of public systems for managing mentally ill offenders.

CONCLUSION

Oregon's PSRB system holds promise as a viable approach for managing a subgroup of mentally ill offenders. It has brought uniformity and predictability to decisions about management of this population. By centralizing supervision in a single board, it has ended the chaotic and often ineffective monitoring by judges throughout the state who had neither the resources, time, nor expertise to supervise insanity acquittees. The PSRB system also has provided community treatment and support programs for chronically mentally ill and dangerous offenders, and it has provided the community with adequate security from those on conditional release. By facilitating conditional release, the system has helped to ease hospital overcrowding.

The multidisciplinary, independent, and part-time structure of the PSRB helps to insulate the decision makers from political and institutional pressures. It distributes responsibility among disciplines, while simultaneously centralizing accountability. The Oregon system has been endorsed by a broad spectrum of professional and lay groups within the state and is the object of increasing attention and cautious emulation in other states. It is too early to say whether the optimism of the first five years will continue to be warranted; longer-term studies are needed. Nevertheless, the Oregon model already has assumed a prominent and promising role in the continuing national debate about the insanity defense.

Academy of Psychiatry and the Law, 12(4):383-403 (1984).

A Review of Research on the Insanity Defense

By RICHARD A. PASEWARK

ABSTRACT: Since the attempted assassination of President Reagan by John Hinckley, Jr., avid attention has again focused upon the supposed deficiencies and abuses of the insanity plea, and the nation has witnessed many attempts in various jurisdictions either to alter or to abolish the plea. Unfortunately, these efforts have been conducted within a context where little empirical data on the operation of the plea is available to guide policymakers. The present article represents an effort to summarize the information that is currently available concerning the frequency with which the plea is made, the characteristics of defendants involved, and the subsequent psychiatric and criminal histories of these individuals.

Richard A. Pasewark received the bachelor's degree from the City College of New York and the master's and doctorate degrees from New York University. Currently, he serves as chairperson of the Department of Psychology, University of Wyoming, Laramie. He has been director of the Wyoming Division of Mental Health and psychologist at Embreeville State Hospital, Pennsylvania. He has also served as a consultant to a state hospital and prison, the Air Force, the Peace Corps, the National Institute of Mental Health, and the American Psychological Association. His major research interest focuses upon the interface between the mental health and criminal justice systems.

CONSIDERING that throughout its long history the defense of insanity has been beset by controversy, it is surprising that relatively little empirical research exists regarding the actual operation and use of this defense. Lacking a systematic base of empirical information, there exists no common factual foundation upon which various discussions, debates, and proposals for reform can be based. Not surprisingly, therefore, much of the discussion on this topic tends to be based upon philosophical, ideological, and doctrinal concerns. Unfortunately, the discussion is also in reaction to and influenced by those few highly select and dramatic cases that typically receive considerable media attention.

Lack of an adequate research base is particularly unfortunate at a time when, stirred by negative public reactions occasioned by the acquittal on grounds of insanity of John W. Hinckley, Jr., for his attempted assassination of President Reagan, many states have passed or are contemplating legislation designed to alter dramatically or even to abolish this special defense.

Although there were a few earlier empirical studies of the insanity defense, it has only been within the last 15 years that any measure of systematic information has begun to become available. Reflecting the nascent state of research in this area, most studies have been confined to assembling data about (1) opinions and attitudes held by various groups about the defense; (2) the frequency of its use and success; (3) characteristics of insanity defendants; and (4) the post-adjudication follow-up of insanity acquittees to ascertain later outcomes. Research has also been restricted to a few jurisdictions and to limited periods of time. Consequently, it proves difficult to generalize from the empirical data that have been thus far generated.

This article will review and summarize selected areas of the extant empirical research on the insanity defense.[1] Discussed will be research pertaining to (1) opinions about the insanity defense; (2) the frequency of the use and success of the plea; (3) characteristics of defendants who use the defense; (4) characteristics of persons who have been adjudicated not guilty by reason of insanity (NGRI); and (5) follow-up studies concerning the later outcomes for insanity acquittees.

OPINIONS ABOUT THE INSANITY DEFENSE

Results of most opinion studies on the insanity plea have revealed generally negative views. In a 1981 nationwide survey of 1601 randomly selected telephone subscribers, 87 percent of the respondents expressed the view that "too many accused of murder are using the insanity defense to keep from going to prison." Similarly, 69 percent opined that "the rules should be changed so that people charged with murder cannot use an insanity defense."[2]

In New York, for a sample of prosecutors, defense attorneys, and judges, Burton and Steadman found that, except

---

1. Other reviews have appeared elsewhere, including Richard A. Pasewark, "Insanity Plea: A Review of the Research Literature," *Journal of Psychiatry and Law*, 9:357-401 (1981); idem, "Insanity Plea: Facts, Fictions, and Unknowns," *Journal of Crime and Justice*, 6:81-99 (1983); Henry J. Steadman and Jeraldine Braff, "Defendants Not Guilty by Reason of Insanity," in *Mentally Disordered Offenders: Perspectives from Law and Social Science*, ed. John Monahan and Henry J. Steadman (New York: Plenum, 1983).

2. Associated Press - National Broadcasting Company, "Insanity Defense Poll" (6 Oct. 1981).

for judges, respondents believed the American Law Institute (ALI) insanity test being used operated poorly. Among the cited problems were poor statutory definitions and vagueness in the law resulting in uneven application; lack of understanding of the law by juries and the public; overreliance on psychiatric testimony that was imprecise and superficial; and the perceived lack of judicial review over release of defendants acquitted on grounds of insanity.[3] In Illinois, Cavanaugh and his colleagues found that only 16 percent of 129 responding psychiatrists supported that state's ALI insanity rule. They noted that "overutilization of the insanity defense, and abuses in determinations of lack of criminal responsibility were frequently mentioned by respondents."[4]

In Wyoming, significant segments of a variety of surveyed groups—resulting in a sample size of 785—believed that the insanity plea was overused and abused. These negative opinions were expressed by 49 percent of the sample of mental health professionals working in mental health centers, 54 percent of state hospital professional staff, 87 percent of responding state legislators, 90 percent of the community residents, 91 percent of police officers, and 94 percent of the college students and state hospital aides. Interestingly, all groups grossly overestimated both the number of persons who pleaded insanity as well as the number actually adjudicated NGRI.[5]

The Wyoming investigations suggest that negative reactions to the insanity defense might, at least in part, result from inaccurate information and associated perceptions and attitudes. Lending some credence to this suggestion is a study by Steadman and Cocozza.[6] Investigating attitudes toward the "criminally insane" in 417 randomly selected households in Albany, New York, they found that such individuals were depicted as more "harmful," "violent," "dangerous," and "bad," compared to the referent group of "most people." Of the persons listed more than once as "criminally insane" by respondents, none could accurately be so classified; all, however, had been convicted of some violent and highly publicized crime such as murder, kidnapping, or bombing. The researchers attributed such misidentification to the nature of media publicity given to notorious criminal cases.

The only published study reporting favorable attitudes toward the insanity defense involved Wyoming attorneys.[7] Of the 51 attorneys who had entered the insanity plea on behalf of clients, 97 percent indicated satisfaction with the ALI rule, despite the fact that only 2 percent of the defendants had actually been adjudicated NGRI.

---

3. Nancy M. Burton and Henry J. Steadman, "Legal Professionals' Perceptions of the Insanity Defense," *Journal of Psychiatry and Law*, 6:173-87 (1978).

4. James L. Cavanaugh, Jr., Richard R. Rogers, and Bonnie Price, "The Insanity Defense in Illinois—A Psychiatric Perspective," *Bulletin of the American Academy of Psychiatry and the Law*, 8:59 (1980).

5. Richard A. Pasewark and Mark L. Pantle, "Insanity Plea: Legislators' View," *American Journal of Psychiatry*, 136:222-23 (1979); Richard A. Pasewark, Deborah Seidenzahl, and Mark L. Pantle, "Opinions about the Insanity Plea," *Journal of Forensic Psychology*, 8:63-72 (1981).

6. Henry J. Steadman and Joseph J. Cocozza, "Selective Reporting and the Public's Misconceptions of the Criminally Insane," *Public Opinion Quarterly*, 41:523-33 (1978).

7. Richard A. Pasewark and Paul L. Craig, "Insanity Plea: Defense Attorneys' View," *Journal of Psychiatry and Law*, 8:413-40 (1980).

The role of media coverage has also been noted by others in seeking an explanation for the seemingly erroneous beliefs and perceptions that large segments of the public seem to have about the insanity defense.[8] Even though the incidence of shocking headline cases is infrequent, the considerable and often fairly sustained coverage, progressing from arrest through trial and disposition, may well lend greater salience to these cases. Thus, it is probable that such coverage will tend to instill in the public a belief that the plea is utilized much more frequently than it actually is and that these reported cases are representative of all defendants using the defense.

Related to the issue of media publicity, Jeffrey and Pasewark surveyed 75 community residents and 150 students enrolled in introductory psychology classes.[9] As in previous Wyoming investigations, respondents grossly overestimated both the number of NGRI pleas and NGRI acquittals. However, when presented with the actual statistics, a significant change occurred in the opinions of respondents about the plea. For example, of community residents, 92 percent originally agreed with the statement "The insanity plea is used too much," and 89 percent agreed that "too many people escape responsibility for crimes by pleading insanity." After being presented with the actual statistics, agreement with these statements decreased to 52 percent and 42 percent, respectively. Although this somewhat dramatic alteration in opinion resulted from knowledge of the low frequency— 104 of 12,307 indictments—and success of the plea—4 of 104—a substantial number of respondents continued to adhere to the belief that the plea was overused and abused. Thus, it would seem that although there are many individuals whose adverse opinions derive from misinformation, there is nevertheless a large segment to whom the plea is abhorrent despite its very low base rate.

FREQUENCY AND SUCCESS
OF THE INSANITY DEFENSE

No national statistics are available for the United States concerning the frequency of the insanity plea that are comparable to those generated for Great Britain.[10] This is probably because, in the United States, most crimes are matters of state, rather than federal, jurisdiction. Moreover, within most states there is no centralized collection of information, and accurate data on the number of insanity pleas and acquittals is not available from a central source. Further, in many states, to determine the number of insanity pleas that were entered, it would probably prove necessary to examine records in each of the state's courts.

Periodic efforts have been made to generate national statistics in the United States regarding the frequency and success of the plea. For example,

8. *Myths and Realities: Report of the National Commission on the Insanity Defense* (Arlington, VA: National Association of Mental Health, 1983); Saleem A. Shah, "Criminal Responsibility," in *Perspectives in Forensic Psychiatry and Psychology,* ed. W. J. Curran, A. L. McGarry, and S. A. Shah (Philadelphia: F. A. Davis, forthcoming).

9. Richard W. Jeffrey and Richard A. Pasewark, "Altering Opinions about the Insanity Plea," *Journal of Psychiatry and Law,* 11:29-40 (1983).

10. Nigel Walker, *Crime and Insanity in England* (Edinburgh: Edinburgh University Press, 1968), vol. 1; Nigel Walker and Sarah McCabe, *Crime and Insanity in England* (Edinburgh: Edinburgh University Press, 1973), vol. 2.

initially Scheidemandel and Kanno, and later Steadman and his colleagues, surveyed the various states to obtain information about institutionalized mentally disordered offenders, including insanity acquittees.[11] Steadman and his colleagues reported that in 1978 there were a total of 1625 admissions of NGRI cases to security hospitals. They were unable, however, to provide information on the number of NGRI cases that were accorded post-adjudication dispositions other than hospitalization—such as conditional or outright release to the community.[12]

Most recently, Pasewark and McGinley surveyed the mental health authorities and alternate sources in the 50 states and the District of Columbia to determine the frequency of NGRI pleas and verdicts.[13] The disappointing results underscore the general unavailability of even this basic information about the plea. Of the 47 responding jurisdictions, only 10, or 21 percent, were able to provide complete information; 17, or 36 percent, indicated only the number of defendants adjudicated NGRI; 1, or 2 percent, was able to provide only the number of insanity pleas entered; and 19, or 40 percent, were unable to provide any data.

From the information currently available, it would appear that (1) the plea is seldom made; (2) the rate at which the plea is used varies widely among states and even within the counties of a given state; and (3) once entered, the success rate for the plea varies among jurisdictions, for presently unknown reasons. For example, among states reporting in the Pasewark and McGinley survey, Michigan indicated 1082 NGRI pleas and 54 NGRI acquittals. The respective figures reported for Montana were 45 and 4; Ohio, 845 and 122; Vermont, 200 and 53; Rhode Island, 4 and 4; and Wyoming, 64 and 0. Some states were able to report information only about insanity acquittals. Some illustrative figures include 6 insanity acquittals in Alabama, 250 in California, 32 in Colorado, and 15 in Virginia.

In earlier reports dealing with single jurisdictions, comparable low incidence and high variability in insanity acquittals have been indicated for California, Connecticut, the District of Columbia, Hawaii, Maryland, Michigan, Missouri, New Jersey, New York, Ontario, Oregon, and Wyoming.[14]

11. Patricia L. Scheidemandel and Charles K. Kanno, *The Mentally Ill Offender: A Survey of Treatment Programs* (Washington, DC: American Psychiatric Association, Joint Information Service, 1965; Henry J. Steadman et al., "Mentally Disordered Offenders: A National Survey of Patients and Facilities," *Law and Human Behavior*, 6:31-38 (1982).

12. For a more recent survey of forensic facilities, see Charlotte A. Kerr and Jeffrey A. Roth, "Populations, Practices, and Problems in Forensic Psychiatric Facilities," this issue of *The Annals* of the American Academy of Political and Social Science.

13. Richard A. Pasewark and W. Hugh McGinley, "Insanity Plea: National Survey of Frequency and Success," *Journal of Psychiatry and Law* (in press).

14. For California, see Arthur R. Matthews, Jr., *Mental Disability and the Law: A Field Study* (Chicago: American Bar Association, 1970); for Connecticut, Betty L. Phillips and Richard A. Pasewark, "Insanity Plea in Connecticut," *Bulletin of the American Academy of Psychiatry and the Law*, 8:335-44 (1980); for District of Columbia, Richard Arens, "The Durham Rule in Action: Judicial Psychiatry and Psychiatric Justice," *Law and Society Review*, 1:41-84 (1967); for Hawaii, Kenneth Fukunaga, *The Criminally Insane in Hawaii* (Honolulu: State of Hawaii, Department of Health, 1977); for Maryland, Michael K. Spodak, Stuart B. Silver, and Christine V. Wright, "Criminality of Discharged Insanity Acquittees: Fifteen Year Experience in Maryland Reviewed," *Bulletin of the American Academy of Psychiatry*

CHARACTERISTICS OF INSANITY DEFENDANTS

Little is known about the characteristics of individuals who raise the defense of insanity. The only extant studies systematically reporting characteristics of defendants derive from the previously cited Wyoming investigations and span different time periods from 1967 to 1979. In Wyoming, the portrait of the NGRI defendant has remained relatively stable over time.[15]

Fairly typical is the picture derived from the work of Randolph and Pasewark, who, over a ten-year period, tracked the 68 defendants who entered the plea in 1967 and 1968.[16]

The typical NGRI defendant in Wyoming is young, single or divorced, and male. Randolph and Pasewark found their defendants to have a mean age of 31.7 years; 44 percent of the sample was single, 24 percent was divorced, and 91 percent was male. The defendant usually has limited education and is employed mainly in unskilled or semiskilled occupations, characteristically in a sporadic fashion. Although the group studied was mainly white, minorities were not underrepresented. The defendants were a relatively transient group; 47 percent had resided in Wyoming for less than a year. Alcohol abuse was present in 59 percent and 14 percent had drug problems. Previous psychiatric hospitalizations had been experienced by 28 percent. Of the subjects, 67 percent had incurred a prior arrest, 54 percent for a felony. Those with arrests averaged 3.9 prior apprehensions. The alleged NGRI offenses ranged from bad checks, for 17 percent, to homicide, for 16 percent. Offender-victim relationships paralleled those in non-NGRI cases. During the court-ordered psychiatric evaluation, 15 percent received psychotic diagnoses and 14 percent had personality disorders. Eighteen percent were evaluated as incompetent to stand trial and 7 percent as insane.

Upon return to court following evaluation at the hospital, only 10 percent retained the insanity plea—perhaps as a result of nonsupportive hospital findings. Only 3 percent were adjudicated NGRI, but this NGRI statistic probably

---

and the Law (in press); for Michigan, Michael Criss and D. Robert Racine, "Impact of Change in Legal Standards for Those Adjudicated Not Guilty by Reason of Insanity," *Bulletin of American Academy of Psychiatry and the Law*, 8:261-71 (1980); for Missouri, John Petrila, "The Insanity Defense and Other Mental Health Dispositions in Missouri," *International Journal of Law and Psychiatry*, 5:81-101 (1982); for New Jersey, Anne C. Singer, "Insanity Acquittal in the Seventies: Observations and Empirical Analysis of One Jurisdiction," *Mental Disability Law Reporter*, 2:406-17 (1976); for New York, Richard A. Pasewark, Mark L. Pantle, and Henry J. Steadman, "The Insanity Plea in New York State, 1965-76," *New York State Bar Journal*, 52:186-89, 217-25 (1979); for Ontario, Cyril Greenland, "Crime and the Insanity Defense, an International Comparison: Ontario and New York State," *Bulletin of the American Academy of Psychiatry and the Law*, 7:125-38 (1979); for Oregon, Jeffrey L. Rogers and Joseph D. Bloom, "Characteristics of Persons Committed to Oregon's Psychiatric Security Review Board," *Bulletin of the American Academy of Psychiatry and the Law*, 10:155-64 (1982); for Wyoming, Richard A. Pasewark and Bruce W. Lanthorn, "Dispositions of Persons Utilizing the Insanity Plea in a Rural State," *Journal of Humanics*, 5:87-98 (1977).

15. For investigations on Wyoming, see Pasewark and Lanthorn, "Dispositions of Persons Utilizing the Insanity Plea"; Robert L. Randolph and Richard A. Pasewark, "Characteristics, Dispositions and Subsequent Arrests of Defendants Pleading Insanity in a Rural State," *Journal of Psychiatry and Law*, 11:345-60 (1983); Richard A. Pasewark and Robert L. Randolph, "Effects of Three Changes of Insanity Plea Statutes in Wyoming," *Journal of Psychiatry and Law* (in press).

16. Randolph and Pasewark, "Characteristics, Dispositions, and Subsequent Arrests."

understates the influence of the plea in the criminal process. While the general Wyoming rate of dismissals and decisions not to prosecute was 10 percent, fully 32 percent of the insanity defendants had their cases disposed of in this fashion.

In the 10 years following trial, 58 percent were rearrested and 44 percent had at least one felony arrest. The number of posttrial arrests did not differ from that in the 10 years prior to the NGRI offense.

Although of interest, the preceding information concerns only a single jurisdiction. Obviously, many other investigations in various jurisdictions are needed to determine the manner, if any, in which insanity defendants might differ from the general criminal defendant population.

CHARACTERISTICS OF NGRI ACQUITTEES

Several reports have been published concerning the characteristics of defendants adjudicated NGRI.

NGRI offenses

While a wide range of offenses including misdemeanors are reported, more serious offenses against the person, such as homicide, rape, and assault, are overrepresented in all studies reporting on this.[17]

Despite this general overrepresentation of serious crimes against persons, pronounced differences occur between jurisdictions. Thus, while 44 percent of New York State NGRI acquittees had been charged with homicide or attempted homicide,[18] in Missouri homicides were involved in only 9 percent of the cases.[19] In Essex County, New Jersey, Ontario, Oregon, and Michigan, the respective figures for homicide charges were 26, 63, 8, and 30 percent. As was the case with NGRI defendants in Wyoming, the victim-offender relationship in NGRI acquittal cases in New York paralleled that in general criminal cases.[20]

Sex

Insanity acquittees, like criminal defendants generally, tend primarily to be males. Nevertheless, a question remains as to whether females are overrepresented. Comparing NGRI acquittees to prison inmates in New York, there was an overrepresentation of females. In a much smaller Connecticut NGRI population, however, females comprised 8 percent of the acquittees and 5 percent of the prison admissions.[21]

Age

NGRI acquittees have been found in some jurisdictions to be somewhat older than the general offender population.[22] In Missouri the average age was 34.[23] In New York it was 36 years. However, in

---

17. See note 14 for studies dealing with each state.

18. Henry J. Steadman, "Insanity Acquittals in New York State, 1965-1978," *American Journal of Psychiatry*, 137:321-26 (1980).

19. Petrila, "Insanity Defense and Other Mental Health Dispositions in Missouri."

20. See references cited for the particular states in note 14.

21. Michael Hawkins and Richard A. Pasewark, "Characteristics of Persons Utilizing the Insanity Plea," *Psychological Reports*, 53:191-95 (1983).

22. Ibid.

23. William R. Morrow and Donald B. Peterson, "Follow-up of Discharged Offenders—'Not Guilty by Reason of Insanity' and 'Criminal Sexual Psychopaths'," *Journal of Criminal Law, Criminology and Police Science*, 57:31-34 (1966).

Connecticut, the average age of 28 years did not differ significantly from prison inmates.[24] In Ontario and Oregon, the mean ages were 27.5 and 30.8 years, respectively. In all jurisdictions, the age range is quite dispersed. In New York it was 16 to 77 years.[25]

Race and ethnicity

Surprisingly, few studies have reported on the ethnic and racial characteristics of acquittees. In Michigan, 54 percent of the acquittees were white and 45 percent were black; in New York, 65 percent were white and 27 percent were black; in Connecticut, 80 percent were white and 20 percent were black. In Connecticut and New York, whites were found to be markedly overrepresented in the NGRI population as compared to prison inmates.[26]

Education

Criss and Racine reported a low education level for acquittees in Michigan. In Connecticut and New York the mean educational levels were significantly below those of prison inmates. However, in New York, a relatively bimodal distribution was obtained. Acquittees tended to have either a high educational level or hardly any formal schooling.[27]

Employment

In Michigan, 38 percent of acquittees were unemployed while 53 percent were unskilled workers and 8 percent were skilled workers. In Hawaii, it is the rare

24. Hawkins and Pasewark, "Characteristics of Persons Utilizing the Insanity Plea."
25. For particular references for each state, see note 14.
26. Ibid.
27. Ibid.

individual, either pleading insanity or so adjudicated, who is employed at the time of the alleged offense.[28] From the educational and employment information that is currently available, it seems evident that references to the insanity plea as a "defense of the rich" are quite erroneous.

Previous arrests

For many insanity acquittees, the NGRI offense does not represent their first contact with law enforcement agencies. In New York, males were considerably more likely to have incurred prior arrests than were females; 47 percent of the males had prior arrests, whereas only 15 percent of the females did. This sex differential has been observed in all jurisdictions reporting this information. The 113 NGRI males in New York with prior police contacts had a total of 524 arrests, varying from misdemeanors to felonies. In Michigan, Cooke and Sikorski reported that 25 percent of the NGRI cases had previous convictions, but these researchers did not indicate arrest information. In Missouri, 66 percent of NGRI acquittees had a previous arrest, while in Connecticut this figure was 64 percent. In Ontario 50 percent of the male and 6 percent of the female acquittees had prior arrests. For a later Missouri group, Petrila documented that 39 percent of the NGRI cases had prior convictions.[29]

28. For Michigan, see Gerald Cooke and Cynthia Sikorski, "Factors Affecting Length of Hospitalization of Persons Adjudicated Not Guilty by Reason of Insanity," *Bulletin of the American Academy of Psychiatry and the Law,* 2:251-61 (1974); for Hawaii, see Richard A. Pasewark and Howard Gudeman, "Insanity Plea in Hawaii" (in progress).
29. For New York, see Pasewark, Pantle, and Steadman, "Insanity Plea in New York State"; for

Previous hospitalizations

In six studies, the proportion of acquittees having prior mental hospitalizations ranged from 35 percent to 79 percent.[30] In investigations differentiating between the sexes, males were much more likely to have been previously hospitalized. No data have been reported on other mental health contacts, such as visits to clinics or private practitioners.

It is difficult to evaluate precisely what these statistics mean. First, it is possible—although not typically stated—that in most studies, reported hospitalizations represent only admissions to state facilities in the particular jurisdictions examined because of the difficulty in documenting private hospitalizations and public sector hospitalizations in other states. On the one hand, this problem might underestimate recorded hospitalizations. However, because of the low socioeconomic status of most defendants, private hospitalization might not be a significant factor. A second problem concerning the interpretation of hospitalization data is the possible inclusion in some reports of hospitalizations that are associated with criminal charges, such as pretrial psychiatric evaluations.

Diagnoses

Diagnoses given to NGRI acquittees vary among jurisdictions. As would be anticipated, a large proportion of cases were classified as psychotic, but even this proportion differs markedly among states. Whether such variation reflects differences in the application of insanity statutes in various jurisdictions, the time at which diagnoses were rendered—for example, in court evaluation or during hospitalizations—the unreliability of psychiatric diagnoses, or some combination of these factors is unknown. In New York State during the period 1965-76, 68 percent of the acquittees received a diagnosis of psychosis. During 1978 in Missouri, fully 78 percent of the NGRI cases were diagnosed as psychotic. In Oregon, Connecticut, Michigan, and Ontario, the respective percentage figures were 67, 40, 73, and 55.[31]

Most studies, except Petrila's of Missouri, report a fairly large proportion of nonpsychotic personality disorders. In Connecticut fully 44 percent of the insanity acquittees were diagnosed as having personality disorders.[32]

Differentiating successful and unsuccessful NGRI defendants

Only two published studies attempt to differentiate between defendants who were successful—that is, who were adjudicated NGRI—and those who were unsuccessful with their insanity defense. Of 202 defendants who used the plea in Erie County, New York, 51, or 25 percent, were acquitted by reason of insanity. Of the many variables examined, successful and unsuccessful defendants could be discriminated on only three. Less likely to be found NGRI were those in the 25-29 age bracket and those with fewer than five prior hospi-

---

Michigan, Cooke and Sikorski, "Factors Affecting Length of Hospitalization"; for Missouri, Petrila, "Insanity Defense and Other Mental Health Dispositions"; for Ontario, Greenland, "Crime and the Insanity Defense."

30. See Hawkins and Pasewark, "Characteristics of Persons Utilizing the Insanity Plea"; and Criss and Racine, "Impact of Change in Legal Standards."

31. See note 14 for references for specific states.

32. For Missouri, see Petrila, "Insanity Defense and Other Mental Health Dispositions"; for Connecticut, see Phillips and Pasewark, "Insanity Plea in Connecticut."

talizations. Most strongly associated with an NGRI adjudication was the opinion on the issue of insanity formulated by the examining psychiatrist or psychiatrists. Of 66 defendants evaluated as insane at the time of the offense, 46, or 70 percent, were adjudicated NGRI and 9 cases, or 14 percent, were dismissed. Only 11, or 17 percent, evaluated as insane were convicted. In contrast, only 3, or 2 percent, of the 131 individuals evaluated as sane received NGRI verdicts.[33]

In a group of 115 Chicago defendants evaluated in conjunction with their insanity plea, Rogers and his colleagues found that an evaluation of insanity by the forensic mental health examiners was associated with completion of a high school education and a prior history of schizophrenia, while a subsequent court NGRI adjudication was significantly related to the psychiatric evaluation of insanity.[34]

Steadman, Rogers, and researchers working with them attributed this strong relationship between findings of the forensic evaluation and court decisions to the potent influence of psychiatric recommendations. Fukunaga and his coauthors, reporting similar findings for Hawaii, suggested that, while this interpretation might be valid, an alternative explanation is also plausible. Given the same evidence, the two groups—the legal triers of fact and mental health examiners—may well reach similar conclusions. Unfortunately, studies that specifically focus upon the direct influence of psychiatric findings are not available, although the mock-jury study of Klein and Temerlin lends some credence to the potency of psychiatric testimony.[35]

FOLLOW-UP STUDIES OF INSANITY ACQUITTEES

Given the current climate of dissatisfaction with the insanity defense, it is surprising that only a few investigations have examined the course of NGRI acquittees after their adjudication. These investigations have focused on post-adjudication mandatory hospitalization, and the subsequent psychiatric hospitalizations and arrests following release.

Hospitalization of NGRI acquittees

Extremely variable periods of involuntary hospitalization have been reported following NGRI acquittals. This is the case even for persons receiving insanity acquittals for the same type of offense. For example, in New York State, hospitalization periods for 34 males, who had been acquitted by reason of insanity for homicide or attempted homicide charges, ranged from 1 to 2326 days, with a mean of 488 days.[36]

To some individuals such findings are disturbing. It is difficult for them to accept that a person acquitted for murder on grounds of insanity might be hospitalized for a relatively brief period.

---

33. Henry J. Steadman et al., "Factors Associated with a Successful Insanity Defense," *American Journal of Psychiatry*, 140:401-4 (1983).

34. Richard Rogers, William Seman, and Jan Stampley, "A Study of Socio-Demographic Characteristics of Individuals Evaluated for Insanity," *National Journal of Offender Therapies and Comparative Criminology*, 28:3-10 (1984).

35. Kenneth Fukunaga et al., "Insanity Plea: Interexaminer Agreement and Concordance of Psychiatric Opinion and Court Verdict," *Law and Human Behavior*, 5:325-28 (1981); Helen E. Klein and Maurice K. Temerlin, "On Expert Testimony in Sanity Cases," *Journal of Nervous and Mental Disease*, 149:435-38 (1969).

36. Pasewark, "Insanity Plea: A Review of the Research."

However, as will be discussed later, such variable periods of confinement should be anticipated given the philosophical and legal bases for the special defense of insanity. The post-acquittal hospitalization of NGRI cases is premised on the need for continued treatment for their mental disorder and also for protection of the community. This rationale for post-acquittal confinement bears no theoretical or doctrinal relationship to the nature or seriousness of the offense charged, although hospital staff and courts certainly seem sensitive to such concerns.

In New York State, Pasewark and his associates compared periods of institutionalization for NGRI acquittees and felons who had committed the same types of criminal acts, pleaded guilty, and been imprisoned. In the first period examined, 1965-71,[37] NGRI acquittees were mandatorily hospitalized at a facility operated by the Department of Corrections. Acquittees and convicted felons did not differ significantly in the length of their confinement, although females in both groups were institutionalized for significantly shorter periods than their male cohorts. During a later time frame, 1971-73,[38] during which acquittees were hospitalized in public civil facilities, NGRI males were found to have been institutionalized for significantly shorter periods of time than the comparable felons—533 versus 837 days. No significant difference was found between the female groups, who were again determined to have shorter hospitalization periods than their male counterparts.

In a parallel study in Connecticut, comparable results were found during the period 1970-72.[39] During this period, 25 NGRI acquittees were mandatorily hospitalized at a civil hospital, following the NGRI verdict. In contrast to New York, Connecticut law provided that this hospitalization period could not exceed the maximum prison term prescribed for the offense of which the defendant was acquitted. Results indicated that NGRI acquittees were institutionalized for significantly shorter periods than were their felon cohorts— 639 versus 1142 days. Further, they spent significantly fewer days hospitalized than the minimum sentences imposed upon the felon group—639 versus 1171 days.

Reporting on 167 insanity acquittees in Michigan, Cooke and Sikorski indicated that individuals with shorter periods of hospitalization tended to be nonwhite, married or widowed, and urban residents; they tended to have higher educational and occupational levels. More often than not, they had been charged with nonhomicide offenses, had not previously been hospitalized, did not have prior criminal records, and had been diagnosed as suffering from personality disorders.[40] The results of this study are subject to question, however, as the data analyses employed a variety of procedures and accepted as significant any variable found to be significant by any of the methods applied.

37. Mark L. Pantle, Richard A. Pasewark, and Henry J. Steadman, "Comparing Institutionalization Periods and Subsequent Arrests of Insanity Acquittees and Convicted Felons," *Journal of Psychiatry and Law*, 8:305-16 (1980).

38. Richard A. Pasewark, Mark L. Pantle, and Henry J. Steadman, "Detention and Rearrest Rates of Persons Found Not Guilty by Reason of Insanity and Convicted Felons," *American Journal of Psychiatry*, 139:892-97 (1982).

39. Phillips and Pasewark, "Insanity Plea in Connecticut."

40. Cooke and Sikorski, "Factors Affecting Length of Hospitalization."

In a more recent study seeking to predict length of hospitalization for New York State insanity acquittees, a stepwise regression procedure was employed.[41] Of the 21 variables examined, only three maintained significance in the equation and contributed more than an additional 1 percent of the observed variance: severity of the offense, being male, and being presently unmarried. Even these three variables accounted for only 8 percent of the variance.

A number of other items have also appeared in the literature reporting on smaller samples of insanity acquittees or on particular sections within a jurisdiction. For example, Lewin reported shorter hospitalization periods for NGRI acquittees with attorneys, while Singer observed shorter hospitalization periods following a court decision mandating a hearing on the issues of present mental illness and dangerousness before mandatory hospitalization.[42]

It was noted earlier that, in theory, the nature and severity of the offense charged should not have an influence on the length of the insanity acquittees' involuntary hospitalization—unless it can be demonstrated that mentally disturbed persons who commit serious crimes are less responsive to psychiatric treatment for their mental disorder than those committing minor offenses. The post-acquittal involuntary hospitalization is designed to provide necessary treatment for the mental disorder that may continue to exist, and also to protect the community from persons who may pose a danger due to their mental disorder. Yet, usual concerns and criticisms pertaining to the relatively short periods of post-acquittal hospitalization seem to relate such periods of confinement to the nature of the offense charged and the penal sentences that can be imposed following conviction. Additionally, critics often fail to consider that the judicial process is frequently rather lengthy. For example, two, three, or even four years may elapse between commission of the offense and the subsequent trial and insanity verdict. During this interval, some defendants may have been hospitalized for care and treatment if found incompetent to stand trial. In any event, during this interval it is quite likely that the mental disorder of many acquittees will have abated or even disappeared; hence, there may not be any sound legal basis for their continued or prolonged confinement.

What seems also to be overlooked is that for some NGRI acquittees the periods of hospitalization can be extremely long—far in excess of the duration of the incarceration that might have followed conviction. For example, in 1916 in New York a 16-year-old youth murdered his teacher and was adjudged insane. As of 1976, he was still hospitalized. Although prolonged periods of hospitalization for insanity acquittees used to be fairly common, this situation appears to have changed during the past decade or so as courts have imposed durational limits on such indeterminate confinement. In comparing the disposition of insanity acquittees with persons who have been convicted, it needs to be remembered that even conviction for a felony does not necessarily result in a prison term. The defendant may plea-bargain to a lesser offense and may even

41. Henry J. Steadman et al., "Hospitalization Length of Insanity Acquittees," *Journal of Clinical Psychology,* 39:611-14 (1983).

42. Travis H. Lewin, "Disposition of the Irresponsible: Protection Following Commitment," *Michigan Law Review,* 66:721-36 (1966); Singer, "Insanity Acquittal in the Seventies."

receive a period of probationary supervision in the community. In a study I am conducting, cases have been identified in which persons convicted of homicide have received probation. Other defendants indicted for homicide were later convicted of assault and the abuse of a corpse.

Post-release hospitalization

Little information is available regarding the later hospitalization of acquittees following their NGRI institutionalization. In New York, of 107 discharged acquittees, 23, or 22 percent, experienced 47 rehospitalization episodes. Of these, 43 were civil and 4 were associated with additional criminal charges. In Connecticut, 44 percent of the released acquittees had subsequent hospitalizations.[43]

Subsequent arrests

Some studies tracking NGRI acquittees following their release indicate a relatively high rate of criminal recidivism. Others report a low rate.

Morrow and Peterson found that, three years after discharge, 37 percent of 44 Missouri acquittees had been convicted of at least one felony.[44] This rate was comparable to the 35 percent recidivism for a federal prison sample.

Spodak and his associates reported on 86 males adjudicated NGRI and hospitalized in Maryland from August 1967 to June 1976 and followed until mid-1982. Median time in the community was 9.5 years. Of the 86 released acquittees, 48, or 56 percent, incurred 130 post-hospitalization arrests. Of these arrests, 47 percent resulted in convictions. The number of subjects convicted is not reported. Only 11 persons, or 13 percent, were incarcerated upon conviction. Spodak and his colleagues argued that incarcerations perhaps serve as a better index of criminal behavior in patients as they reflect behavior that is dangerous or potentially dangerous. Often arrests "do not truly reflect recurrent significant criminality. [Offenders] may be subject to arrest on lesser suspicion when a significant offense occurs . . . additionally arrests may reflect community bias."[45] This position must, however, be regarded as speculative. Many non-mentally-ill individuals charged with dangerous crimes, such as aggravated assault and robbery, are given nonprison sentences. Moreover it is not known whether an NGRI acquittee is more or less subject to arrest than any other individual.

Individuals adjudicated NGRI in New York from 1971 to 1976 evidenced a high rate of criminal recidivism by 1981. Of 111 released males, 35, or 32 percent, had accumulated 120 arrests and 26—23 percent—had at least one felony arrest. Of the 22 females, 3, or 14 percent, had post-release arrests.[46]

In two New York studies cited previously, NGRI acquittees were compared with felons who had pleaded guilty to the same criminal charge and had been imprisoned.[47] The initial study contained 46 persons adjudicated NGRI

43. For New York, see Pasewark, Pantle, and Steadman, "Insanity Plea in New York State, 1965-76"; for Connecticut, see Phillips and Pasewark, "Insanity Plea in Conneticut."

44. Morrow and Peterson, "Follow-up of Discharged Offenders."

45. Spodak, Silver, and Wright, "Criminality of Discharged Insanity Acquittees," p. 15 of manuscript.

46. Richard A. Pasewark et al., "Criminal Recidivism among Insanity Acquittees," *International Journal of Law and Psychiatry*, 5:365-75 (1982).

47. Pantle, Pasewark, and Steadman, "Comparing Institutionalization Periods"; Pasewark,

from 1965 to 1971 and 46 matched felons. During this period, NGRIs were hospitalized in a facility administered by the Department of Corrections. By the time the study terminated in 1976, 30 male and 7 female NGRI acquittees had been discharged. Of the 37, 9—24 percent—had incurred a total of 30 posthospitalization arrests. Of the 37 comparable felons who had been released from prison, 10—27 percent—experienced 15 subsequent arrests. All arrestees in both groups were males. The second New York study compared NGRI acquittees and felons who had been institutionalized from 1971 to 1973, when acquittees were involuntarily hospitalized at civil facilities. By 1976, comparable arrest rates were again demonstrated for the acquittee and felon groups. Similar results were obtained in a parallel study in Connecticut.[48]

These results are discouraging in their indication of relatively high recidivism rates for the acquittees, comparable to those for the released felons. Equally discouraging is a later follow-up study of New York acquittees that found that NGRIs who escaped during their mental hospitalization had rearrest rates comparable to those who had been discharged because they had presumably recovered from their mental disorders and were no longer considered dangerous.[49]

In contrast to these reports, Canada and Oregon report a relatively low post-release recidivism rate for acquittees. Unfortunately, the Canadian study by Quinsey, Preusse, and Fernley is somewhat contaminated as it included a number of defendants found unfit to stand trial.[50] Of 56 dischargees, only 3 were rearrested. This low rate is perhaps due to lengthy hospitalization periods, which averaged eight years. Upon discharge the acquittees were probably older and hence at lower risk for criminal recidivism.

The follow-up study by Bloom and his colleagues in Oregon is of particular interest as it presents outcome information on an innovative mechanism, the Psychiatric Security Review Board, established by statute in 1978 to supervise NGRI acquittees.[51] Subjects were 36 acquittees granted conditional release following trial and 90 acquittees granted conditional release following hospitalization by the board from 1978 to 1980. During this period, another 138 acquittees were not conditionally released. Of the 126 conditionally released, 40 were returned to the hospital for "some breach of the conditional release plan or for deterioration in their mental condition";[52] 6 were "charged with new crimes."

On the one hand, these data might, as the authors suggest, attest to the success of the Psychiatric Security Review Board by indicating a relatively low recidivism rate. On the other hand, the findings prove difficult to evaluate. First, the cut-off date of the follow-up period is not provided nor is the average

---

Pantle, and Steadman, "Detention and Rearrest Rates."

48. Phillips and Pasewark, "Insanity Plea in Connecticut."

49. Pasewark et al., "Criminal Recidivism among Insanity Acquittees."

50. Vernon L. Quinsey, Manfred Preusse, and Robert A. Fernley, "A Follow-up of Patients Found 'Unfit to Stand Trial' or 'Not Guilty Because of Insanity'," *Canadian Psychiatric Association Journal*, 20:461-67 (1975).

51. Joseph Bloom, Jeffrey Rogers, and Spero M. Manson, "After Oregon's Insanity Defense: A Comparison of Conditional Release and Hospitalization," *International Journal of Law and Psychiatry*, 5:391-402 (1982).

52. Ibid., p. 399.

release time of subjects given. Even if the follow-up had been to the time the initial paper was presented in 1982, it represents a much shorter period than that generally reported in other studies. Second, criminal recidivism is provided in terms of "crimes charged," without explanation of this term. The term might very well mean that legal action proceeded past the stage of arrest to indictment or arraignment. If so, it would represent something quite different from the legal action denoted by "arrest."[53]

COMMENT

In examining the history of the insanity defense, I am always astonished by the sporadic, almost cyclical occasions of intense emotional reactions—even outrage—periodically generated by this defense.[54] Typically preceding these public reactions there have been some crimes of notoriety committed by mentally disturbed persons who have pleaded or have been adjudicated NGRI. This was the case in England in 1843 when Daniel McNaughtan shot Sir Robert Peel's secretary. It was also the case following the recent acquittal on grounds of insanity of John W. Hinckley, Jr., who attempted to assassinate President Reagan in 1981.

Because the relative and even the absolute number of insanity defendants and acquittees is rather minuscule compared to the huge volumes of serious criminal cases coming to the attention of the criminal justice system, one is at a loss to explain the public and political reactions to the insanity defense. We might wonder if such reactions reflect a continuing apprehensiveness about and socially rejecting attitudes toward mental illness and the mentally ill. It may also be that the insanity defense serves, much like a lightning rod, to divert attention from the more intractable and pervasive problems within our criminal justice system.

Although one cannot question the right of citizens and professionals to advocate changes in the law, nor the right and duty of legislators to revise statutes, there does seem to be reason to be concerned at the rapidity with which policymakers seek major changes in the absence of adequate knowledge about the operation of the present system or the results that the proposed reforms might actually produce. The special defense of insanity has evolved over almost a thousand years, and its precipitous abrogation because of a few dramatic cases can legitimately be decried.

53. For further data on the Oregon system, see Jeffrey L. Rogers, Joseph D. Bloom, and Spero M. Manson, "Oregon's Psychiatric Security Review Board: A Comprehensive System for Managing Insanity Acquittees," this issue of *The Annals* of the American Academy of Political and Social Science.

54. Richard A. Pasewark and Mark D. Pasewark, "Insanity Revised: Once More over the Cuckoo's Nest," *Journal of Psychiatry and Law*, 6:481-98 (1978).

The Insanity Defense: Problems and Prospects for Studying the Impact of Legal Reforms

By HENRY J. STEADMAN and JOSEPH P. MORRISSEY

ABSTRACT: Cries for reform of insanity defense statutes are often associated with notorious cases involving heinous offenses. In fact, little research exists on the reforms sparked by such cases. Reforms initiated without data on their likely impacts may lead to illusory or unintended results. A strategy to assess such changes, and any other type of insanity defense reform, is articulated in this article. This approach is substantially different from the approaches of any published reports. It rests upon a multistate scope, a systemic focus, an assessment of impacts on the entire criminal process, and a longitudinal data base. Some of the impediments to implementing such research designs and ways by which they can be overcome are discussed.

Henry J. Steadman is director of the Bureau of Evaluation Research of the New York State Office of Mental Health and adjunct professor of sociology at the State University of New York (SUNY), Albany. He has published widely, on the interface of mental health and criminal justice, most recently Mentally Disordered Offenders: Perspective from Law and Social Science *(1983), coedited with John Monahan.*

Joseph P. Morrissey is a research scientist with the New York State Office of Mental Health and adjunct professor of sociology at SUNY, Albany. He has published widely on the sociology of mental hospitalization and mental health service delivery, including The Enduring Asylum *(1981).*

IN his classic discussion, "The Diffusion of Sexual Psychopath Laws," Sutherland identified three factors consistently present when such laws were developed: (1) fear aroused in the community by a few serious sex crimes; (2) agitated action by the community in connection with the fear; and (3) the appointment of a committee to gather information and implement change.[1] Although, as Sutherland notes, the community's fear often subsides in a brief time, the committee has the formal duty to follow through until some remedial action is taken.

Sutherland's scenario also appears to depict accurately both historical and contemporary efforts to reform the insanity defense. Certainly this pattern was followed in 1843 after Daniel McNaughtan's acquittal on grounds of insanity. Following his acquittal and the subsequent public outrage, along with Queen Victoria's very displeased reaction, there was much discussion in the House of Lords. The lords eventually decided to ask the 15 common-law judges to act as a committee to explain the relevant law in response to five general questions that were put to them. What became known as the McNaughtan test for exculpatory insanity was contained in the response of the judges to the combined second and third questions.[2]

More recently, it was the public reaction to the case of Michael Hightower—a 32-year-old Vietnam veteran who raped two women, was acquitted by reason of insanity, was released after one year of treatment, subsequently shot a nurse, and was convicted of assault with intent to kill—that led to Idaho's 1982 abolition of the insanity defense.[3] Similarly, the extensive media coverage and strenuous lobbying efforts by the Reagan administration after the insanity acquittal of John Hinckley, Jr., led to congressional hearings and heightened efforts to revise federal legislation. Further reverberations of the Hinckley case are apparent in the actions of many state legislatures to impanel special committees to revise their insanity defense statutes.

Interestingly, the literature on reform in the mental health system tends not to focus on the type of reform sparked by these infamous cases. While response to the issues these cases present is most often in the form of movements for legislative reforms, the majority of the research on the impacts of legal interventions on mental health systems has focused on the role of litigation and resulting case law in bringing about change. These studies have examined the effects of some of the landmark mental health cases of the late 1960s and early 1970s on the clients and on the systems of care. The core question, as Lottman has observed, is whether a number of "stunning paper victories . . . actually result in constitutionally and professionally adequate care and treatment for their intended beneficiaries."[4]

The earliest research in this genre emanated from the first major mental health case in the United States decided on constitutional grounds, *Baxstrom* v. *Herold*.[5] This landmark decision

1. Edwin H. Sutherland, "The Diffusion of Sexual Psychopath Laws," *American Journal of Sociology,* 56:142-48 (Sept. 1950).
2. Richard Moran, *Knowing Right from Wrong: The Insanity Defense of Daniel McNaughtan* (New York: Free Press, 1981).

3. John Leo, "Is the System Guilty?" *Time,* pp. 26-27 (July 1982).
4. Michael S. Lottman, "Enforcement of Judicial Decrees: Now Comes the Hard Part," *Mental Disability Law Reporter,* 1:69-76 (1976).
5. *Baxstrom* v. *Herold,* 383 U.S. 107 (1966).

resulted in the mass transfer of 967 allegedly dangerous mental patients from two New York State maximum-security correctional mental hospitals to 27 regular civil hospitals between March and August 1966. It also resulted in a four-year follow-up of these patients that examined the impact of this decision on the patients and the mental hospitals to which they were transferred.[6] In 1970, a remarkably similar decision in Pennsylvania[7] produced another mass patient transfer and another follow-up research project to assess the impact of the decision.[8] These two decisions, pertaining to criminal commitment cases, contributed to a burgeoning mental health advocacy movement, but the major scene of class action suits in the early 1970s shifted to civil commitment issues. No decision was more important than *Wyatt v. Stickney*.[9] In its breadth and in its insertion of the judiciary into the operation of state mental hospitals this decision has had few parallels. Numerous attempts were made to assess *Wyatt*'s impacts.[10] These analyses tended to concentrate on the extent to which the decision produced real change in the Alabama state hospital system.

This research on the major issues of the civil law produced "evidence . . . to date [that] is mixed, at best."[11] A law

6. Henry J. Steadman and Joseph Cocozza, *Careers of the Criminally Insane* (Lexington, MA: Lexington Books, 1974).

7. *Dixon v. Attorney General of the Commonwealth of Pennsylvania*, 383 F. Supp. 969 (1971).

8. Terence P. Thornberry and Joseph E. Jacoby, *The Criminally Insane* (Chicago: University of Chicago Press, 1979).

9. *Wyatt v. Stickney*, 125 F. Supp. 781 (M.D. Ala. 1971).

10. L. Ralph Jones and Richard R. Parlour, eds., *Wyatt v. Stickney: Retrospect and Prospect* (New York: Grune & Stratton, 1981).

11. Lottman, "Enforcement of Judicial Decrees."

review pointed out that "despite the doctrinal advances, the implementation record in mental health legislation has not been impressive. . . . The difficulty of enforcing far-reaching remedial decrees has raised serious doubts about the utility and desirability of litigation as a means of systemic reform in the mental health field."[12]

Despite these sobering assessments, the impact of mental health litigation "has clearly been substantial, particularly when measured against the modicum of real change that follows new legislation."[13] In fact, there is little research that demonstrates the superiority of one type of action over the other for producing actual change. Some work on the impact of major mental health statutory revisions in California and Massachusetts suggests that certain legislation has had significant impact. Urmer has reported that, as intended by its sponsors, the Lanterman-Petris-Short Act of 1969, which revised California's civil commitment code, had measurable impacts on the census and average lengths of stay in the state mental hospitals and shifted some responsibility for the care and management of the mentally ill to the police and correctional facilities.[14] McGarry and his colleagues found that the Massachusetts Mental Health Act of 1970 did lead to a number of the changes sought by the legislature in that due-process protections were expanded, effective

12. Harvard Law Review, "Mental Health Litigation: Implementing Institutional Reform," *Mental Disability Law Reporter*, 2:221-23 (1977).

13. Ibid., p. 222.

14. Michael Urmer, *A Study of California's New Mental Health Law* (Chatsworth, CA: ENKI Research Institute, 1972); idem, *The Burden of the Mentally Disordered Offender on Law Enforcement* (Chatsworth, CA: ENKI Research Institute, 1973).

periodic review of involuntary commitments was initiated, and the use of mental hospitals by criminal courts was diminished. On the basis of their research, they concluded that "despite various imperfections in implementation, in large measure the drafters of the statute appear to have substantially accomplished their objectives."[15] Accordingly, the limited empirical research directly on mental health legislation seems somewhat more optimistic about the prospects of producing actual change from legislative reform than some of the proponents of litigation have observed it to be.

INSANITY DEFENSE REFORMS: MISPERCEPTIONS AND WASTED RESOURCES

Whatever the limits of statutory revisions to produce real change, proposals for insanity defense reform have tended to proceed furiously after each recent, notorious insanity defense case. Appelbaum has noted that "until recently [late 1960s and early 1970s], the insanity defense was the focus of relatively little concern."[16] He suggests that this lack of concern was due to acquittees' historically receiving indefinite commitments to maximum-security facilities that usually far exceeded any criminal sentence they would have received. With the advent of the mental health advocacy movement in the late 1960s and early 1970s, however, commitment and release practices were changed, and due-process protections were extended to all classes of the mentally ill. Thus, the public could no longer be assured of long-term secure detention of insanity acquittees.

These changes helped to produce a situation in which 87 percent of the public believes too many murderers are using the insanity plea and 70 percent of the public would ban insanity pleas in all murder cases.[17] Because of sporadic, but infamous, cases such as those of John Hinckley, Jr., David Berkowitz, and Mark David Chapman—the last being a case in which insanity was expected to be the plea, but was not—the perceptions of the public and legislators regarding the insanity defense are badly distorted. Pasewark and Seidenzahl found that college students overestimated the number of insanity pleas by a factor of 800;[18] Pasewark and Pantle found that legislators overestimated the number by a factor of 400.[19] In fact, for 1978, the most recent year for which national data are available, there were only 1625 admissions of insanity acquittees to security hospitals in the entire United States, and only 3100 acquittees were hospitalized on any given day.[20] In New York there were only two insanity pleas for every 1000 felony arrests in 1978 and in California, there were only five acquittals for every 1000 felony convictions in 1980.[21] Further, the popular

15. A. Louis McGarry et al., *Civil Commitment and Social Policy* (Washington, DC: Government Printing Office, 1981), p. 146.

16. Paul Appelbaum, "The Insanity Defense: New Calls for Reform" *Hospital and Community Psychiatry,* 33:13-14 (Jan. 1982).

17. David Lauter, "Why Insanity Defense is Breaking Down," *National Law Journal,* 4(34):1, 11-13 (May 1982).

18. Richard A. Pasewark and Deborah Seidenzahl, "Opinions Concerning the Insanity Plea and Criminality among Mental Patients," *Bulletin of the American Academy of Psychiatry and the Law,* 1:199-202 (1980).

19. Richard A. Pasewark and Mark L. Pantle, "Insanity Plea: Legislator's View," *American Journal of Psychiatry,* 136:222-23 (1979).

20. Henry J. Steadman et al., "Mentally Disordered Offenders: A National Survey of Patients and Facilities," *Law and Human Behavior,* 6(1):31-38 (1982).

21. For New York, see U.S., Congress, House, Committee on the Judiciary, Subcommittee on

perception that all insanity acquittees are heinous murderers is erroneous. In New York and Michigan murder and attempted murder do comprise 51 percent and 57 percent of all insanity acquittals. However, in New Jersey, Missouri, and Oregon murder accounted for only 26 percent, 5 percent, and 5 percent of insanity acquittals, respectively.[22] Clearly, the actual offenses of persons acquitted on grounds of insanity are markedly different from public perceptions.

The policy significance of such misperceptions is at least threefold. First, these inaccurate ideas are likely to result in statutes that produce a detention and treatment system that is both inappropriate and damaging for the vast majority of insanity acquittees. The criminal justice mental health standards developed by the American Bar Association, which call for special and more restrictive commitment procedures for insanity acquittees involved in murder, rape, manslaughter, robbery, and arson, are designed precisely to prevent the general and indiscriminate use of such procedures for all insanity acquittees.[23]

Second, reforms initiated in the absence of scientific information about their likely consequences may lead to illusory change. One example is Michigan's guilty-but-mentally-ill (GBMI) statute, which was enacted in 1975. According to Smith and Hall, "the primary purpose behind the Michigan GBMI verdict was to decrease the number of insanity acquittals. Michigan legislators hoped to use the new verdict to prevent the early release of dangerous NGRI [not guilty by reason of insanity] acquittals by offering Michigan juries a substitute for the insanity verdict."[24] In the three years prior to the introduction of a GBMI plea, there was an average of 60 findings of NGRI per year. In the seven years after the GBMI statute, 1976 through 1982, there was an average of 54 NGRI acquittals each year and an average of an additional 33 GBMI verdicts.[25] Thus, as opposed to the goal of reduction, the number of insanity acquittals has remained fairly constant. Further, the number of insanity pleas more than doubled over the same period.[26] The effect of Michigan's legal

---

Criminal Justice, *Insanity Defense in Federal Courts,* Testimony by Henry J. Steadman, serial no. 124 (Washington, DC: Government Printing Office, 1982), pp. 78-87; for California, see Michael Jordan, "The Insanity Defense," *Western Law Journal,* 3:2 (Fall 1982).

22. For data on murder and attempted murder in New York, see Henry J. Steadman, "Insanity Acquittals in New York State, 1965-1978," *American Journal of Psychiatry,* 137:321-26 (Mar. 1980); for Michigan, see Gerald Cooke and Cynthia Sikorski, "Factors Affecting Length of Hospitalization in Persons Adjudicated Not Guilty by Reason of Insanity," *Bulletin of the American Academy of Psychiatry and the Law,* 2:251-61 (1974); for New Jersey, see Anne Singer, "Insanity Acquittal in the Seventies: Observations and Empirical Analysis of One Jurisdiction," *Mental Disability Law Reporter,* 2:406-17 (1978); for Missouri, see John Petrila, "The Insanity Defense and Other Mental Health Dispositions in Missouri," *International Journal of Law and Psychiatry,* 5:81-101 (1982); for Oregon, see Jeffrey L. Rogers and Joseph D. Bloom, "Characteristics of Persons Committed to Oregon's Psychiatric Security Review Board," *Bulletin of the American Academy of Psychiatry and the Law,* 10:155-64 (1982).

23. American Bar Association, *Proposed Criminal Justice Mental Health Standards* (Washington, DC: American Bar Association, 1982).

24. Gore A. Smith and James A. Hall, "Evaluating Michigan's Guilty but Mentally Ill Verdict: An Empirical Study," *Journal of Law Reform,* 16(1):75-112 (Fall 1982).

25. Jim Romans, director, Forensic Services, Department of Health, State of Michigan, personal communication (Sept. 1982).

26. Lynn W. Blunt and Harley V. Stock, "Guilty but Mentally Ill: The Michigan Experi-

reform appears to have been to create a new category of mentally ill offender, the incumbents of which would be identified for treatment within the prison system rather than the state mental hospital system. While this statutory change served to placate the public's demands for true justice, the uses and any potential abuses of the NGRI plea do not appear to have been affected to any discernible degree.

Third, insanity defense reforms often result in a disproportionate investment of scarce resources not only in the reform process itself, but also in the creation of institutional arrangements that will draw critical resources away from the larger mental health system, which is already fiscally distressed and underfunded. A crucial policy issue is whether insanity defense reform is cost effective, given the press of other service demands on the mental health and criminal justice systems. In fact, cost issues are a major rationale for undertaking research on insanity defense reforms. The low base rate of insanity acquittals has led the American Psychiatric Association's Insanity Defense Work Group to conclude, "While philosophically important for the criminal law, the insanity defense is empirically unimportant [involving a fraction of one percent of all felony cases]."[27] Some comparative statistics help to place NGRI cases in proper perspective. In 1978, for example, there were 1625 NGRI admissions in the United States.[28] However, four times as many cases were found incompetent to stand trial, and six times as many persons were mentally ill prisoners. Most dramatically, the number of involuntary civil commitments to U.S. mental hospitals—about 220,000 in 1980—was about 135 times larger than the number of insanity acquittees.

Nonetheless, consideration of insanity reforms consumes enormous time and effort for congressional and other legislative committees, state mental health agency staff, and special committees of various professional associations. Moreover, the reforms result in placing demands on overtaxed or insufficiently equipped systems. GBMI statutes, for example, mandate mental health treatment in the prison system, although it is widely recognized that correctional institutions often have deficits in professional staff and related resources for providing such care. State mental hospital authorities, in turn, are now faced with the mandate to reallocate institutional resources to community-based mental health services. Yet, lengthening periods of hospitalization for NGRI acquittees will surely add to the demands by specialized institutional facilities for those same resources.

Many of these provisions and expenditures represent unanticipated costs of both public and political overreactions to the perceived problems associated with the insanity defense. That is, costly systems of care are being created to deal with one or another set of perceived problems without due regard to their longer-term consequences for the system as a whole. Hence, like many earlier reforms, those regarding the insanity defense are likely to fail. One recent example of such insufficiently considered reform is the experience with determinate sentencing laws. In responding to public fears about crime in the

---

ence" (Paper delivered at the Annual Meeting of the American Academy of Psychiatry and the Law, Portland, OR, Oct. 1983).

27. American Psychiatric Association, Insanity Defense Work Group," American Psychiatric Association Statement on the Insanity Defense," *American Journal of Psychiatry*, 140:681-88 (June 1983).

28. Steadman et al., "Mentally Disordered Offenders."

streets and public insistence on tougher policies toward offenders, many state legislatures adopted more restrictive sentencing statutes. While these provisions may have helped to soothe public outrage, they soon led to considerable prison overcrowding. In New York State, for example, the prison system is at 116 percent of capacity as a direct result of tougher sentencing laws, and the public is now faced with the need to invest more than $1 billion in the construction of a new generation of prisons to accommodate the inflow of prisoners.

In examining the impact of insanity defense reform one must be particularly cognizant of the symbolic role of the insanity defense. Stone has suggested that exculpation on the grounds of serious mental disease or defect is ultimately valuable not due to the number of actual acquittals, which is relatively small, but because the acquittals are the exceptions that prove the rule.[29] That is, if only these very few are not responsible, all other persons charged with crimes are to be held criminally responsible and appropriate subjects for whatever punishment society metes out to them. In a similar vein, Abel has suggested that a major problem with research assessing the impact of laws with explicit reformist objectives is that it "neglects the symbolic meanings of law, which is particularly unfortunate since the significance of reformist laws is often largely symbolic."[30] This observation seems especially germane to insanity defense reforms, which actually impact on very few individuals directly

29. Alan Stone, *Mental Health Law: A System in Transition* (Washington, DC: Government Printing Office, 1975).
30. Richard L. Abel, "Redirecting Social Studies of Law," *Law and Society Review*, pp. 805-29 (Spring 1980).

but do serve major symbolic functions for legislators trying to assuage public fears and outrage. What this suggests is considerable care and caution in establishing the goals of any proposed reform. Researchers must ascertain what symbolic goals may be driving the reform movements and how these may be met simply by the passage of legislation, regardless of the actual impact the legislation has on the volume, characteristics, or treatment of persons acquitted by reason of insanity.

NEEDED RESEARCH APPROACHES

If further research is to be at all useful to the policymaking process, while also making a significant contribution to current knowledge about the uses and abuses of the insanity defense, it must incorporate several design considerations. The research must

—be multistate in scope;

—adopt a systemic focus;

—assess the impacts of all types of insanity defense reforms;

—allow for a comprehensive assessment of each reform as it affects the entire criminal process, that is, from the plea stage through postverdict disposition and subsequent outcome; and

—generate a longitudinal data base so that relevant information before and after the reform can be contrasted and analyzed.

The need for multistate studies

In the past decade, a much wider variety of data on NGRI cases has become available. As recently summarized by Steadman and by Sales and Hafemeister, information has been developed by various investigators on the characteristics of insanity acquittees, their criminal and hospitalization histories, the types of their offenses, their institutional careers, and their recidivism following release.[31] Without exception, each study has been conducted on a single jurisdiction. Certainly many investigators have compared their findings to other research, yet in no instance have groups of insanity defendants or acquittees been studied across jurisdictions by the same research team. When simple description is the goal—the logical first step in new research areas—the limitations of single-site studies are not overly problematic. However, as we move toward policy-relevant questions or more sophisticated substantive inquiries about the insanity defense, comparative research designs are needed. Unless longitudinal data bases are developed across jurisdictions, we will be unable to reach the level of generalization required both for middle-range theorizing and for informed public policy choices.

There are clear trade-offs between single-state and multistate studies. Certainly, as the number of states in any one study increases, the possibilities of logistical problems in data collection or interpretive difficulties are often introduced. Also, the availability and reliability of comparable data varies greatly from state to state. As a result, almost inevitably some precision in measurement is lost as each additional state is added. Nonetheless, the severe limitations on generalizability and the slow cumulative development of findings from single-state studies would tend to override the problems of multistate research methods. Moreover, there are clear and pressing needs for research projects that can determine the extent to which any given set of insanity defense reforms succeeds in altering the flow of NGRI cases, and whether one type of reform is more successful for particular purposes than others. These issues can be adequately addressed only in multistate studies that use the same sampling, data collection, measurement, and analytical procedures.

This is not to discount totally the utility of intensive, single-state studies for certain types of research questions. Such designs might be especially appropriate to issues surrounding the dynamics of a particular piece of legislation: in drafting, moving through the legislative process, enacting, and later implementing the insanity reforms. The complexities of the political process and the number and often low visibility of key actors and interest groups almost preclude multistate studies, unless the studies are done prospectively. The work of Bardach on California's civil commitment legislation, the Lanterman-Petris-Short Act, exemplifies the complexity of an in-depth analysis, especially when done retrospectively.[32] Hence, to the extent that research on insanity defense reform focuses on details of the political process involved in the legislation, single-state studies may be useful. At this point in time, however, such efforts are of secondary utility in addressing the major policy questions, which require empirical data

31. Henry J. Steadman, "Empirical Research on the Insanity Defense," *The Annals* of the American Academy of Political and Social Science, 477:58-71 (Jan. 1985); Bruce D. Sales and Thomas Hafemeister, "Empiricism and Legal Policy on the Insanity Defense," in *Mental Health and Criminal Justice*, ed. Linda Teplin (Beverly Hills, CA: Sage, 1984), pp. 253-78.

32. Eugene Bardach, *Skill Factor in Politics: Repealing the Mental Commitment Laws in California* (Berkeley: University of California Press, 1972).

on the range of actual impacts of various types of legislative reforms.

The need for a systemic focus

In moving forward with more comprehensive research designs, it also seems advisable to recognize the need for a systemic conceptualization of insanity defense reforms. Although legal scholars may be interested in changing the insanity test simply on jurisprudential grounds, the public and the legislators are not. The dominant concerns are to tighten the system; to make it harder to get in—that is, to reduce the number and rate of insanity acquittals—and harder to get out—by, for example, increasing the duration of confinement and making eventual release more difficult to obtain. Courts as well as hospital officials are often faulted for allowing insanity acquittees to return to the community after relatively short periods of hospitalization. The larger policy and pragmatic questions revolve around how the judicial, mental health, and correctional systems can be adjusted to protect the community more effectively from individuals who have demonstrated their dangerousness and/or who are perceived as dangerous. Statutory reforms concerning the insanity defense really reflect attempts at system-level change. Unless the various discrete stages in this processing system—plea, adjudication, disposition, and outcome —are studied simultaneously, significant changes, whether intended or unintended, may go unrecognized.

An emphasis on system-level studies further highlights the need for multiple-state research designs in order to attain any level of generalization. Any given state is likely to implement only one or two of the major potential reforms in the insanity defense such as a change in the insanity test, the burden of proof, the standard of proof, the introduction of a GBMI statute, or more restrictive post-verdict dispositional arrangements. No single-state study can adequately address the impact of the full range of reforms, and, for a given type of reform, the results may constitute little more than a case study. The latter situation, of course, makes generalization extremely hazardous. Yet, this is precisely the situation we are in with regard to the insanity defense research conducted over the past decade.

A systemic focus in no way precludes a more intensive scrutiny of individual cases. By disaggregating the stages or components, the data can be analyzed at the individual case level as well as the overall system level. For example, the individual case can be the unit analysis in examining the sociodemographic, clinical, and offense characteristics of successful insanity pleas as well as the differences between persons found NGRI and those found GBMI in jurisdictions where both verdicts are possible. Aggregating the data at the systemic level allows for comparisons between, as well as within, states in terms of the overall number and composition of pleas, NGRI acquittals, GBMI verdicts, straight criminal convictions, and post-verdict institutionalization in mental hospitals or prisons. Thus, multiple questions can be answered on the basis of a comparative system-level study of insanity defense reforms.

Viewing insanity defense processes as a system does not imply that the components are smoothly coordinated. Rather it acknowledges that there are a number of sequential processes that are set in motion with an insanity plea and that a change in any one might have ramifications for the other components. For example, if a more restrictive procedure is introduced for release from post-acquittal hospitalization, the anticipated outcome is an increased length of hospitalization. Such prolonged confinement may well serve to discourage use of the insanity defense. However, as judges and juries become more comfortable with NGRI verdicts, which assure prolonged periods of confinement, this change may also increase the proportion of NGRI acquittals. Thus, while the number of insanity pleas may be reduced, the rate of acquittals may increase. Stated differently, a reform at the back end of the system may have substantial impact at the front end as well.

For all these reasons, the most efficient way to direct research resources to advance both substantive understanding and informed public policy is to make some significant changes in our research approaches to the insanity defense. Multistate studies are essential. A focus on how insanity defense reforms actually impact on all the relevant components of the criminal justice and mental health systems is highly desirable. A broad systemic conceptualization can help to reduce the likelihood of inaccurate assessments of the actual impacts of reform. The empirical data on the insanity defense have expanded in scope and in quality in the past decade. Those advances now point toward some major new approaches to answer pressing policy and substantive questions about the insanity defense adequately.

IMPEDIMENTS TO RESEARCH

The scarcity of empirical data on the operations of the systems established to treat and detain insanity acquittees becomes particularly acute when the demand for reform intensifies, as it has during the last few years. Sutherland noted that a key juncture in the process of statutory reform was a meeting to publicly review the reform proposals by the committee or task force empowered to recommend the change. Most often, this public review was organized "in the name of science and without critical appraisal." In fact, however, it proceeded on the basis of anecdote, opinion, and political expediency.[33]

Current deliberations on insanity defense reform can have little more than the pretense of science and rationality in the face of the paucity of relevant empirical evidence and the strong ideological, political, and other pressures for reform. The score of states with recent and impending reforms in the insanity defense presents an opportunity to undertake a comparative, longitudinal study of the systemic impacts of these changes. In the absence of such evidence, future reforms are likely to perpetuate inappropriate, cosmetic, or even illusory changes that temporarily assuage public outrage, but fail to address what may be fundamental flaws in the law, in the institutional and administrative provisions of the mental health and criminal justice systems.

It is far easier to conceptualize what research would be productive than it is actually to implement that research. The work that is needed includes various types of impact assessment that are all dependent on records of ongoing system operations. Also required is information about how many persons are using the insanity plea, how many are successful, the characteristics of both those

33. Sutherland, "Diffusion of Sexual Psychopath Laws."

pleading insanity and those successful with the plea, and what happens to both groups following adjudication—whether conviction or insanity acquittal—and disposition. The sources of such information are prosecutorial office records, court records, state mental health agency records, and state correctional agency records. At each juncture it is some type of record that is the primary data source. It is precisely this feature of research on insanity defense reform that makes reform efforts so difficult.

Glaser has enumerated some of the major reasons that operational records are unsatisfactory for research.

1. They vary greatly in their completeness.
2. They vary in their terminology for describing the same items, in the aspects of the item they emphasize, or in the dimensions they employ to indicate an item's magnitude or quality.
3. They are often bulky and inefficient for the retrieval of information.
4. They were not designed for research and therefore often do not include the type of information researchers need.[34]

To this list should be added two other problems: the essential information is not centralized, and the events in question are infrequent. The raw data are rarely available in one place in a state, and compilations of data on the individual events are not often produced, even periodically, through the routine operation of any single state agency.

For various reasons, it is generally the case that the forensic mental health information network in any state is less developed than the general mental health or correctional management information systems. Whatever can be found in regular reports or can be generated about patient census, discharge rates, average lengths of stay, crime rates, and so forth, the researcher generally will be unable to ascertain information about insanity acquittees, defendants found incompetent to stand trial, or mentally ill prison inmates. Apparently, because these forensic populations cut across both the mental health and criminal justice agencies, information systems tend to become the stepchildren of both types of agencies insofar as regularly available operational reports are concerned. As a result, each research effort, almost regardless of its ambitiousness, must start from scratch by going back to individual case records or facility logs. These characteristics of the information systems mean in practical terms that a researcher interested in insanity defense pleas must typically obtain data in each county in the state. Furthermore, the infrequency of the plea makes locating the universe of cases even more difficult.

In the 62 counties of New York State, for example, there are approximately 120,000 felony arrests but only an estimated 400 insanity pleas. Thus, for every 300 felony arrests there is 1 insanity plea. Locating the one or two cases that occur annually in the smallest counties is relatively easy, as such cases are memorable—by virtue of their infrequency—and identified by court officers. In counties with moderate or large numbers of insanity pleas, the inverse is the case and complete enumeration requires poring through an entire year's log book or case files of every arrest and plea. This work is labor intensive and extremely costly.

34. Daniel Glaser, *Routinizing Evaluation: Getting Feedback on Effectiveness of Crime and Delinquency Programs* (Washington, DC: National Institute of Mental Health, 1973).

Should the research project also include the next stage in the insanity defense process—confinement following acquittal—the research becomes a little less complex in that most states place all acquittees, at least initially, into one high-security state mental hospital. This would suggest that the acquittee becomes part of a statewide information system that would permit tracking and provide basic descriptors for each person; however, such record keeping is rarely the case. Few states, without special programming or on-site work by the researchers, are able to provide routine data on specific forensic populations. In even fewer instances are any regular reports produced on these populations. Moreover, many states have such poor centralized management information systems that every state facility's records need to be searched individually to obtain a full list of transactions for each research subject.

None of these difficulties prohibit the necessary research from being conducted, but the necessary data must be assembled by the research team. Such assembly is labor intensive and costly and establishes no routinized system from which future reports can be produced. Obviously, creative procedures can be developed to use the mail and telephones in lieu of extensive travel to counties or facilities. However, in counties with a larger volume of cases, research staff will need to review records on site, either because of local staff limitations or in order to ensure the reliability of the data abstracted. This on-site work, of course, adds to the travel and staffing costs of any project.

A more efficient solution to many of these informational and data-collection difficulties would be the development by states of more comprehensive forensic management information systems. Unfortunately, the critical information needed to inform public policy questions surrounding the insanity defense cannot await the development of such systems, the prospects for which are not strong. Policymakers are rushing, often blundering, forward, urging reforms to placate public fears with little in the way of reliable evidence on which to posit the effects of the proposed changes and without much interest in ascertaining the burdens they may impose on the systems of detention and care and on the insanity acquittees themselves. Just as Lottman was concerned about the possible hollowness of the "stunning paper victories" of mental health litigation,[35] so too research needs to be conducted to measure the real outcomes of the symbolic reforms that tend to characterize movements to legislate changes in the insanity defense.

In addressing all the questions about the insanity defense, its administration and its reform, there is a clear and urgent need to develop management information systems. Amazingly simple questions that are often posed cannot be answered in a timely fashion. Research projects can supply significant information, but this should be an adjunct to forensic management information systems. For broad questions or for special topics, research may be appropriate and can be designed to overcome the impediments discussed here. However, more limited questions about the volume and characteristics of persons pleading insanity and being acquitted on those grounds should be answerable from ongoing information systems. Such a development would reduce many problems now faced by efforts to reform the insanity defense and would greatly expand the prospects for the type of research identified here.

35. Lottmann, "Enforcement of Judicial Decrees."

Populations, Practices, and Problems in Forensic Psychiatric Facilities

By CHARLOTTE A. KERR and JEFFREY A. ROTH

ABSTRACT: This is a study of the public facilities to which mentally disordered offenders are committed or transferred so that they may be securely confined while simultaneously participating in programs designed for treatment of their mental disorders. The study focuses principally on the nature and characteristics of these facilities: their patient populations, staff, security conditions, treatment programs, and operational programs. We identified and surveyed 231 facilities. The information from the survey, legal research, and site visits to 11 programs has been integrated and used to address four major issues: the types of facilities mentally disordered offenders are institutionalized in for treatment of their mental disorders; the legal, diagnostic, and demographic characteristics of the residents of these facilities; the forms of treatment and levels of staffing available in these facilities; and the common problems faced by facility administrators with respect to facility management, treatment, and release decisions.

Ms. Kerr is currently pursuing her doctorate in criminology at the University of Maryland. She is a senior research analyst in the Office of Research and Evaluation at the Federal Bureau of Prisons.

Dr. Roth received his Ph.D. in economics from Michigan State University in 1971. He is currently senior staff officer to the National Research Council's Committee on Research on Law Enforcement and the Administration of Justice.

NOTE: The research reported in this article was performed while both authors were employed at Westat, and was supported by contract no. 278-80-0012 (SM) from the Center for Studies of Antisocial and Violent Behavior, National Institute of Mental Health. The complete report of the Study of Facilities and Programs for Mentally Disordered Offenders will be available from the center. The authors wish to thank Thomas F. Courtless, Christopher Dunn, and Elyce Zenoff for helpful advice. The views reflected in this article are solely those of the authors and should not be attributed to Westat, the National Research Council, or the Federal Bureau of Prisons.

THIS article updates and extends information published more than a decade ago based on two comprehensive surveys of facilities organized to house and treat mentally disordered offenders.[1] Conceptually, the term "mentally disordered offenders" refers to alleged and convicted offenders whose adjudication or confinement is handled differently from standard criminal justice processes owing to potential or evident mental disorder. There are a number of legal conditions or statuses that subject alleged or convicted criminal offenders with mental disorders to specialized procedures and dispositions that can lead to involuntary confinement in prisons, mental hospitals, or program units within such facilities for treatment for mental disorders.

Thus, included under the rubric "mentally disordered offenders" for purposes of this study are defendants found not guilty by reason of insanity; defendants found incompetent to stand trial; persons adjudicated under special statutes, for example, sexual psychopath or defective delinquent; persons adjudicated guilty but mentally ill; convicted offenders who display symptoms of serious mental illness while serving a sentence, some of whom are transferred to a hospital for treatment of mental illness; juveniles who are convicted of, or found involved in, crimes and are committed for treatment of mental illness; defendants being evaluated for competency to stand trial; and defendants being examined for criminal responsibility.

This is a study of the public facilities to which mentally disordered offenders are committed or transferred so that they may be securely confined while simultaneously participating in programs designed primarily for treatment of their mental disorders. The study's focus is principally on the nature and characteristics of these facilities: their patient populations, their staff, their security conditions, their treatment programs, and their administrative or operational problems. It is not focused on the possible relationships between crime and mental illness nor on the criminal justice or other legal processes per se that lead to confinement in such institutions. Although these latter topics are important and interesting, the present study restricts its focus by intent and design to the institutions and programs in which mentally disordered offenders are primarily confined for treatment. Among the reasons for this is the necessity to update and improve upon information reported about such institutions and programs over a decade ago.

PREVIOUS STUDIES

In 1969, under the auspices of the Joint Information Service of the American Psychiatric Association and the National Association for Mental Health, Scheidemandel and Kanno made the first effort to obtain a nationwide inventory of the facilities available to meet the needs of this special group of persons, often dubbed the mad and the bad.[2] Based on the 1967 *Guide Issue* of

1. Patricia L. Scheidemandel and Charles K. Kanno, *The Mentally Ill Offender: A Survey of Treatment Programs* (Washington, DC: Joint Information Service of the American Psychiatric Association and the National Association for Mental Health, 1969); William C. Eckerman, *A Nationwide Survey of Mental Health and Correctional Institutions for Adult Mentally Disordered Offenders*, National Institute of Mental Health, Department of Health, Education, and Welfare pub. no. (HSM) 73-9018 (Washington, DC: Government Printing Office, 1972).

2. Scheidemandel and Kanno, *Mentally Ill Offender*.

the American Hospital Association, which is a list of facilities given statutory responsibility for such persons, and an identifying questionnaire sent to all state mental hospitals, they compiled a comprehensive list of facilities admitting substantial numbers of mentally disordered offenders. Of 153 such facilities identified, 98 responded in usable form, a rate of 64 percent. Based on these responses, Scheidemandel and Kanno reported statistics on auspices, location, size, admissions policies, and level of security of facilities; the composition of admissions by sex, legal status, diagnosis, and crime type; number, composition, and training of staff; treatment programs; other activities; and cost.

A few years later, Eckerman surveyed 73 facilities offering comprehensive, special programs for mentally disordered offenders, of which 68, or 93 percent, provided usable responses.[3] Based on these responses, Eckerman published both a directory and a monograph reporting information that included security features, activities for patients, and staffing patterns in the facilities; capacity; population size; diagnostic classification; and legal status composition.

In 1978, an inventory of 48 facilities was compiled by Sheldon and Norman.[4] Although they produced no statistical report, they gave the following characteristics of each facility: capacity, average population, accreditation status vis-à-vis the Joint Commission on Accreditation of Hospitals, primary modes of therapy, staff composition, security measures, room accommodations, and visitation procedures. During 1978, Steadman and others surveyed a more comprehensive population of facilities—all facilities housing any mentally disordered offenders—in preparation for a study of transfer of such persons between correctional and mental health facilities.[5]

STUDY METHODOLOGY

The present study was conducted in three interrelated phases: identification of the population of facilities to be surveyed; execution of a national mail survey, with more intensive telephone follow-up of selected respondents; and on-site observation involving two-day visits to 11 facilities that seemed likely, based on their survey responses and legal or organizational settings, to provide clear examples of programmatic responses to common or emerging administrative problems.

The first stage was intended to locate all facilities, regardless of organizational auspices, that could be expected to operate long-term treatment programs for one or more of the categories of mentally disordered offenders listed previously. In some states service-delivery systems for these groups were thought to have changed since the time of the earlier surveys, incorporating alternatives to the traditional large-scale security hospitals on which those surveys focused. Therefore, the merged facility lists from those surveys served as a departure point for the current survey, augmented by lists obtained from federal and state correctional and mental health administrators and from Steadman's work on transfer.

---

3. Eckerman, *Nationwide Survey of Mental Health and Correctional Institutions.*

4. Robert B. Sheldon and William Barry Norman, "Comprehensive Survey of Forensic Psychiatric Facilities in the United States," *Bulletin of the American Academy of Psychiatry and the Law,* 4:93-104 (1978).

5. Henry J. Steadman et al. "Mentally Disordered Offenders: A National Survey of Patients and Facilities," *Law and Human Behavior,* 6:31-38 (1982).

The augmented list was then screened by telephone to remove private facilities, those not providing residential treatment of mentally disordered offenders beyond the initial evaluation stage, and prison isolation units intended solely for short-term stabilization of acting-out prisoners. In general, screening was also intended to assure that included facilities either housed exclusively mentally disordered offenders, operated specialized treatment programs serving at least four mentally disordered offenders, or provided the only available treatment within the geographic catchment area. A few large hospitals not segregating mentally disordered offenders from other residents because of overcrowding or treatment philosophy were also included, provided that mentally disordered offenders made up 10 percent of their populations.

The screening effort reduced the augmented list from 518 names to 231 potentially eligible facilities. Besides traditional security hospitals, these included systems of satellite evaluation and treatment centers; small units providing specialized treatment to juveniles, sex offenders, and other groups with special needs; and nonresidential psychiatric units in prisons treating inmates on an outpatient basis.

A two-part questionnaire was developed and pretested at five facilities. The first part, generally to be completed by a facility staff member maintaining records, was intended to collect data that could be compared to the earlier surveys, as well as other objective data on facility population characteristics and flows, available treatment modalities, security practices, staffing levels, and training practices. The second part, generally to be completed by a senior administrator, was influenced heavily by a review of recent developments in pertinent statutory and case law and by a review of existing literature on issues in treatment, administration, and compliance with legal mandates. The reviews identified a number of developments that had affected, or were expected to affect, facility programs, activities, and conditions. The questionnaire probed for respondents' awareness of these developments and issues, perceptions of their day-to-day effects, and responses to those effects. It also sought administrators' views of the most pressing problems for facilities, their responses to those problems, and their priorities in research and statistics.

The questionnaires were mailed in October 1981. By March 1982, extensive telephone follow-up had yielded 128 completed responses, self-exclusions of 55 ineligible facilities and 10 closed or duplicate facilities, and 38 refusals, some of which may have reflected ineligible or closed facilities. These returns constituted a net response rate of 84 percent of eligible respondents, if ineligible and closed facilities occurred at the same rates among responding and refusing facilities.

Follow-up telephone interviews were conducted with 60 administrators of facilities responding to the mail survey. These interviews provided amplification and interpretation of answers to the mail survey, more detailed assessments of the site-specific effects of legal changes and other influences, respondents' views of treatment needs specific to legal status, and their interpretations of various legal mandates and standards. The interviews also aided in the selection of candidate facilities for the case studies.

The efforts that have been described identified a number of legal requirements, residents' needs, and organizational or political influences that commonly impinge on day-to-day operations of facilities for mentally disordered offenders or are likely to do so in the future. Of these influences the following emerged as especially prevalent or significant: burdens associated with litigious and legislative activity, effects of statewide budget cutbacks and changes in administrative structure at the state or facility level, effects of fluctuations in population size, and needs for enhanced pre-release preparation and post-release follow-up.

On the basis of available information, 11 facilities that appeared to have dealt successfully with one or more of these influences were selected for two-day visits. During each visit, a two-person team conducted structured interviews with administrative, clinical, and security staff at all levels. For each facility, the interviews addressed historical context, admissions procedures and criteria, staffing issues, treatment programs, release programs, community relations, impinging legal issues, and program cost. Although the site visits were not evaluative, they did provide information not available elsewhere on the intensity and individuation of treatment, and they captured a diversity of impressions of the issues facing each facility and the adequacy of facility responses to them. Based on each site visit, a case study report was drafted, presented to facility administrators for comment, and revised as appropriate to reflect facility comments.

FINDINGS

Information from the survey data, legal research, and case studies has been integrated and used to address four major questions:

1. In what kinds of facilities are mentally disordered offenders institutionalized for treatment of their mental disorders?
2. What are the legal, diagnostic, and demographic characteristics of the residents of these facilities?
3. What forms of treatment and levels of staffing are common to these facilities?
4. What are the common problems faced by facility administrators with respect to facility management, treatment, and release decisions?

In the next sections, answers to these questions are summarized and compared to previous research. Then, recommendations are presented for future research.

Characteristics of responding facilities

As was the case more than a decade ago, care and treatment of mentally disordered offenders is primarily the responsibility of state mental health departments. Of 127 respondents reporting their auspices, 79 report themselves to be mental health facilities, 30 are under correctional auspices, and 18 are under other auspices, primarily social service agencies, youth authorities, or joint mental health and correctional authority. This distribution is quite similar to that reported by Scheidemandel and Kanno for a group of what they called primary facilities: 77 under mental health, 22 under corrections, and 15 under other auspices.[6] The resident populations are most heavily concen-

6. Scheidemandel and Kanno, *Mentally Ill Offender*.

trated in mental health facilities, with approximately 70 percent housed there, 23 percent in correctional facilities, and only about 7 percent in social service or other facilities. Approximately 60 percent of responding facilities under all auspices are units of larger institutions. Moreover, the overwhelming majority of facilities—121—are under state jurisdiction, with only five federal facilities and one local one.

Only four of the responding facilities are dedicated to mentally disordered female offenders, although females are eligible for admission to 46 others—a distribution similar to that reported by Eckerman.[7] Halleck has noted that the paucity of specialized facilities for females usually exists because the state has not felt there were sufficient numbers of females to justify the construction of a special unit.[8] Therefore, female mentally disordered offenders in most states are housed with males, or with mentally ill female non-offenders, or with other female prisoners. Thus, the female mentally disordered offender appears to be an example of the general point made by Resnick and Shaw that due to the small numbers of females there is a lack of specially dedicated facilities, which "limits the ability either to classify women into many different categories, or, once classified, to place them in facilities designed for their needs."[9]

Of the 127 responding facilities, only 17 are dedicated to juveniles, that is,

7. Eckerman, *Nationwide Survey of Mental Health and Correctional Institutions*, p. 29.

8. Seymour Halleck, *The Mentally Disordered Offender* (Rockville, MD: National Institute of Mental Health, forthcoming).

9. Judith Resnick and Nancy Shaw, "Prisoners of Their Sex: Health Problems of Incarcerated Women," in *Prisoners' Rights Sourcebook,* ed. I. P. Robbins (New York: Clark Boardman, 1980), p. 324.

persons detained by order of a juvenile court. Another 12 facilities accept both juveniles and persons sentenced by adult court, while the vast majority—98—limit admissions to adults. The existence of any juvenile-only facilities is a change from 1969, when Scheidemandel and Kanno, despite intensive efforts, were unable to locate any.[10] Such facilities may have been established in response to statutory and judicial activity during the 1970s extending to juveniles many due-process guarantees—including both the question of competency to stand trial and the insanity defense—previously reserved for adults.

As shown in Table 1, facility design capacities vary widely—from three units with capacities of 10 persons or fewer to one facility, dedicated to the mentally disordered offender, that has a capacity of 1254. For free-standing institutions, the median capacity category is reported to be 101-250, while the corresponding category for separate units of larger institutions—such as psychiatric units of prisons and forensic units of mental hospitals—is 51-100. In general, institutions with capacities exceeding 101 are slightly more predominant under correctional than other auspices.

At least two facility characteristics seem to be related to size. First, estimated length of stay among released residents is only about two months in facilities with capacities of 10 or fewer, and it increases rather steadily with capacity, reaching approximately 16 months in facilities with capacities exceeding 501. Thus, the larger facilities tend to provide more long-term housing and treatment. Possible explanations for this relationship include the fact that some of the smaller facilities—such as

10. Scheidemandel and Kanno, *Mentally Ill Offender,* p. 1.

TABLE 1
RESIDENT POPULATION CONCENTRATION BY CAPACITY OF FACILITIES
OR UNITS FOR MENTALLY DISORDERED OFFENDERS

Facility Capacity in Number of Residents	Number (and Percentage) of Facilities		Percentage of Resident Population
10 or fewer	4	(3.8)	0.1
11-25	11	(10.4)	1.1
26-50	21	(19.8)	4.3
51-100	22	(20.8)	8.6
101-250	30	(28.3)	25.8
251-500	10	(9.4)	17.7
501 or more	8	(7.5)	42.6
Total	106*	(100.0)	100.2†

SOURCE: Center for Studies of Antisocial and Violent Behavior, National Institute of Mental Health.
*Does not total 128 due to item nonresponse.
†Does not total 100.0 due to rounding.

those in Ohio and New York—are geographically dispersed institutions performing both treatment and psychiatric evaluations, which require less time than does treatment of mental illness. Others are psychiatric units of prisons, with the goal of stabilizing behavior sufficiently to permit the inmate to function in the general prison population, a more limited and less time-consuming goal than fundamental behavioral change preceding release to the community.

Second, the survey data show several rather clear-cut relationships between facility population and the frequency of certain critical incidents: escapes and suicides occur disproportionately frequently in small facilities, and other deaths disproportionately frequently in large facilities. The latter relationship is probably associated with older populations, in light of the longer length of stay in large facilities. The former effects may reflect acute psychotic episodes among residents of small units, the success of suicide prevention programs in larger facilities, and escape opportunities presented by work or school release for juveniles in the smaller facilities.

Characteristics of residents

As shown in Table 2, the responding facilities house both adjudicated mentally disordered offenders and persons being evaluated for competency or responsibility. For adjudicated mentally disordered adult offenders, the distribution of legal categories generally resembles that reported by Steadman for all such persons in the United States as of 1978.[11] According to both surveys, this group is approximately equally divided among the following categories: persons found incompetent to stand trial, persons found not guilty by reason of insanity, persons sentenced under special statutes, and mentally ill inmates of correctional facilities transferred to special prison units or mental health facilities for treatment of mental illness. The slight differences between the composition reported in the present survey and the compositon reported by Steadman

11. Steadman et al., "Mentally Disordered Offenders: A National Survey," pp. 31-38.

may be due to inclusion of different facilities, to random fluctuations, or to reporting errors by respondents. The two most notable differences, however, are consistent with hypotheses related to recent legal changes: we found a smaller proportion of persons found incompetent, which could reflect increasing success of treatment-to-competency programs established in response to the mandate of *Jackson* v. *Indiana*,[12] and an increase in the proportion of mentally ill inmates held in correctional rather than mental health facilities, perhaps related to the tightening of due-process standards for transfer of prisoners to mental hospitals mandated by the decision in *Vitek* v. *Jones*.[13]

Demographically, compared to the general federal and state prison systems, the entire set of responding facilities houses a population containing about twice as many youths under 17, more residents aged 65 and over, and somewhat more whites. The overrepresentation of youths disappears when juvenile-only facilities are excluded from the comparison; in fact, youths who have been tried as adults constitute only 1.6 percent of the population of adult-only facilities for mentally disordered offenders, compared to 2.6 percent in the general prison population. The predominance of elderly residents, however, occurs in adult-only facilities under all auspices.

*Treatment practices
and staffing levels*

Among responding facilities, some form of individualized treatment planning is generally institutionalized, with over 90 percent of responding facilities reporting preparation and regular review of individual treatment plans. Psychotropic medication is the most universal form of treatment, being available in 97.6 percent of responding facilities and reportedly administered to a median of 61 percent of residents. According to staff interviews—but not record checks—performed during site visits, psychotropic medications are administered for immediate crisis intervention, short-term stabilization of inappropriate behavior, and long-term control therapy. In addition, antidepressants and anticonvulsants are administered as needed. However, reports suggest that discretion is used in administration of all medication. One facility visited had obtained a grant for a special program to educate residents about the purposes and side effects of medication. Another facility selected for a site visit had instituted a procedure for residents' reporting of excessive side effects followed by phased reduction of medication levels.

About 90 percent of responding facilities report offering group and individual therapy at least weekly, to medians of 60 percent and 34 percent of their residents, respectively. This level of availability is somewhat greater than that reported by Scheidemandel and Kanno,[14] but somewhat less than that reported by Eckerman.[15] Also, compared to the earlier surveys, the use of electroconvulsive therapy and other somatic therapies—for instance, Indoklon and insulin shock—has virtually disappeared. Although electroconvulsive therapy is reportedly available in 19.2 percent of facilities, the median participation rate is 0.0 percent; other

12. *Jackson* v. *Indiana*, 406 U.S. 715 (1972).
13. *Vitek* v. *Jones*, 445 U.S. 480 (1980).

14. Scheidemandel and Kanno, *Mentally Ill Offender*, p. 48.
15. Eckerman, *Nationwide Survey of Mental Health and Correctional Institutions*, p. 45.

TABLE 2
LEGAL-STATUS COMPOSITION OF ADULT AND JUVENILE RESIDENT POPULATION,
BY AUSPICES AND AGE JURISDICTION (Percentage)

Legal Status	Corrections				Mental Health				Social Services and Other				Total			
	Adults and juveniles (N = 77)	Juveniles only (N = 154)	Adults only (N = 3,449)	Total (N = 3,680)	Adults and juveniles (N = 1,664)	Juveniles only (N = 251)	Adults only (N = 9,509)	Total (N = 11,424)	Adults and juveniles (N = 242)	Juveniles only (N = 265)	Adults only (N = 678)	Total (N = 1,185)	Adults and juveniles (N = 1,983)	Juveniles only (N = 670)	Adults only (N = 13,636)	Total (N = 16,289)§
Adults																
Being evaluated for competency	0.0	0.0	0.8	0.7	4.2	0.0	9.0	8.1	0.4	0.0	7.8	4.5	3.6	0.0	6.9	6.2
Being evaluated for responsibility	0.0	0.0	0.6	0.6	1.0	0.0	8.8	7.5	0.8	0.0	3.7	2.3	0.9	0.0	6.5	5.6
Guilty but mentally ill	0.0	0.0	1.4	1.3	0.6	0.0	0.6	0.6	0.0	0.0	0.6	0.3	0.5	0.0	0.8	0.7
Incompetent to stand trial	0.0	0.0	0.5	0.5	2.8	0.0	17.4	14.9	4.1	0.0	8.6	5.8	2.8	0.0	12.7	11.0
Not guilty by reason of insanity	0.0	0.0	0.0	0.0	3.8	0.0	21.5	18.4	17.8	0.0	7.5	7.9	5.4	0.0	15.4	13.6
Penal transfers	28.6	0.0	60.7	57.5	19.1	0.0	10.9	11.9	0.0	0.0	16.8	9.6	17.1	0.0	23.8	22.1
Sex offenders	13.0	0.0	14.3	13.7	2.6	0.0	12.2	10.5	0.8	0.0	40.4	23.3	2.8	0.0	14.1	12.1
Civilly admitted*	0.0	0.0	0.0	0.0	57.9	0.0	14.0	20.1	74.4	0.0	11.6	21.8	57.7	0.0	10.3	15.7
Other	0.0	0.0	21.7	20.3	4.6	0.0	5.6	5.3	0.0	0.0	3.0	1.7	3.9	0.0	9.5	8.4
Juveniles																
Being evaluated for competency	0.0	0.0	0.0	0.0	0.4	12.8	0.0	0.3	0.0	0.0	0.0	0.0	0.3	4.8	0.0	0.2
Incompetent to stand trial	0.0	0.0	0.0	0.0	0.2	0.8	0.0	0.0‡	0.0	0.4	0.0	0.1	0.2	0.5	0.0	0.0‡
Not guilty by reason of insanity	0.0	0.0	0.0	0.0	0.0	0.0	0.0	0.0	0.0	0.0	0.0	0.0	0.0	0.0	0.0	0.0
Sentenced to treatment	58.4	100.0	0.0	5.4	1.1	18.7	0.0	0.5	0.0	92.1	0.0	20.6	3.2	66.4	0.0	3.1
Civilly admitted*	0.0	0.0	0.0	0.0	1.4	61.4	0.0	1.8	1.2	0.4	0.0	0.3	1.3	23.2	0.0	1.1
Other	0.0	0.0	0.0	0.0	0.2	6.4	0.0	0.2	0.4	7.2	0.0	1.7	0.2	5.2	0.0	0.2
Total	100.0	100.0	100.0	100.0	99.9†	100.1†	100.0	100.1†	99.9†	100.1†	100.0	99.9†	99.9†	100.1†	100.0	100.0

SOURCE: Center for Studies of Antisocial and Violent Behavior, National Institute of Mental Health.
*In some states, includes persons who are involuntarily civilly committed after a finding that they are unlikely to regain competence to stand trial.
†Does not total 100.0 due to rounding.
‡Indicates nonzero population less than 0.05 percent of total population.
§Total differs from overall total of 19,543 due to item nonresponse.

somatic therapies are reportedly available in only 3.2 percent of facilities, but they are used extensively in those few facilities.

The facilities selected for telephone follow-up and case studies—that is, those facilities at which some impression could be formed of the quality of treatment—are in no sense representative of the population of facilities for mentally disordered offenders, or even of the responding facilities. Nevertheless, several recurrent themes worth noting emerged from these efforts.

First, in general, facilities with populations larger than about 50 seem to offer more highly structured treatment programs than do smaller facilities. This might be expected, because the larger facilities are likely to house sufficient numbers of residents with a given need so that a special program to meet that need becomes cost effective.

Second, in the one facility observed in which psychiatric technicians faced a licensure requirement, several desirable effects were noted that did not appear in the other facilities visited. The technicians articulate uniquely high levels of understanding of the treatment process, and there is an awareness among senior technicians of their roles as trainers and examples for more junior technicians. In addition, they demonstrate initiative in establishing therapeutic groups to meet the needs of special subsets of residents, and they reflect high morale as a result of respect demonstrated by facility administrators. These observations suggest that professionalization of technicians produces desirable effects.

Third, many treatment staff mentioned that distance, as well as organizational and resource limits, mitigates against follow-up to ensure ongoing adherence to the treatment plan following release, even when release is to the general prison population. Informally, a number of staff members expressed the view that this lack would lead to the eventual return of those released to the institution.

Fourth, statutes in some states permit mental hospitals to reject potential penal transferees on a treatability criterion. This was seen as an important aid to effective treatment, not only because it provides a safety valve for controlling population size, but also because it permits the facility to reject those who might later disrupt or refuse group therapeutic processes, thereby lowering the effectiveness of the programs for other residents. While the availability of this rejection criterion could theoretically lead to denial of treatment to certain unalluring but seriously disturbed persons, it is used rather effectively at one facility to transfer untreatable patients to a unit where medication is used extensively and to keep them separate from treatable persons receiving verbal therapy in the other unit.

With respect to security practices, approximately one-third of responding facilities classify themselves as maximum security. Another 19 percent are classified as medium security, 10 percent as minimum security, and 16 percent as comprising all three levels. About 60 percent of all facilities house all residents in closed wards.

Among the 35 percent of responding facilities operating under multiple levels of security, the criteria for security-level assignment emphasize patient behavior and elapsed time during the present institutionalization, rather than historical or explicitly predictive criteria. The most commonly cited criteria are assaultive behavior, in 25.2 percent of the facilities, and time in the facility, adjustment to the program, or both, in 23.6 percent. Substantially less common is a psychiatric or clinical determination, which occurs in 14.2 percent of the facilities, and still fewer respondents cite historical factors such as legal status, offense charged, and prior escape history.

Overall, responding facilities report a median of 136.5 staff members per 100 residents, a ratio that varies from 121.5 in facilities housing both adults and juveniles, to 133.0 in adult-only facilities, to 219.0 in juvenile-only facilities. By organizational auspices, the number of staff per 100 residents is reportedly 65.5 in correctional facilities, 175.5 in mental health facilities, and 147.5 in social services and other facilities. Besides these differences in levels of staffing, differences are also apparent with respect to the mix of staff. Within correctional facilities, treatment staff outnumber security staff by a ratio of about 1.75 to 1.0. Among mental health and social service and other facilities, the corresponding ratios are about 11.0 to 1.0 and 13.0 to 1.0, respectively.

As Table 3 shows, staffing levels differ in rather interesting ways with respect to population. For administrators, treatment personnel, and ancillary therapists, economies of scale seem to exist in the sense that their numbers per 100 residents generally decline as facility population increases. In contrast, the number of security staff per 100 residents increases with population, possibly because security problems are more acute in larger facilities, or because the larger facilities are more likely than others to be correctional facilities, which are considered to be more security conscious.

Common administrative problems

The concerns of managing the organizational aspects of the facility were observed on site to be related to, although separate from, treatment monitoring. This section discusses the organization and administration of the programs including the auspices under which the facility operates as well as staffing and staff-training issues.

Many programs combine the dual therapeutic and corrections mandate of the facility by training line staff to function as both security guards and therapists. The major problem associated with this dual role is that sometimes a conflict is felt between the two roles of therapist and guard. Traditional roles of therapist and guard are almost antithetical to each other—the former is based on interaction and the other discourages it.

Another concern of facility management is the prevention of staff burnout. Some of the programs visited had instituted structured times for staff to discuss problems with residents or other staff or both. It was recognized that these facilities can be highly charged and that dealing with persons both mad and bad is extremely stressful. In addition, the multidisciplinary nature of the staff sometimes contributed to interprofessional conflicts in dealing with certain types of residents. This structured time not only portrayed to staff that the administration was supportive of them, but it allowed the administration to be aware of potential problems and bring them to closure before they escalated.

The administration of treatment programming also includes both the provision and the assessment of treatment activities. As stated earlier, the mail survey data showed that about 90 per-

TABLE 3
STAFF-TO-RESIDENT RATIOS, BY FACILITY POPULATION (Median ratio of staff per 100 residents)

Staff Category	10 or fewer (N = 3)	11-25 (N = 17)	26-50 (N = 24)	Facility Population 51-100 (N = 20)	101-250 (N = 29)	251-500 (N = 11)	501 or more (N = 8)	Total (N = 112)
Senior administrators	17.0	9.0	5.5	2.4	1.6	1.1	0.5	2.5
Other administrators and clerical staff	17.0	7.7	9.5	9.5	8.0	5.3	4.5	8.0
Treatment staff								
Psychiatrists	10.0	6.3	3.4	1.4	1.7	2.3	0.5	2.3
Other graduate-level therapists	10.0	15.0	12.5	5.5	6.9	4.0	2.5	7.3
Senior medical staff	18.8	27.0	23.0	14.5	9.0	8.2	3.5	12.8
Technicians and aides	20.0	120.0	65.5	42.5	23.2	6.0	2.5	50.0
Ancillary therapists	4.2	0.4	3.0	1.5	1.6	0.8	0.3	1.4
Educators	0.0	0.2	2.5	0.5	1.4	1.1	0.5	0.8
Security staff								
Armed	0.0	0.0	0.1	0.8	0.1	0.1	0.2	0.0
Unarmed	25.0	2.1	5.5	9.5	26.0	25.0	2.5	9.0
Maintenance staff	0.0	7.6	3.5	10.5	5.8	7.2	6.0	6.5
Total staff	300.0	229.0	201.0	147.0	118.0	106.0	71.5	136.5

SOURCE: Center for Studies of Antisocial and Violent Behavior, National Institute of Mental Health.
NOTE: Staffing data reflect full-time equivalents actually on staff rather than authorized levels.

cent of the facilities responding to the survey prepared individual treatment plans. On site it was learned that some of these plans are developed and maintained orally in at least a few institutions. In other facilities, staff noted that the variation in the actual treatment plans is not sufficient to warrant their being deemed individual. However, in still other facilities the individual treatment plans are reviewed comprehensively in case conferences, with goals and success measures negotiated by the treatment team. The resulting plan is then presented to the resident and his or her willingness to participate in treatment negotiated. Such a procedure is likely to lead not only to more complete and individualized treatment plans, but also to more acceptance of treatment by residents.

Observations on site found that some facilities classify ward meetings that discuss general living arrangements as group therapy. In other facilities, the groups have a structured syllabus with topics, a rationale for the group, as well as measures of success. In most of the facilities, due to budget pressures, the groups are led by ward aides or psychiatric technicians. In some of the facilities, these staff have the opportunity to develop groups addressing special needs and using methods they consider important. Interestingly, the same staff are among the most highly motivated observed in any facility visited.

Another aspect of treatment programming administration is the evaluation of ongoing treatment and the use of evaluation results to suggest improvements in the treatment program. Based on information obtained from the site visits, it appears that several facilities have established research departments within the facility. Although the structures and procedures exist for the conduct of research, very few facilities have established a feedback loop for utilizing research results to improve actual treatment programming. The conduct of research and the use of research results are seen as two fairly separate structures.

Another concern related to the therapeutic activities within a facility is that of control of critical incidents. Critical incidents include patient suicides, homicides, and escapes. Interestingly, although both suicides and escapes are reported to occur with disproportionate frequency in smaller facilities, administrative concern about suicide, at least, is more widespread in the larger facilities. All facilities that were visited had experienced at least one critical incident and had established directives for dealing with such incidents.

Another type of patient management concern voiced by one-third of the respondents housing both males and females includes problems associated with that mix. Specific examples cited by respondents include both sexual acting-out and the need for procedures to protect privacy. However, only one program visited had changed from mixed-sex to single-sex housing units because of such problems. During its first year of operation, there had been several incidents between male and female residents that led to elimination of coed units. However, the therapy groups continue to be coed, and, according to one staff member, the patients appear to be more at ease in the single-sex housing units.

Release decisions for convicted sex offenders and mentally ill inmates generally fall within the purview of parole authorities rather than mental health professionals. When an incompetent defendant has been restored to competency, the disposition decision is shifted to the courts, and eventually, unless the defendant is found not guilty, to parole authorities. The release decision for civilly committed persons whose competency has been judged unrestorable remains dependent on input from the staff of a facility for mentally disordered offenders. Moreover, as noted by Wexler, a successful insanity defense can lead to commitment to a secure mental hospital.[16] Thus, both for persons whose competency is unrestorable and for persons found not guilty by reason of insanity, responsibility for recommending release is likely to remain with the staff of a facility for mentally disordered offenders.

National survey results indicate that problems associated with release to the community are nearly universal and that impacts are observable in the establishment of pre-release services, transitional release programs, and efforts to provide post-release follow-up. Over 90 percent of the responding facilities report releasing residents directly to the community, and 83 percent of the facilities report offering pre-release services. The most common form of pre-release service is counseling and testing, reported by 59.1 percent of the facilities. In addition, 33.9 percent report, in their own words, "negotiating terms of treatment with community agencies." The respondents' choice of this terminology presumably reflects a more aggressive stance than that of another 21.3 percent of facilities reporting "referral to community agencies." Community mental health centers are the most commonly named community agency other than courts. During telephone follow-ups and site visits, staff members frequently expressed frustration with the perceived reluctance of the centers or other community agencies to accept supervisory responsibility for mentally disordered offenders following their release.

In addition to pre-release services, 74 percent of the facilities report operating one or more transitional release programs. Of these, 31.4 percent report partial release, 40.5 report release for work or education, and 26.3 percent report some other special release program. During telephone follow-up and site visits, administrators and treatment staff expressed substantial concern over the conflict between transitional release programs and community security. Specifically, resident activity outside the walls is presumed to facilitate successful post-release transition to the community, but it requires the supervision of sufficient staff to protect the community during such activities. Besides this real conflict between competing goals, administrators see themselves confronted with a public relations problem: the reduction of perhaps unwarranted community fear concerning such programs. Several facilities visited had received occasional adverse publicity about their transitional release programs and had initiated public informational activities to counter this publicity.

Transitional release programs were observed in 3 of the 11 facilities visited during case study preparation. In all 3 programs, residents progress in stages from full institutionalization to release; in 1 of these, responsibility for authorization to progress from one stage to the next is shared by facility staff and the court. Administrators of all 3 programs expressed acute awareness of the high-risk nature of these programs.

16. David Wexler, *Civil Commitments and Dangerous Mental Patients: Legal Issues of Confinement, Treatment, and Release,* Department of Health, Education, and Welfare pub. no. (ADM) 77-331 (Washington, DC: Government Printing Office, 1976), p. 48.

Nearly half the facilities releasing residents to the community report postrelease follow-up with the former resident and about 60 percent report follow-up with community agencies. Follow-up with the releasee is usually to provide support and information about community adjustment and to evaluate adjustment to the community. Follow-up with agencies is typically to monitor referrals and to evaluate adjustment. During telephone interviews and site visits, a commonly expressed concern of facility treatment staff was the lack of supervision in the community, especially with respect to maintenance of medication. This gap is apparently seen as a frequent cause of failure, or recidivism by the releasee. It is worth noting that this lack of control over follow-up extends to mentally ill inmates returned to the general prison population following stabilization. Even staff of a psychiatric hospital, under correctional auspices and located on the grounds of the correctional facility to which most of its mentally ill inmates are returned, expressed frustration over their lack of ability to monitor follow-up of the postrelease treatment plan.

With respect to the decision to release mentally disordered offenders—particularly insanity acquittees—to the community, Wexler wrote that *"psychological studies suggest that if a legal decision-making structure could be designed in which release responsibility is shared or diffused, the decision to release might be made with fewer inhibitions."*[17] To remove the inhibitions, he suggested the court as an appropriate locus for the decision. However, vesting the release decision responsibility in the judge would appear to diffuse the responsibility of treatment staff in formulating release recommendations, thereby reducing their accountability. An innovative example of shared release responsibility, which achieves the benefit of insights from a variety of perspectives without the loss of accountability, is provided by Oregon's Psychiatric Security Review Board, a five-member panel independent of the institution.[18] The board becomes responsible for the individual once he or she has been acquitted of criminal charges by reason of insanity and is placed by the court under the jurisdiction of the board. The board then assumes responsibility for determining whether the person needs to be confined in a security hospital, released into the community on certain conditions, or later discharged from its jurisdiction. The hospital staff are, therefore, relieved of responsibility for the release decision and the conflict between roles as a provider of treatment and evaluator of treatment progress, on the one hand, and decision maker concerning readiness for release, on the other.

RECOMMENDATIONS FOR
FUTURE RESEARCH

As indicated in the preceding sections, the phased quantitative and qualitative research conducted in the present study provides a fairly comprehensive picture of facilities for mentally disordered offenders—their organizational structure, size, treatment and security practices, and staffing levels. In addition, the complete study provides a series of descriptions of facility residents

17. Ibid., p. 54 (italics in original).

18. See Jeffrey L. Rogers, Joseph D. Bloom, and Spero M. Manson, "Oregon's Psychiatric Security Review Board: A Comprehensive System for Managing Insanity Acquittees," this issue of *The Annals* of the American Academy of Political and Social Science.

in terms of legal status, psychiatric diagnosis, age, and ethnicity.[19] However, considerations of the respondents' burden and resource constraints placed a number of limits on both the detail of the data and the resulting achievable depth of analysis. Because of these limits, a number of interesting research questions remain.

While the national survey data do enumerate the availability of treatment and the level of resident participation, the survey could not attempt to determine the quality of treatment, which we believe can only be assessed, if at all, by systematic observation of patient-staff interactions in host institutions. For example, during site visits to a nonrepresentative subset of facilities, it was found that group therapy is defined by some administrators to include the weekly ward meeting where the issues are ward management and maintenance, a type of interaction not widely considered therapeutic, even though the meeting is regularly scheduled for one hour each week and has a 100 percent participation rate. Groups with well-defined therapeutic goals, subjects, and processes are, however, included in the same category by other responding facilities. Consequently, the variation in the definitions accorded to "treatment" is a major impediment to any survey attempting to assess the status of treatment nationwide.

As another example, we were not able to collect detailed national data on the credentials of the group leaders. Site visits and follow-up telephone calls to 60

19. Charlotte A. Kerr and Jeffrey A. Roth, with Thomas F. Courtless and Elyce Zenoff, *Survey of Facilities and Programs for Mentally Disordered Offenders: Final Report* (Rockville, MD: National Institute of Mental Health, forthcoming).

facilities revealed that the majority of the group leaders are psychiatric technicians or, at most, psychiatric nurses or social workers.

As a final example, we were not able to determine the type and quality of individual treatment planning. On site the questions were posed to discover whether a review of individual charts would show individualized approaches to treatment, and responses were mixed. Our data do not allow us to assess the thoroughness or extent of treatment plan review. Therefore, an important research question not addressed by the current effort is an assessment of the quality of treatment planning and an analysis of factors associated with quality.

Finally, a number of interesting questions relating individual residents' criminal histories, legal status, diagnoses, and treatments to institutional and postrelease behaviors cannot be examined using our data. To limit the respondents' burden, our questions concerning residents were limited to those that could be answered from existing reports rather than those requiring micro-level analysis of individual records. Therefore, we could not address questions such as the extent of use or success of a given treatment mode for residents of a particular diagnostic subset, or an analysis of the relationship between psychiatric diagnosis and the probability of violent behavior. These remain important topics for future research.

Another research gap not filled by the present effort is the measurement of average length of stay for persons in residence. To our knowledge, no facility regularly computes or reports average length of stay for the population in residence as of a given day. This is understandable, as the computation would require extraction of admission dates from the entire set of patient records, an arduous task with a manual records system. Some facilities do periodically report average length of stay for residents released during the period, a somewhat easier task. However, because any cohort of released residents will overrepresent short-stay residents—such as persons being evaluated—relative to the facility's entire population, the average for those released will understate the average for the population in residence. These underestimates, when misinterpreted by the media, legislatures, or public, may provide unwarranted support for claims that mentally disordered offenders are treated relatively leniently.

We were also limited in our analysis of the true legal status of civilly committed residents of responding facilities. We could determine the number of individuals committed through the criminal courts and the number committed through civil commitment procedures. However, to separate statistically persons voluntarily or involuntarily civilly committed through other routes—such as dangerous mental patients or unrestorable incompetents—would necessitate a detailed analysis of individual records. This is another issue for further research.

Law and Psychiatry: Scandinavia in the 1980s

By LEIF ÖJESJÖ

ABSTRACT: The major policies and practices with regard to the civil and criminal commitment of the mentally ill in the Scandinavian countries during the 1970s and 1980s are described and discussed. Deinstitutionalization, community work, and outpatient treatment within geographically defined sectors have been introduced in all the Nordic countries. At the same time, criminally committed mental patients constitute an increasing proportion of the involuntarily hospitalized population. The special defense of insanity and tests such as McNaughtan are not used in the Scandinavian countries. The handling and disposition of severely mentally ill criminal defendants is closer to the notions of guilty but mentally ill in some U.S. jurisdictions, although in Scandinavia such persons are hospitalized and do not receive penal sentences. Even though forensic psychiatry has come under much criticism, there is still a need for psychiatric evaluations for courts and there is still a need for the provision of mental health treatment, rehabilitation, and follow-up for mentally disordered offenders.

Leif Öjesjö is medical director at the Center for Social and Forensic Psychiatry, Linköping, Sweden. He received his M.D. degree from Lund University, and he has been a research associate of the New School for Social Research, New York City, and a visiting research scholar in the Department of Anthropology, Brown University, Providence, Rhode Island. His major research interests are in forensic psychiatry and psychiatric epidemiology.

THE preceding articles provide a description and discussion of various aspects of the interactions between the legal and mental health systems in the United States. This article will examine some Scandinavian policies and practices pertaining to the civil and criminal commitment systems for the mentally ill. Because the organization of the mental health laws and systems differs considerably in the five Nordic countries—Denmark, Finland, Iceland, Norway, and Sweden—no uniform picture can be provided. It does appear, however, that criminal commitments account for an increasing proportion of the involuntarily hospitalized mentally ill population.

Due to the nature of my own experience, this discussion will be focused mainly on Sweden. Comparisons will be made with the other Scandinavian countries.[1]

The incidence rates for crime and mental disorders have generally been rising. This trend appears to be related to increasing levels of work shortages, unemployment, alienation, and problems of drug and alcohol abuse. The social welfare system is facing severe problems, and community service agencies are finding it hard to obtain sufficient resources to handle their growing client populations. Sweden, as well as its neighbors, is acutely aware of the interconnections between certain social and medical problems; moreover, the laws encourage judges to use special care provisions for alcoholics, drug addicts, and mentally disturbed persons.[2]

1. Sweden is often cited as an example of future trends in social and criminal policy and is often praised—or criticized—for the high standards of living. Paul C. Friday, "Sanctioning in Sweden: An Overview," *Federal Probation,* 40:48-55 (1976).
2. Harold K. Becker and Einar O. Hjellemo, *Justice in Modern Sweden* (Springfield, IL: Charles C Thomas, 1976).

CIVIL COMMITMENT POLICIES AND PRACTICES

The existing legislation providing for compulsory psychiatric care in Sweden was introduced in 1967. Ideologically, however, it can be traced back to the nineteenth century, when the treatment of serious mental disorders as illnesses was introduced. Patients were removed from their ordinary surroundings and were placed in geographically isolated institutions. Closely allied with this notion of isolation was a conviction that the mentally ill were dangerous, socially inept, and disruptive.

As in other Western countries, the old mental hospitals were distinguished by the comprehensive nature of the care that they provided, as well as their compulsory features. Mental health care was developed and handled by a separate organization, with its own legislative authority. A change came in the 1950s, when mental health care began to be provided on a voluntary basis and when treatment with psychoactive drugs was introduced. During the sixties, seventies, and eighties the planning of psychiatric care acquired a new direction in favor of more open—that is, less institution-based—forms of care, rooted in an increased awareness of the interactions of biological, social, and psychological factors underlying the development of mental disorders.

Although declining, the number of psychiatric admissions, voluntary as well as involuntary, is still quite high. In 1982, there were 348 psychiatric beds per 100,000 population in Sweden, and admission rates were 1345 per 100,000. A fairly large proportion of these admissions—248 per 100,000—were compulsory. This is a much higher rate of compulsory hospitalization than for the other Scandinavian countries. Within

Sweden, regional differences have been and continue to remain large. The number of persons receiving compulsory psychiatric care can be up to five times greater in one county council area than in another.[3]

The development in the West toward more open psychiatric institutions and community mental health care has created a general unwillingness on the part of hospitals to receive the more disturbed and aggressive patients. Unfortunately, psychiatrists have long been ambivalent about including the bad and the mad among their patients, because the former were hard to treat and also because they tended to destroy the image of the more deserving and treatable patients.[4] Mental health practice in Scandinavia does not differ in any important way from this general trend, but, as elsewhere, not enough is known about criteria for accepting patients, for enforcing treatment, and for the discharge and aftercare of the patients.[5]

In Sweden, compulsory psychiatric care may be provided for a person if he or she suffers from a mental illness or mental abnormality of such severity that institutional care is considered to be imperative and if, in addition, certain special indications also exist. The relevant law provides that mentally disordered persons may involuntarily be hospitalized if they:

—are lacking insight into their illness, and/or are dependent on drugs, and may have their state of health considerably improved with care and/or aggravated without care;

—are dangerous to themselves or others;

—are unable to take care of themselves;

—have a way of life that is severely disturbing to others; or

—constitute a danger to the property of others or to some other interest protected by law.

The last criterion concerns only mentally disordered offenders sentenced by criminal courts.[6]

Under the present system, compulsory hospitalization of the mentally ill requires an order by two physicians, one of whom must be a psychiatrist. Generally, no judicial proceedings are involved, unless the commitment is being contested. In such cases, appeals are considered by a special discharge committee chaired by a judge. Compulsory hospitalization is basically for an indeterminate period; however, since 1 January 1983 the rule has been that the need for continuing compulsory hospitalization must be reported to the discharge committee after three months, and every six months thereafter.

It is worth mentioning that in Sweden and Denmark—as also in most U.S. jurisdictions—voluntarily admitted patients can be retained involuntarily once they have been hospitalized, if they meet the necessary requirements. Such conversion of voluntary patients to involuntary status is not possible in Norway.

In the 1700-bed Aarhus Psychiatric Hospital, supposedly typical of Danish

3. Social Affairs Commission, *Psychiatry, Compulsion and Legal Security* (Stockholm: Allmanna förlaget, 1984), p. 469.

4. David Ingleby, "London International History of Psychiatry Conference," *New Ideas in Psychology,* 3(1):109-14 (1985).

5. Keith Soothill et al., "Compulsory Admissions to Mental Hospitals in Six Countries," *International Journal of Law and Psychiatry,* 4:327-44 (1983).

6. Swedish National Law Code, Mental Health Act §293 (1966).

mental hospitals, the main source of admissions was from the patients' homes, and about 70 percent of the patients had prior histories of mental health care. Schizophrenia and affective psychosis were the most common disorders; however, alcohol- and drug-dependency syndromes and personality disorders also ranked high, coming to approximately one-third of the total sample. Psychopharmacological medications were the most frequent treatment given, while individual psychotherapy was rare. On the other hand, Denmark seems to have developed a relatively broad network of aftercare facilities.[7]

The trend now in all the Nordic countries is in favor of outpatient mental health care in geographically defined sectors. Increasingly, care is provided at psychiatric clinics affiliated with general medical hospitals through centrally financed community council programs and unified health insurance schemes.[8] The changes in mental health policies also concern compulsory care. The regional differences that were mentioned earlier indicate that such services are governed not only by legislation, but also by organizational factors, attitudes, and budgetary considerations. Experiences from other countries, notably the democratic psychiatry movement in Italy, have shown that the need for compulsory hospitalization can very markedly be reduced as a function of legislated changes in such public policies.[9] By dealing with problems well before the persons come to the clinic, and dealing also with the family and work situation as the foci of needed interventions, hospitalization could well be prevented in many—if not most—cases.

In order for a real reform of mental health services to be feasible, the county councils, which are responsible for health and medical services, and the municipalities, which are responsible for various social services, must share the burden for ensuring that the necessary measures are taken.

CRIMINAL COMMITMENTS
AND EVALUATIONS

Penal and legal philosophies have developed out of a general welfare ideology that maintains that the correctional approach should focus on the reintegration and rehabilitation of the offender and should stress the socialization process. Correctional experts—for example, criminologists, psychiatrists, psychologists, sociologists, and lawyers—have been sought for advice, but not for making final decisions and major policies.[10] Specialized institutions

7. Soothill et al., "Compulsory Admissions to Mental Hospitals."

8. In Sweden, for instance, all residents are covered by a compulsory health insurance system; a sick person is guaranteed a daily allowance during illness. The aim is to provide about 90 percent of lost income. Health insurance also covers all hospitalization, which, in principle, is free of charge. Visits to physicians at outpatient clinics cost a uniform amount, approximately $5.00. Medications prescribed by a physician cost a maximum of approximately $6.00 on any single occasion, and certain essential medications—such as insulin—are available free of charge.

9. Franco Basaglia, "Problems of Law and Psychiatry. The Italian Experience," *International Journal of Law and Psychiatry*, 3(1):17-37 (1980); Shulamit Ramon, "Psychiatrica Democratica: A Case Study of an Italian Community Mental Health Service," *International Journal of Health Services*, 13(2):307-24 (1983); Carlo Perris and Dargut Kemali, "Focus on the Italian Psychiatric Reform," *Acta Psychiatrica Scandinavica*, supp., 316(71):9-157 (1985).

10. Becker and Hjellemo, *Justice in Modern Sweden*; Friday, "Sanctioning in Sweden"; John Fry, ed., *Limits of the Welfare State* (Westmead: Saxon House, 1979).

for chronic offenders, alcoholic criminals, and psychopaths have been established. Olof Kinberg and other psychiatrists involved themselves very early and actively in the administration of these reforms in penal law, believing that it was possible to control criminal behavior through a medical approach.[11] However, during recent years the pendulum has swung back. As Borup Svendsen has observed, "Psychiatrists can't explain crime as such, as some psychiatrists 'overselling' themselves have claimed, and their treatment results have not been convincing."[12]

In Sweden, forensic psychiatry is an independent medical specialty on a par with general psychiatry and child psychiatry, whereas in Denmark, Finland, Norway, and possibly also Iceland, it is a subspecialty of general psychiatry. It should also be noted that, although forensic psychiatric work is predominantly directed and carried out by physicians—namely, psychiatrists—other mental health professionals—psychologists, social workers, nurses, and other staff—are increasingly involved.

Scandinavian law, unlike Anglo-American law, does not have a special defense of insanity, hence the practices in Scandinavia may be viewed as being closer to the guilty-but-mentally-ill policies and provisions in about 12 U.S. jurisdictions.[13] But, unlike the U.S. practice, persons found to be both guilty and severely mentally ill cannot be sentenced to penal institutions; rather, they receive care and treatment in security hospitals.

It is an important principle in Swedish criminal law that defendants are assumed to be responsible for their actions and thus should stand trial.[14] In the case of persons who are considered by the court to be too mentally impaired, the criminal proceedings may be delayed pending the defendants' treatment and recovery. In less serious cases the criminal charges may be dropped and the case disposed of by diversion to the mental health system. When, under Swedish criminal law, it would be considered unfair and unjust to regard the defendant as having intended to commit the offense, he or she may be adjudged not guilty. However, in my experience, such adjudications are extremely rare.

According to the Swedish Penal Code, psychiatric care may be a recommended disposition for a person who has been convicted by a court of law and who is considered to have committed the offense "under the influence of" mental disorder and/or to be in need of treatment at the time of sentencing. Such persons are considered guilty and,

---

11. Olof Kinberg, *Basic Problems of Criminology* (Copenhagen: Munksgaard, 1935); George K. Stürup, *Treating the Untreatable* (Baltimore, MD: Johns Hopkins University Press, 1968).

12. Borup B. Svendsen, "Declining Interest in Forensic Psychiatry: Recent Developments in Denmark," *Bulletin of the American Academy of Psychiatry and the Law,* 1:20-28 (1977); idem, "Present Status of Forensic Psychiatry in Denmark," *Acta Psychiatrica Scandinavica,* 55:176-80 (1977).

13. The legal definitions of exculpatory insanity, based on the McNaughtan right-or-wrong test or other such tests in the U.S. jurisdictions, are largely unknown in the Nordic countries, with the possible exception of Finland. The several guilty-but-mentally-ill laws in the United States probably provide a much more familiar concept to the Scandinavians. See, for example, "Guilty but Mentally Ill: A Historical and Constitutional Analysis," *Journal of Urban Law,* 53:471-96 (1976); Saleem A. Shah, "Criminal Responsibility," in *Perspectives in Forensic Psychiatry and Psychology,* ed. W. J. Curran, A. L. McGarry, and S. A. Shah (Philadelphia: F. A. Davis, forthcoming).

14. Hans Danelius, *Human Rights in Sweden* (Lund: Swedish Institute, 1981).

if any of the statuses mentioned in the code are found to exist—namely, mental illness, mental retardation, or other mental abnormality considered equal to a mental illness—the court may, according to provisions of Chapter 33, Section 2, award only certain specifically prescribed sanctions. These sanctions are institutional psychiatric care, noninstitutional psychiatric care, probation, or a fine. For alcohol and drug addicts and for juveniles, alternative sanctions are available.

According to Svendsen and his colleagues, the number of forensic reports have been at least four times higher in Sweden than in the other Nordic countries: approximately 45 per 100,000 population versus 5-11 per 100,000.[15] Psychiatrists are appointed by the courts. In Norway the reporting psychiatrist ordinarily has to appear in court, but in the other countries this is rarely the case. The forensic psychiatrist is viewed as an impartial clinical expert who can advise the court concerning the disposition of the case. Direct, cross-, and redirect examination of these expert witnesses, as is common in the United States, is rare in the Scandinavian countries.

The psychiatrist's written reports may be reviewed later in the legal process by a medical-legal council. Such reviews take place in Finland and Norway in all cases; in Denmark in about two-thirds of the cases, these being the more doubtful or serious cases; while in Sweden only about 10 percent of the reports are reviewed.

The organization of forensic psychiatry at the posttrial stage—that is, correctional psychiatry—differs considerably in the five countries. Nevertheless, some comparative remarks seem appropriate.[16] Activities at the posttrial stage generally take place in four settings: (1) in the probation system and prisons where psychiatrists are visiting physicians; (2) in mental health departments, administered by psychiatrists, within the penal system; (3) in special, or security, hospitals for mentally disordered offenders; and (4) in the general hospital system.

In Finland, mentally disordered offenders are traditionally treated rather conservatively. There is heavy reliance on inpatient confinement and care, and outpatient treatment and aftercare programs have very limited resources. In this regard, the progress of penal psychiatry is lagging behind with respect to the principles of modern general psychiatry.[17] A relatively large number of Finnish offenders are placed in security hospitals, while in Norway and Iceland only a small number of mentally disordered offenders are handled in this manner.[18] A dominant trend in all

15. Borup B. Svendsen et al., "Present Functions of Forensic Psychiatry in Scandinavia," *Acta Psychiatrica Scandinavica,* 55:165-75 (1977).

16. See ibid. In Sweden only a small portion of people convicted in criminal cases are currently hospitalized: only about 4 percent of those in prisons and 2 percent of those on parole status. On the other hand, of those involved in the most violent crimes—for example, criminal homicide—the majority may have been hospitalized. Special interest has been devoted to the heterogenous group considered to be afflicted with the equivalent of mental disease. Many of these persons suffer from personality disorders, such as so-called psychopathy and other conditions; many are alcoholics and/or drug addicts. Often the need for care and treatment has been differently judged by the hospital physicians and by the examining psychiatrists. See, for example, Henry Werlinder, *Psychopathy: A History of the Concepts* (Stockholm: Almquist and Wiksell, 1978).

17. Matti Touvinen, "Present Status of Forensic Psychiatry in Finland," *Acta Psychiatrica Scandinavica,* 55:181-82 (1977).

18. P. Anchersen and Kjele Noreik, "Present Status of Forensic Psychiatry in Norway," *Acta*

Scandinavian countries, however, has been the tendency to abolish punishment for persons in certain categories, such as young offenders and alcoholics. These persons are generally integrated into the regular social services system.

In Sweden, forensic psychiatric evaluation is widespread in the prison system and was developed in close relationship with the prison system, while its inclusion in civil law cases—divorce, child custody, testamentary capacity, and the like—has been less common. These activities have now been reorganized into regional units under the national Board of Health and Welfare. Among the problems faced by these regional units have been long waiting times for patients, heavy emphasis on assessment and diagnosis, and fewer resources for and less emphasis on a range of treatment services.[19] A more recent trend, however, is in the direction of limiting diagnostic assessments at the pretrial stage and utilizing them only when indicated, rather than more routinely, for dispositional decisions. Thus, treatment, rehabilitation, and various aftercare programs could then become integral parts of modern forensic mental health services.[20]

Dangerousness assessments

The main issues in which dangerousness assessments are typically involved are compulsory hospitalization and psychiatric reports on offenders prepared for the courts. The findings from a study coordinated by the World Health Organization showed that an "offence-oriented" response to dangerousness—in which the purview over certain types of crime is seen as being at the boundary between the mental health system and the penal system—predominated in the two industrialized European countries that were involved in the study, Denmark and Switzerland. In two-thirds of the sample violence was a feature of the criminal offense.[21] These findings are supported by data from Karsudden, Sweden's largest maximum-security hospital. This facility has been designed for the treatment of behavioral or personality disorders; it is widely used for young male offenders and for transfers from other psychiatric hospitals, jails, and prisons.

As was shown in earlier studies by Steadman in New York State,[22] in the majority of cases from Karsudden the dangerousness standard was applied to persons who had engaged in serious acts of violence. It was particularly interesting that the data did not show that psychiatric diagnoses and substance abuse problems could differentiate between the "dangerous" group and the "non-dangerous" comparison group.[23] These findings support the view that

---

Psychiatrica Scandinavica, 55:187-93 (1977); Thordur Möller and Gisli Thorsteinsson, "Present Status of Forensic Psychiatry in Iceland," ibid., 55:183-86 (1977).

19. Anita Meyerson and K. E. Törnquist, "Present Status of Forensic Psychiatry in Sweden," *Acta Psychiatrica Scandinavica,* 55:194-98 (1977).

20. Leif Öjesjö, "Developing Forensic Psychiatric Services for the 1980's: The Linköping Experiment," *International Journal of Law and Psychiatry,* 4:213-18 (1981).

21. Timothy Harding and Hans Adserballe, "Assessments of Dangerousness: Observations in Six Countries. A Summary of Results from a W.H.O. Coordinated Study," *International Journal of Law and Psychiatry,* 6:391-98 (1983).

22. Henry J. Steadman, "Some Evidence on the Inadequacy of the Concept and Determination of Dangerousness in Law and Psychiatry," *Journal of Psychiatry and Law,* 1:409-26 (1974).

23. Bo Ertmann and Leif Öjesjö, "Dangerousness at Karsudden," *International Journal of Law and Psychiatry,* 6:125-29 (1983).

security hospitals function to remove and retain certain types of deviant persons who not only have engaged in violent offenses but who are also considered to be mentally disturbed. In view of the heavy emphasis on the secure confinement of such persons, security mental hospitals more closely resemble penal rather than psychiatric institutions.

FORENSIC PSYCHIATRY UNDER ATTACK

The Scandinavian theory and practice of forensic psychiatry have received considerable discussion during the past decade or more in academic and professional circles as well as in the mass media. For example, critical attacks on the psychiatric reports to the courts and on the Herstedvester Detention Center for Criminal Psychopaths, in Denmark, and the Reitgjerdet Special Hospital, in Norway, have received much publicity. Moreover, criminologists have strongly criticized the treatment ideology,[24] and they have argued that the role of the forensic psychiatrist tends to conflict with the basic and traditional role of the physician.[25]

In Denmark attacks on forensic psychiatry have been particularly heavy, and there has been a definite decrease in the involvement of forensic psychiatrists in the aforementioned evaluation activities for criminal courts. The special psychiatrically administered detention centers for criminal psychopaths, so famous in past decades, were reorganized some years ago and special psychiatric sanctions—that is, indeterminate periods of confinement—were abolished. Indeterminate periods of confinement were also abolished in youth prisons and labor camps. The evaluation tasks of forensic psychiatry continue within the Danish Ministry of Justice, but to a more limited extent. And, as has been the case for almost ten years at Maryland's Patuxent Institution, which was originally modeled after the Herstedvester facility, mental health evaluation and treatment are now offered to incarcerated prisoners and probationers on a purely voluntary basis and for the determinate periods of their criminal sentences. As George Stürup described it, Herstedvester became a more general psychiatric unit for treatment of all types of "difficult offenders," short-term as well as long-term prisoners. Thus, even persons awaiting trial may be found at this facility together with some of the most "dangerous" and mentally disturbed offenders who are serving long prison sentences.[26]

Thus, although realizing that times have changed and past ideologies and trends are no longer very acceptable, most experts seem to agree that there is still a need and an appropriate role for forensic psychiatry in the Scandinavian countries. For example, psychiatric evaluation and treatment is necessary and appropriate for offenders who are severely mentally ill or retarded.

RESEARCH

Though not a major focus of this article, some relevant recent research

---

24. I. Anttila, "Conservative and Radical Criminal Policy in the Nordic Countries," *Scandinavian Studies in Criminology*, 3:9-21 (1971).

25. Nils Christie, "Law and Medicine: The Case against Role Blurring," *Law and Society Review*, 5:357-65 (1971).

26. George K. Stürup, "Changing Patterns of Treatment in Herstedvester: Forensic Psychiatric Considerations in Retrospect and Prospect," *Bulletin of the American Academy of Psychiatry and the Law*, 6:176-94 (1978).

will be mentioned. Danish and Swedish twin, adoption, and other genetic studies have received international attention.[27] Several biologically oriented studies relevant to the fields of criminology and forensic mental health have been published from the Karolinska Institute in Stockholm.[28] Also available in English are a number of psychologically oriented studies.[29] Some descriptive studies have dealt with the handling and treatment of mentally disordered offenders.[30]

Contemporary emphasis on brief hospitalization and community-centered treatment serves to emphasize the need for studies that could clarify the links between socially disruptive behavior and the follow-up status of expatients. Indeed, it is only through longitudinal studies that we will be able to differentiate between individuals who appear to be best dealt with by the criminal justice system and those who are determined to be in need of care and treatment and thus are better handled in the mental health system.

Due to the different ideological traditions in different countries and to the frequent methodological weaknesses in many of the studies, it has been difficult to compare findings across study populations. Nevertheless, in a prospective study of a cohort of psychiatric remand patients, George Smidelik and I have been able to confirm many findings reported in the research literature in other countries.[31] We found, for example, that fully two-thirds of the former psychiatric remand patients were rearrested during the three-year follow-up period. Persons whose life histories indicated a pattern of repetitive trouble were most likely to fail to remain deinstitutionalized. Approximately one-third

27. See, for example, Fino Schulsinger, "Psychopathy: Heredity and Environment," in *Genetics, Environment and Psychopathology*, ed. S. A. Mednick et al. (Amsterdam: North Holland, 1974); Sarnoff A. Mednick and K. O Christiansen, *Biosocial Bases of Criminal Behavior* (New York: Gardner Press, 1977); Mikael Bohman, "Some Genetic Aspects of Alcoholism and Criminality," *Archives of General Psychiatry*, 35:269-75 (1978); Sören Sigvardsson, "Alcohol Abuse and Criminality: A Cross-Fostering Study of Gene-Environment Interaction" (Umeå University Medical Dissertations, n.s. 82, Umeå University, 1982); Alice Theilgaard, "Aggression and the XYY Personality," *International Journal of Law and Psychiatry*, 6:413-21 (1983).

28. See, for example, R. D. Hare and D. Schalling, eds., *Psychopathic Behavior* (Chichester: John Wiley, 1978); Lars Lidberg et al., "Homicide, Suicide, and CSF 5-HIAA," *Acta Psychiatrica Scandinavica*, 71:230-36 (1985).

29. See, for example, Hans Olof Akesson, "Historic and Contemporary Views on Incest in Sweden," *Nordisk psykiatrisk tidskrift*, 33:176-81 (1979); Bert Kutchinsky, "The Effect of Easy Availability of Pornography on the Incidence of Sex Crimes: The Danish Experience," *Journal of Social Issues*, 29:163-81 (1973); Matti Viukari, Ranan Rimon, and Seppo Söderholm, "Attitudes towards Criminals and Other Patients," *Acta Psychiatrica Scandinavica*, 59:24-30 (1979).

30. See, for example, Bengt Ekblom, *Acts of Violence by Patients in Mental Hospitals* (Uppsala: Svenska bokförlaget, 1970); Eva Johansson, *Background and Development of Youth Prison Inmates* (Stockholm: Almquist and Wiksell, 1974); idem, "Recidivistic Criminals and Their Families: Morbidity, Mortality and Abuse of Alcohol," *Scandinavian Journal of Social Medicine*, supp. 27 (1981); Kjeld Reiter, "Mortality and Causes of Death in Men Found to Be Mentally Abnormal by Forensic Psychiatrists," *Scandinavian Journal of Social Medicine*, 2:1-3 (1974); Matti Virkunen, "On Arson Committed by Schizophrenics," *Acta Psychiatrica Scandinavica*, 50: 152-60 (1974); idem, "Psychomotor Epilepsy and Violence," *American Journal of Psychiatry*, 140: 646-47 (1983); Matti Virkunen, Arto Nuutila, and Seppo Huusko, "Brain Injury and Criminality: A Retrospective Study," *Diseases of the Nervous System*, 38:907-8 (1977).

31. Leif Öjesjö and George Smidelik, "A Prospective Study of 123 Forensic Patients in Sweden" (manuscript, Rättspskiatriska Stationen, Linköping, 1985).

of these subjects had been able to improve their situation and had made satisfactory adjustments in the community. These persons attributed their success to reduced substance use and abuse, new relationships, Alcoholics Anonymous, and the treatment they had received. These findings suggest that treatment directed at mental disorders and at substance abuse can lead to reduced criminal recidivism and a more successful adjustment in the community. Recent follow-up studies in the United States of forensic patients who have been offered community care and treatment have shown similar findings.[32]

The Lundby study in Sweden has provided unique opportunities for the use of general population data for analyzing the occurrence of mental disorder, alcoholism, and criminality. It was found that the histories of 9 percent of the total number of male alcoholics included a registered violent crime.[33] In another Swedish epidemiological study, drug-related criminality was studied by following up criminal charges for stratified samples of unselected groups from the general population for a period of five to nine years. The most common drug-related crimes were against property, against the Narcotic Drug Penal Act, and against the Road Traffic Offense Act. It was estimated that 25-50 percent of the criminals in the unselected groups of young men were drug abusers.[34]

CONCLUDING REMARKS

Traditionally, forensic psychiatry in Scandinavia has been limited to evaluations for courts and to provision of treatment within penal and security mental institutions. It has been suggested that several other types of services should also be provided—for example, community work, aftercare, crisis intervention, and outpatient treatment. Any system that is concerned with issues at the interface of the legal and mental health fields needs mental health staff. The question that continues to be a subject of debate is, At what points in the process are the services of these professionals most needed and for what purposes?[35]

Ten years ago a World Health Organization working group conducted a critical appraisal of forensic psychiatry in what was perceived as a time of great social and legal change throughout Europe.[36] It had become clear that lawyers often expected psychiatrists to assist them in many ways by giving opinions about the mental functioning of the individual involved and by answering various questions. Criminologists,

32. Joseph D. Bloom, Jeffrey L. Rogers, and Spero M. Manson, "After Oregon's Insanity Defense: A Comparison of Conditional Release and Hospitalization," *International Journal of Law and Psychiatry*, 5: 391-402 (1982); Richard Rogers, Michael Harris, and Orest E. Wasyliw, "Observed and Self-Reported Psychopathology in NGRI Acquittees in Court-Mandated Outpatient Treatment," *International Journal of Offender Therapy and Comparative Criminology*, 27:143-49 (1983).

33. Leif Öjesjö, "Prevalence of Known and Hidden Alcoholism in the Revisited Lundby Population," *Social Psychiatry*, 15:81-90 (1980); idem, "Alcohol, Drugs and Forensic Psychiatry," *Psychiatric Clinics of North America*, 6:733-49 (1983).

34. G. Benson and M. B. Holmberg, "Drug-Related Criminality among Young People," *Acta Psychiatrica Scandinavica*, 70:487-502 (1984).

35. Borup B. Svendsen, "Is the Existence of a Forensic Psychiatry Justified?" *Acta Psychiatrica Scandinavica*, 55:161-64 (1977); Öjesjö, "Developing Forensic Psychiatric Services"; idem, "Forensic Psychiatry and Beyond" (Paper delivered at the Eleventh International Conference on Law and Psychiatry, Florence, Italy, 1985).

36. World Health Organization, *Forensic Psychiatry: Report of a Working Group* (Copenhagen: WHO Regional Office for Europe, 1977).

sociologists, and offenders' advocacy organizations had, on the other hand, been very critical of the forensic psychiatric contributions. Indeed, there was a widespread view that psychiatrists "were in a well-intentioned but misguided way helping to uphold the evil of incarceration" and were departing from their basic medical role and related ethical guidelines.[37] The participating forensic psychiatrists in the World Health Organization group, however, pointed out that even if physicians relabeled themselves, lawyers and persons facing criminal prosecution would still seek their consultation.

Recently, in 1984, a Swedish task force presented its view of the existing legislation on compulsory psychiatric care. The recommendations were designed to transform psychiatry by markedly reducing commitments and by reinforcing the legal rights of mental patients.[38] The task force urged that the current Compulsory Psychiatric Treatment Act be replaced by the proposed Emergency Compulsory Mental Care Act. The suggested new law provides for the compulsory care and treatment of mentally disturbed persons in acute or crisis situations and when the possibilities of providing treatment in noninstitutional and voluntary facilities have been exhausted. The opening sections of the proposed new act provide that care must be provided with the patient's consent.[39]

The task force also realized the difficulties faced by disruptive offender patients in trying to obtain adequate services in a community-oriented forensic mental health system; it concluded that some special arrangements would need to be made. The basic intention is that special sanctions—namely, compulsory treatment—should be applied very restrictively and less frequently than under the existing legislation. By introducing the concepts of determinate maximum and minimum periods of involuntary treatment, the task force also sought to balance care and punishment, the offenders' interests and social control considerations.

The reactions to the foregoing proposals of the Swedish task force have been fairly predictable—given the social roles and functions of the different parties involved. State agencies and the medical establishment are not at all pleased by this type of legislative activism and they have strongly opposed the proposed reforms. These groups are offended by the task force's negative views of psychiatry; moreover, they do not see that they may be part of the very problems they are called upon to solve. Delayed treatment and seemingly unnecessary bureaucratic procedures are some other problems that have received major criticism. The patients' rights movement, the workers' organizations, and possibly the now-governing Social Democratic party favor the proposed reforms. Finally, the important national and county council health services are concerned about the cost issues, and they want to wait to see if they will receive sufficient funds to do what has been proposed.[40]

37. Ibid.
38. Social Affairs Commission, *Psychiatry, Compulsion, and Legal Security;* Margit Kjerrström, "Psychiatry, Compulsion, and Legal Security: A Report from the Social Affairs Commission in Sweden," *International Journal of Law and Psychiatry* (in press).
39. Social Affairs Commission, *Psychiatry, Compulsion and Legal Security.*

40. Eva Johansson, "Psychiatry, Compulsion, and Legal Security: Critical Points of View," *International Journal of Law and Psychiatry* (in press); Leif Öjesjö, "Comments on Psychiatry, Compulsion, and Legal Security," ibid. (in press).

Book Department

	PAGE
INTERNATIONAL RELATIONS AND POLITICS	155
AFRICA, ASIA, AND LATIN AMERICA	163
EUROPE	171
UNITED STATES	174
SOCIOLOGY	180
ECONOMICS	185

INTERNATIONAL RELATIONS AND POLITICS

DOUGHERTY, JAMES E. *The Bishops and Nuclear Weapons: The Catholic Pastoral Letter on War and Peace.* Pp. 225. Hamden, CT: Shoe String Press, 1984. $22.50.

JOHNSON, JAMES TURNER. *Can Modern War Be Just?* Pp. 215. New Haven, CT: Yale University Press, 1984. $17.95.

In his memorable 1964 essay on the paradoxes of nuclear strategy, Hans Morgenthau observed that we strive naively for nuclear war with conventional consequences. Add our equally earnest efforts to apply conventional wisdom to unconventional weapons, and we have the grand dilemma that has given rise both to the Catholic bishops' letter on war and peace and to these two valuable books.

Of the two books, James E. Dougherty's casts the broader conceptual net. Indeed, it is mistitled, for it provides ample treatment of just-war doctrines up to and including the times of recent popes; an analysis of the worldviews of today's bishops; and some loving glances at what the French and German bishops have said. Moreover, it develops an interesting thesis: that the nuclear age has given us "a distinct analytical dimension," namely, deterrence; that the bishops had no body of well-defined thought on deterrence to inform them in their deliberations; and that they did precious little to develop such a corpus. While the European bishops were much more comfortable with the idea that holding awful weapons for the purpose of deterrence—all in the context of earnest efforts for peace—is justifiable, their American counterparts "oscillate between contradictory positions" and offer policy recommendations beyond the competence of shepherds.

In eloquent summary, Dougherty suggests that

were St. Augustine and St. Thomas here, they would probably say, "If nuclear deterrence is rational, then it is moral." That is essentially what Pope John Paul II declared.... We had better not start peeling deterrence away, layer by layer, as if it were an onion. One who does that begins with an onion and ends with nothing but tears (p. 201).

The peeling-away is exemplified in proposals for no first use, freeze, conversion to conventional weapons, and pacifism, and especially by those who love wars of national liberation but hate deterrence of the USSR. Throughout, the discussion is marked by the lucidity and scholarship that characterize Dougherty's previous works in international relations theory and nuclear deterrence.

James Turner Johnson asks whether we can still honor the principle of noncombatant immunity. While paying ample attention to subnuclear conflicts, and to the entire range of just-war concepts, his focus inevitably fixes on the implications of that principle for tactical and strategic nuclear doctrine. He affirms—along with the bishops and Dougherty—the moral unacceptability of aiming at cities qua cities and thinks through just what a strict counterforce policy might mean. For him, it boils down to a preference for conventional weapons and then for accurate, limited-yield warheads used as far from cities as possible—but not necessarily avoiding cities, as the war proceeds, if the enemy nests military targets there. This in turn leads him to support cruise missiles, neutron bombs, Star Wars—to keep the devastation away from the planet—and, best of all, a low-yield decapitation strategy.

The two books are eminently discussable, especially when challenged by those who—like Kattenberg, Jervis, and Bundy—ask the hard questions of counterforce doctrine. Can we really have a second-strike counterforce capability that does not smell to the Russians like a first-strike? Are the Russians so eager to swallow Western Europe—despite current indigestions—that they are deterred only by the prospect of coming in last, instead of next to last, in a nuclear war? Dare we forget that when the bishops, Dougherty, and Johnson ask for sufficiency in a counterforce mode they ask for many more weapons, deployed in a more destabilizing manner, than would be the case with a relative handful of invulnerable weapons aimed at cities? And if we ever do manage the significant reductions the bishops yearn for, will we not pass through a stage where old-fashioned, counter-city mutual assured destruction is all we have? And would that not be wonderful? Is, then, the conventional morality as suitable to nuclear weapons as the bishops and the countervailers would like to think?

A second set of pertinent questions is posed by the findings of Paul Bracken and Thomas Powers about who would end up deciding what to fire and what to target in "the fog of war." Readers of Johnson, especially, need to confront two questions that he does not consider. First, what are the consequences for stability—of both the arms-race and crisis varieties—of the particular weapons he espouses? Second, if we decapitate the enemy, who will decide when to stop fighting, and how will the orders be communicated and enforced?

Indeed, the paradoxes are many and mystifying. These two books should advance the conversation.

GORDON L. SHULL
College of Wooster
Ohio

FRANCK, THOMAS M. *Nation against Nation: What Happened to the U.N. Dream and What the U.S. Can Do about It.* New York: Oxford University Press, 1985. Pp. viii, 334. $19.95.

To judge by his latest book as well as his several earlier writings, New York University professor Thomas Franck is one of those United Nations scholars who want to keep the organization going no matter what. Sometimes this goal presents the curious picture of students of the world organization, like Franck, acting as stout defenders and rationalizers of U.N. behavior—or misbehavior—against some of our diplomats with U.N. experience on the firing line—the Kirkpatricks and the Moynihans—who could only be called lukewarm supporters of the United Nations as presently constituted—and politicized.

Yet Franck is not blind to U.N. failures, including the built-in variety. He finds Soviet membership and participation in the world body to be often characterized by propaganda gimmickry and mockery of the Charter. He deplores the clique-like condemnation of Israel in the form of "some Arab nations [that] never cease to project their partisan perspective under the U.N.

imprint." He also mounts predictable criticism of Waldheim for, among other things, finding politically motivated jobs for politically motivated job seekers within the Secretariat. Of de Cuellar—for some unspecified reason—Franck is more hopeful.

Nor does Franck spare the United States from his raking fire against behavior on the part of the higher-paying U.N. members that is not in the spirit of the United Nations. He alleges that, among other things, the United States is far too obsessed with totalitarianism. In the single brief mention of this dire threat of the twentieth and twenty-first centuries, he depicts the whole U.N.-resident controversy over totalitarianism, and its abuse of human rights, to be, he writes, "hypocrisy." The test of a U.N. Assembly resolution condemning totalitarianism was revised, under the pressure of the "U.S. and its friends," so that "it echoes the global aspiration for democracy." At this point, one wonders which friends and what global aspiration. Franck continues that the revision "represents little but hypocrisy, that, as duc de la Rochefoucauld has observed, is the homage that vice pays to virtue." And in a similar vein, Franck faults other U.S. initiatives and certain of its ambassadors, such as Jeane Kirkpatrick. He insists that she only alienated most members of the world body. We had heard something different, however: that she was highly respected, even by the majority clique of United States baiters.

In conclusion, Franck has defended the shell of the United Nations—its founding principles, toward which he shows nostalgia, frequently referring to Mrs. Franklin D. Roosevelt. But he finds the U.N. oyster to be contaminated. Despite this non sequitur, Franck can write that the "situation is not hopeless . . . if Washington. . . ."

For the liberally inclined defenders of the United Nations, it is always Washington that must do this or that. But Washington tried long ago to play both hard- and softball on the East River. The game did not play. Today it is a sport in name only, played by the most ungentlemanly rules imaginable; not even traditional debating procedures are followed any longer. The United Nations is little more than a staging area for East-bloc countries and for Third World posturing against the United States and most northern industrial nations. What peace keeping there is resembles a minor fringe benefit from a huge corporation. U.N. beneficence—in some of its agencies—is, indeed, commendable. But this work could be performed outside the U.N. structure as effectively, or more so, than it is presently performed.

The reader gets the impression that Franck rather enjoys the perpetual fray at Turtle Bay. Both the United States and the USSR occasionally get put in their place, he seems to suggest. Meanwhile, he is totally oblivious of the major confrontation brewing outside the walls of the world organization—in other words, where the action really is.

Annals readers will call this confrontation by differing names; some will rule out a democracy-versus-totalitarian confrontation altogether as propaganda from the American side, as Franck himself suggests. Others, however, might agree with the Shevchenkos and Solzhenitsyns that the Soviet Union threw down the gauntlet before capitalist democracies some time ago and has been stepping up its struggle against anti-Communism in recent years. This effort from Moscow has not only made the United Nations appear like the joker in the deck—whose value is determined largely by the Soviets and their friends or sympathizers—but has made expressions of hope for its success look like the scriptural form of hope that is unseen. In fact, it is nowhere in sight, literally or figuratively.

ALBERT L. WEEKS

New York University

FRASER, T. G. *Partition in Ireland, India and Palestine, Theory and Practice.* Pp. xiii, 225. New York: St. Martin's Press, 1984. $27.50.

The most significant observation of this book, which would otherwise be a chore to read, is literally its last sentence: "Partition provided one way out of the dilemmas [Ireland, India, and Palestine] faced; the underlying problems remained to reappear in different forms, perhaps confirming the view that there are no 'solutions' to human affairs but merely a series of imperfect expedients." That is fine. But to have to wade through a mass of innumerable opinions and commissions' recommendations and caveats dealing with what are essentially well-known stories—without adding anything new of substance—becomes a tedious effort. This is a classic case of not seeing the forest for the trees.

While T. G. Fraser, who teaches at the New University of Ulster, has obviously labored in the archives and has written a good account of what diplomats thought, his is a work of description rather than analysis. There is very little discussion of theory.

Can one learn anything from former British rule in Ireland, India, and Palestine? Fraser does not venture into a realm that one might anticipate from his title. For example, he could have explored the impossibility of ever determining the natural boundaries of any state. Geography is not necessarily destiny, as witness Haiti and the Dominican Republic, or Portugal and Spain. He could also have gone into the hypocrisy with which most countries are afflicted. When Muslims constituted a minority in India, they favored partition; when in a majority in Palestine, they opposed it. He could have noted that appeals to God-given territory founder on the rocks of not knowing to whom God talks. He could have noted that in national conflicts, disputants delve into history only so far as it justifies their interests. He could have shown that there were other cases of British imperial devolution, such as Ghana, Nigeria, and Kenya—all of which had internal conflicts—where the path of partition was not taken, contrary to the countries examined in this book. Each case is unique. It is true, as Fraser does point out, that religious conflict was common to Ireland, India, and Palestine, but in other parts of the world this has been overcome.

In theory, one cannot say that either self-determination—critics always call it balkanization—or a larger political agglomeration—which critics call imperialism or domination—is desirable or natural. Pushed to an extreme, one may have the caricature of atomization or a world tyranny. Whatever the outcome, some group is sure to be dissatisfied. This is an imperfect world that grew organically, not rationally. Continued friction is inevitable.

This book, while giving a basically fair presentation of all sides, may be useful to students of diplomacy, but it suffers from a lack of wider perspectives.

WALLACE SOKOLSKY
Bronx Community College
New York City

GURTOV, MELVIN and RAY MAGHROORI. *Roots of Failure: United States Policy in the Third World.* Pp. viii, 224. Westport, CT: Greenwood Press, 1984. $27.95.

Gurtov and Maghroori have written an interesting and stimulating work. Their main theme is that, in spite of fundamental changes in the world and in U.S. preponderance of power since 1945, U.S. foreign policy has maintained a consistent containment-type approach. Moreover, fear of change and concern with political stability in developing countries led U.S. officials "either to excuse authoritatively imposed order as a necessary expedient for development and/or to mistake it for political stability." Authoritarianism was accepted because it was seen as facilitating "economic modernization" and as having the potential of evolving into democracy. Nationalism and populism were almost always seen as "ultimately dangerous to American interests," while the precept that nationalism and revolution could coexist was rejected, opening the way for justifying U.S. intervention "to restore national independence" to a particular society. In this way, self-determination, ironically, came to be used "to *justify,* rather than limit or prevent, intervention" in the affairs of other states.

The foregoing views are developed in analyzing U.S. foreign policy in chapters on Iran, Nicaragua—by the late Stephen M. Gorman—and Vietnam. On the basis of the information presented, Gurtov and Maghroori conclude that global interdependence has discredited the national interest as an appropriate device. They then list the kinds of changes in international institutions and in U.S. foreign policy that would advance the cause of a new "global vision."

Gurtov and Maghroori earlier argued that realism casts its hold over practically every holder of high office in the national security state since the end of World War II. Pretending to be scientific and objective, it actually was "chauvinistic, elitist, competitive, amoral, violence accepting, fixated on maximizing power, and steeped in pessimism and distrust." We may or may not accept these views—the debate has ranged a long time. The more important point is who will be reading the present text and who will be influenced by it. Gurtov and Maghroori themselves do not provide us with much hope when, before presenting us with their "global-humanist alternative," they emphasize, "For alternative courses of action even to be put on the decision-makers' agenda and debated as 'live options' requires radical alterations of their ideology, values, and attitudes. It also requires major changes in the way foreign-policy bureaucrats perceive and act upon problems." It seems unlikely that the present volume will accomplish or even begin to accomplish this major task.

PAUL W. VAN DER VEUR
Ohio University
Athens

MacFARLANE, S. NEIL. *Superpower Rivalry and Third World Radicalism: The Idea of National Liberation.* Pp. vii, 238. Baltimore, MD: Johns Hopkins University Press, 1985. $24.50.

Among the factors that have shaped the direction and content of contemporary international relations has been that of national liberation movements. Until now, this phenomenon, finding its modern expression primarily in the Third World, has never been studied as a concept, although it has been an issue of theoretical concern, policy objectives, and frequent political commentary by scholars, political leaders, journalists, and others. In the volume under review, we have such a study by S. Neil MacFarlane, who teaches in the Department of Government and Foreign Affairs at the University of Virginia. He has done his work with scholarly distinction.

MacFarlane begins his study by addressing the question of whether, despite their variety of historical circumstances and ideological commitments, national revolutionary movements in the Third World enjoy a "widely shared idea of national liberation." Having maintained an affirmative answer to the question, he proceeds to identify and discuss the common attributes of that idea, the sources of those attributes, the latter's relationship to earlier forms of nationalism and the liberal concept of self-determination as well as the Marxist-Leninist view respecting the nature, emphasis, and goal of social change. Finally, MacFarlane looks at the implications that the spread of national liberation has had and will have for the internal and external policies of states that are products of such movements, for the East-West struggle, for the interests of the East and the West, for the Third World, and, perhaps most important, for the character of the international systems.

The work is timely. It appears at a juncture when Washington—after about four decades of national liberation movements, from China and Vietnam to Algeria, Southern Africa, and Nicaragua—has begun to experience utmost frustration in dealing with the Third World's search for social change; and when Moscow, after a like period of identification with those movements, finds itself confronted by Afghanistan, by strong nationalist sentiments in states like Egypt and Ghana, and by being "lumped with the capitalist north" as a source of oppression to the south. Both capitals should benefit from this study, especially from its focus on the indigenous sources of liberation movements.

There are a few weaknesses such as the book's failure to include Nicaragua or José Martí in its analysis, and there are a few typographical errors such as "relected" on page 162. Such are minor, however.

The study is outstandingly researched, its questions carefully framed, and its discussions characteristically in-depth and balanced. The scholarly community, from bright undergraduate students to specialists in international and global politics, should find it very helpful; so, too, should the informed public, especially journalists.

WINSTON LANGLEY
University of Massachusetts
Boston

MASHAW, JERRY L. *Due Process in the Administrative State.* Pp. xiv, 279. New Haven, CT: Yale University Press, 1985. $24.00.

Due process is one of the most revered principles of Anglo-American jurisprudence, and in a number of landmark cases the U.S. Supreme Court has construed the phrase to forbid any procedure that is shocking to the conscience or that makes impossible a fair and enlightened political system. Although the bulk of the vast literature on this subject concerns the criminal justice system, the book under review explores the extension of due process to the many noncriminal issues raised by the administrative state.

Going beyond his earlier *Bureaucratic Justice,* Mashaw, the William Nelson Cromwell Professor of Law at Yale, has written a work that is both stimulating and provocative, and that makes a major contribution to the ongoing dialogue about due process in public administration. Its purpose, Mashaw writes, is "to lay a firmer foundation for protecting individual rights through due process adjudication." After analyzing three conventional ways of approaching due process, Mashaw offers his own "dignitary theory"—an infelicitous term—as the approach most appropriate to the fundamental principles of American liberal-democratic constitutionalism.

The strengths of the book far outweigh its weaknesses. It is tightly organized, cogently argued, and full of pithy historical illustrations. Moreover, Mashaw has a writing style that is vastly superior to that of most of today's lawyers and professors. No less important, he is unfailingly fair and never drops an argument or thesis without thoroughly examining both its merits and deficiencies.

On the negative side, Mashaw has a tendency to cite an endless number of cases. His quotations are sometimes excessively long. Furthermore, his dignitary theory is not quite as new as he supposes, while the charts in chapter 4 will be more confusing than illuminating to many readers.

Due Process in the Administrative State is actually a plea for philosophizing as a technique for practical decision making. As such, it will put off the general reader but should interest lawyers, social scientists, and philosophers. All in all, this is a sober, solid book, part legal history, part constitutional model-building, and part critical analysis of what the thirty-ninth article of Magna Carta (1215) called the "law of the land." It is surely one of the best such works in many years. If only the price were more reasonable, it could be recommended unreservedly.

FRANCIS M. WILHOIT
Drake University
Des Moines
Iowa

RA'ANAN, URI and ROBERT L. PFALTZGRAFF, eds. *International Security Dimensions of Space*. Pp. 324. Hamden, CT: Shoe String Press, 1984. $32.50.

This book constitutes many of the amended papers presented during the Eleventh Annual Conference of the International Security Studies Program of the Fletcher School of Law and Diplomacy at Tufts University. The title of the book denotes the subject of the conference. As readers of this review know, the subject is currently topical and of pressing and utmost importance as this nation strives for a coherent national space policy. Many of the ideas expressed in the papers have already found their acceptance in developments since President Reagan made his 1983 Star Wars speech.

The 16 essays by experts from government, the armed services, and corporate, technological, and academic communities are organized into six parts that best describe what readers will encounter: "Space as a Military Environment"; "Space as a High Frontier for Strategic Defense"; "Technological and Operational Aspects of Superpower Space Systems"; "Organizational Dimensions of Space Programs, Unilateral and Multilateral"; "National Interests and the Legal Regime in Space"; and "Policy Implications." Appendixes include key events in the evolution of the U.S. military space program, during the period 1945-60, and evolution of the Soviet space program since Sputnik. For the most part, footnotes are at a minimum or entirely absent. The book would have been more useful if the editors had appended a short bibliography at the end of each part to direct interested parties to additional views on the areas involved. This book will be of limited use to the uninitiated.

DANIEL C. TURACK
Capital University
Columbus
Ohio

STEIN, JONATHAN B. *From H-Bomb to Star Wars: The Politics of Strategic Decision Making*. Pp. xiii, 118. Lexington, MA: D. C. Heath, 1984. $20.00.

KARSTEN, PETER, PETER HOWELL, and ART ALLEN. *Military Threats: A Systematic Historical Analysis of the Determinants of Success*. Pp. xiii, 166. Westport, CT: Greenwood Press, 1984. $29.95.

Jonathan Stein's thoughtful book compares the hydrogen bomb and Strategic Defense Initiative (SDI) decisions via two tidy case studies and a brief, cogent conclusion. Stein's thesis is that the arms race originates in domestic political interactions and is not predominantly determined by any technological imperative, but instead, in the cases at hand, actually proceeds in areas of extraordinary technical difficulty, as Professor Bethe would have it, bordering on fantasy. There is much to be learned from the exploration of this timely thesis in the H-bomb and SDI decision-making processes.

In Stein's treatment, and as generally argued by civilian analysts, doctrinal change lagged behind the creation of fusion weapons but has preceded SDI research. SDI reflects a larger policy debate in the United States over the meaning of deterrence and can be interpreted, as is suggested here, as a bid to reestablish unambiguous nuclear superiority of the United States and the North Atlantic Treaty Organization over the Soviet Union. However it is interpreted, the SDI decision may well be as consequential as that leading to the hydrogen bomb. SDI shows a desire to reassert the dominance of defense over offense, hence the appellation "Maginot Line in the sky." Setting SDI in a context of purportedly morally superior deterrence-by-defense arguments, when doctrine has emphasized nuclear war fighting, simply serves to direct attention away from the fact that even in most Western deterrence arguments the capabilities sought for SDI would be crisis destabilizing, not to mention what a worst-case Soviet analysis would make of them.

Facts intrude in the case for SDI; as Stein points out, unless leakproof, ballistic missile defense systems do not cause mutual assured destruction to be superceded, and as Stein kindly does not show, we have not yet even discovered a foolproof defense against that early ballistic missile, the bullet.

Defense policymaking is a chimerical field in which the Manhattan Project took place in Chicago and other locations, Szilard wrote the Einstein letter, and Truman's H-bomb decision seems unstuck in time. Stein is to be congratulated for his well-crafted study, which deals equitably with elusive hardware and doctrinal issues in a great range of diverse source materials. It is suitable for both undergraduates and graduate students if supplemented in the latter case with primary materials.

Karsten, Howell, and Allen present the results of an extremely ambitious data-making venture concerning determinants of successful military threats over more than 2000 years. They have been advised by eminent specialists, and their findings in part echo those of Blechman and Kaplan in *Force Without War,* Bruce Russett, J. David Singer, and Bruce Bueno de Mesquita. The extensive data gathering is potentially of great interest to quantitative international relations specialists and to quantitative historians; as such, it merits separate treatment.

The book's most important contribution may be the discovery that in its historical sample of major power threats, about half were purely compellent while only about one-fourth were purely deterrent. If the predominance of compellence over deterrence is a general phenomenon, it may explain some cases of apparent failure of so-called deterrence strategies. Karsten and his colleagues also find target nations more aware of potential war costs and risks than are the major powers making the threats. In these data there is no propensity for smaller, weaker states to yield to threats more often than larger states; states in deterrence or compellence relations rarely have substantial trade or investment ties; the climate of international opinion evidently influences outcome of threats; and there may exist acts that cannot be deterred or decision makers who cannot be compelled. When failure is defined as war outbreak rather than more generally as failure to achieve any of a variety of objectives, success of one threat is not correlated with success in a latter threat between the same countries. This definition of failure argues, as does *Force without War,* that countries can be rented but they cannot be bought. Shows of force may provoke undesired wars in this context.

Military Threats must be read as a descriptive study. It is a remarkably interesting one, liberally illustrated with examples and quotations. In this study, a stratified nonrandom sample of 83 pre- and post-nuclear cases has been obtained, in a Herculean effort, from the work of major historians, but the basis for selection of each case remains unclear. The authors' contention that their findings are more representative than are findings of studies drawn from fewer cases is not necessarily sustainable, as sample size does not address the question of method of sampling, and as the expectation that the postwar subset is an exhaustive sample seems contradicted in chapter 4. Operational definitions of crisis, threat, success, and failure are set out; however, operational definitions for most of the independent variables chosen are not presented. Information has been discarded in the collapsing of variables such as gross national product—presumably only for the later cases—and population into five-point scales; further, some variable categories— for example, tactical variables—appear to tap indicators of disparate concepts, such as negotiating space and battlefield war capabilities. It is unclear that the structure of the data conforms to the rigorous requirements of the factor analyses conducted.

For these reasons the greatest usefulness of *Military Threats* lies in the data collection, the thought-provoking discussion of parameters of deterrence relations in chapter 1, and the case-based observations in chapters 3 and 4.

THERESA C. SMITH
Mankato State University
Minnesota

AFRICA, ASIA, AND LATIN AMERICA

CAMP, RODERIC A. *The Making of a Government: Political Leaders in Modern Mexico.* Pp. x, 237. Tucson: University of Arizona Press, 1985. $23.50.

Roderic Camp has presented another in his series of very useful studies on twentieth-century Mexican leaders. Any student of Mexico who has sought information on individual Mexican leaders knows the difficulties in coming by such accurate data. The labor of scholars who make it available is therefore especially appreciated.

Previous volumes by Camp include *The Role of Economists in Policy Making: A Comparative Case Study of Mexico and the United States* (1977); *Mexico's Leaders: Their Education and Recruitment* (1980); and *Mexican Political Biographies, 1935-80* (1982). The first of these studies gives at least brief citation to the work of some two dozen Mexican economists and relates their roles to as many or more U.S. economic scholars and practitioners. The second study, *Mexico's Leaders,* analyzes the careers of most of the outstanding political leaders who were active from the 1930s through the 1970s. Data include details on education: where the person was educated, by whom taught, and so forth. Overwhelmingly the elite had the National University as their alma mater. The third study covers the nearly 1000 such persons active in Mexican political life. In *The Making of a Government,* Camp covers about 900 political leaders whose careers extended mainly from the 1930s through the 1970s.

After treating the problem of the socialization of Mexican public figures in general, Camp deals with reasons for their becoming interested in and choosing a career in politics; the role of parents, friends, and pertinent events in socialization; the influence of the school environment; the impact of books; and the significance of teachers as the leaders' socializers. Such teachers are usefully categorized as to their political philosophies.

In their careers, over half of the political leaders took the route of top-level cabinet positions, such as department directors and subdirectors. The second most common pattern was that of a mixed administrative-electoral career.

Throughout, the study shows the overwhelming influence of the national capital—first through education in the National University, compared with other universities, and second through the predominance of experience in the executive branch of the national government, compared with the state governments.

I could have questioned the exclusion of an occasional prominent name, but usually it was the name of an eminent person whose length of political experience was shorter than that of his other experience.

Again, Mexicanists will appreciate the latest of Camp's useful studies of biographical data.

WILLIAM P. TUCKER
Texas Tech University
Lubbock

CLUTTERBUCK, RICHARD. *Conflict and Violence in Singapore and Malaysia 1945-1983.* Pp. 412. Boulder, CO: Westview Press, 1985. $24.00.

In 1973 Clutterbuck, a retired major general in the British army and the author of books on terrorism and on the Communist insurgency in Peninsular Malaya, published *Riot and Revolution in Singapore and Malaya 1945-1963.* Given the relative paucity at the time of studies on the Malayan Communist guerrilla struggle, and on its corollary united front tactics in Singapore, that book was a valuable analysis. It remains so today, and though dated, still is useful for its insights into, for example, the development of the radical Chinese student movement in Singapore and the counterinsurgency tactics employed by the British in Malaya. The volume under review is an attempt to update that earlier study. It incorporates virtually without alteration most of the substance of the 1973 book—about 260 pages—including the footnotes, many of which are now outdated. To these now have been added 93 pages of text in a new section that deals with what Clutterbuck calls the "aftermath" and "prospects" of Malaysia and Singapore, that is, the more than two decades since the formation of Malyasia and the subsequent secession and independence of Singapore. These decades have been the critically formative years of nationhood for the two states and, moreover, there is by now a wealth of scholarly analytical literature about their problems. To see this trailblazing era of early nationhood designated here as seemingly but an "aftermath" of the Communist "Emergency" years probably will strike many Malaysians today as rather droll.

Violence, let alone conflict, not just in Peninsular Malaya—a focus of the 1973 study—but in all of a rapidly modernizing and changing Malaysia and Singapore as well is dealt with in this book in a highly compressed fashion. Such a treatment is so synoptic, superficial, and selective that one is puzzled that the task was undertaken at all. Nodal problems receive rather short shrift in these pages, and others are neglected altogether. The complex vagaries, splits, and policy turns of the Peninsular Malayan Communist insurgency, one of contemporary Malaysia's most enduring forms of violent conflict, merits all of four pages of cursory treatment; the Communist guerrilla resistance in Sarawak, five. Treatment of the latter subject, in fact, appears to end with 1974, though such standard sources as the *Yearbook of International Communist Affairs,* with which Clutterbuck does not seem to be familiar, could not only have brought more current detail but also insights into the etiology of the problem. One reads nothing of perhaps the most threatening source of political instability in recent years in Malaysia, the resurgence of Islamic fundamentalism as reflected, for example, in the so-called *dakwah* ("call to the faith") movement and in the militant Pertubuhan Angkatan Sabilullah (Organization of Holy Fighters).

Instead, Clutterbuck has preferred to concentrate on the 1969 race riots in Kuala Lumpur and on Malaysia's New Economic Policy and its prospects. In the 40 or so pages devoted to Singapore in the past two decades the emphasis falls on the development of social services and, quite rightly, also on the price of success—that is, the political cost to Singaporeans of their highly sanitized, orderly economic growth in a tightly controlled one-party state. As brief, Baedeker-like glimpses of Singapore's and Malaysia's recent history, there is little wrong with these pages, save their omissions and their lack of depth and analysis. There is a bibliography of documents and standard secondary sources, as well as an impressive list of those whom Clutterbuck interviewed. Looking over the latter in the context of the overall quality of the book, one wonders if Clutterbuck should not have pressed his respondents a little harder.

JUSTUS M. VAN DER KROEF
University of Bridgeport
Connecticut

EICKELMAN, CHRISTINE. *Women and Community in Oman.* Pp. xix, 251. New York: New York University Press, 1984. $32.50. Paperbound, $12.50.

PRIDHAM, B. R., ed. *Contemporary Yemen: Political and Historical Background.* Pp. xi, 276. New York: St. Martin's Press, 1984. $29.95.

The two books under review, both outrageously priced considering their length and lack of technical data, have another thing in common. Both deal with countries and societies that are little known in the Western world and particularly in the United States. Although Oman and the two Yemens occupy important strategic positions in terms of American policy and in the Middle East, and Oman is one of the region's major oil producers, there have been few scholarly studies, and fewer works of a general nature, dealing with them. For this reason alone, anyone willing to pay the price will find them a useful addition to the shelf.

Beyond this general usefulness there are important differences in the two books. Eickelman's book is essentially a memoir of her stay with her anthropologist husband and daughter in the small oasis-village of Hamra, in inner Oman. Field notes and interviews from her diary are interspersed within a lengthy but always interesting analysis of the attitudes, values, and behavior of the women of Hamra. The men of the oasis are all but invisible in the book; so is Professor Eickelman, except for a word of appreciation in the preface for his notes, encouragement, and the use of his word processor. This is determinedly and unabashedly a women's book.

Eickelman has organized her study around the simplest of social topics—the organization of households, social interchange, relationships among neighbors, visiting, children, and the growth process to adulthood. Her concluding chapter, "Hamra Past and Present," is an attempt to place the village in the larger context of Omani history. Placing a historical chapter at the end is an unusual order of presentation, but it works here. As she says, "It was only after experiencing the society and community of Hamra for some time that I could interpret the significance of historical change."

Along the way to understanding Eickelman provides us with much detail and interesting information about the Omanis, or at least about Omani women. In many respects they are quite different from their sisters in other Arab states, for example, in the use of the family cluster (*hayyan*), which is a crucial concept in understanding Omani social life and which governs visiting patterns, use of household space, male-female relations, and relationships with outsiders. Omanis also avoid open conflict and display a pervasive civility and tact in all relationships, nor will they point out the mistakes of others, even those of their own children. The emphasis on motherhood, as opposed to being the mother of children, is another unusual feature of Omani life. In sum, what emerges from Eickelman's portrait is a stratified but beautifully organized society, with few rough edges.

Contemporary Yemen is another matter. It a collection of 17 papers presented at a symposium on contemporary Yemen—both Yemens—at Exeter University in 1983. As with all such collections, the papers are uneven in quality. "Towards a Sociology of the Islamisation of Yemen," by Thomas Gochenour, is a useful analysis by environmental zones of the process by which Yemen became a Muslim society. Jon Mandaville provides a brief but interesting analysis of the Ottoman involvement in Yemen. Fred Halliday, Manfred Wenner, and John Duke Anthony, all of whom have previously written on Yemen, deal effectively with various aspects of politics in the two Yemens.

The main difficulty with the book is not that it is a collection of papers, but that it brings together Yemeni and non-Yemeni scholars of decidedly differing viewpoints, with no attempt to synthesize or reconcile on the editor's part. This is most notable in the papers by the participants from the Peoples' Democratic Republic of Yemen. "Education for Nation-building" by A. K. al-Noban, for example, seems largely a whitewash treatment of the Democratic Republic's Marxist-inspired educational system and an unreasonable downgrading of education under the British. S. Bukair's "The PDRY: Three Designs for Independence" suggests a far greater cohesion and early strength for the National Liberation Front than is warranted. Such distortions do not contribute to the avowed purpose of the book.

WILLIAM SPENCER

Gainesville
Florida

GOODMAN, DAVID S., ed. *Groups and Politics in the People's Republic of China.* Pp. v, 218. Armonk, NY: M. E. Sharpe, 1984. No price.

Although this book is a collection of work by 10 scholars, unlike similar publications of collected essays, each and every chapter does confine itself to the declared aim of the editor: "the application of a group perspective to the study of politics in the People's Republic of China." The majority of the essays were workshop papers while others were commissioned productions.

As observed by David Goodman, the architect of the project, studies of groups have been successfully undertaken on the Soviet political system and insofar as China shares with the Soviet Union many of the characteristics of a communist regime, identifiable groups should also exist in China and it is worthwhile to investigate them.

Peter Ferdinand succinctly reasserts the central theme of the book: although "no communist regime accepts that it contains interest groups or that it should accord legitimacy to such groups," "the interest group approach does offer the prospect of insights into the work of Chinese politics."

The chapter by Jürgen Domes on intra-elite group formation and conflict in the People's Republic of China (PRC) considers two phenomena: (1) the formation of intra-elite groups from 1958 to 1976, and (2) the development of elite-level factional conflict during the same period. It is, however, not clear whether the groups discussed by Domes share the same underlying meaning of the categories found to be useful by the editor. In any event, Domes's chapter does not lend itself to ready comprehension, save that Domes arrives at an unexplained, platitudinous one-sentence conclusion: "the political system of the PRC continues to display the characteristic features of a transitional crisis system."

As far as other groups are concerned, Barbara Krug looks at economists; Gerald Segal, the military; Gordon White, teachers; John Burns, peasants; Tony Saich, urban workers; and James Cotton, intellectuals. Each of these chapters is well written and together they provide important insights into the operation of the Chinese political system. However, whether they jointly or individually contribute to reinforce the editor's principal tenet is questionable.

Goodman conceptualizes that the provincial party first secretaries are more likely to be a categorical than an active political group in Chinese politics because they are primarily political brokers or middlemen between the central bureaucracy and their local constituencies. Goodman also launches into a critical attack on the analysis of the role of provincial leaders by another China scholar, Parris Chang.

Michael Waller writes the all-encompassing conclusion to the erstwhile divergent interests of the contributors and he furnishes the golden thread to all the foregoing chapters. To me, Waller's heavy borrowing from the Soviet historical experiences in his analysis of Chinese communist politics seems to gloss over other unique features of the Chinese landscape. That is a common shortcoming of Soviet specialists' works on Chinese politics.

Two complaints of the style of presentation are the absence of an index and the inconsistent usage of translated Chinese terms. Both the Wade-Giles and the *pinyin* pronunciation systems are used.

FRANKIE FOOK-LUN LEUNG
Chinese University of Hong Kong

ISAACS, HAROLD R. *Re-encounters in China: Notes of a Journey in a Time Capsule.* Pp. xii, 192. Armonk, NY: M. E. Sharpe, 1985. $19.95.

Of the many reports of revisits to China that I have read, this book, containing some sober facts and keen insights from a veteran China journalist and researcher, should be palatable to the general reader while not alienating the expert and the political scientist. Harold Isaacs first went to China in 1930, living in Shanghai and Peking for a few years. Shanghai was a good place to study the Chinese revolution in progress. The 1938 edition of his *Tragedy of the Chinese Revolution* has an introduction by Leon Trotsky. He was acquainted with many left-wing leaders in 1933 and 1934. In October 1980 the Chinese Writers Association invited him and his wife to revisit China for a fortnight.

The highlight of this book is Isaac's conversations with his friends, who include the late Soong Ching-ling, Sun Yat-sen's widow, who died in 1981; the late Mao Tun, who also died in 1981, at age 85; Ting Ling, China's best-known woman writer, whose younger husband is Chen Meng; the social scientist Chen Han-seng, at 85 a vivid survivor of the Communist movement, and Liu Tsun-chi, a noted publicist who, like numerous others, spent many years in Communist prisons. This coverage should interest novice students of modern Chinese literature and history.

Important data include the lowest figure—a half million—for deaths during China's Cultural Revolution, which lasted from 1966 to 1976. Other estimates run to the millions. There is comment also on China's overpopulation problem. The modest house in Peking used by Wilma and John Fairbank in the 1930s was occupied in 1980 by 30 people in seven families. The smaller house of the Isaacses was now crowded with five families totaling some 25 souls. The narrow streets and houses had changed little, but a huge number of people had been added. These casual data may be noted by critics of China's population control.

"Of the larger politics," Isaacs learned that the official judgment of Mao Tse-tung, announced on 27 June 1981, was that "Comrade Mao was a great Marxist and a great proletarian revolutionary, strategist, and theorist." He was 30 percent "wrong" and 70 percent "right."

After the daily account, there is one note after another as if to lengthen the book. Actually there are important observations and impressions from the trip in 1980, when some people were still confused and still supporting the ideas of the Cultural Revolution. There was much juvenile crime, robbery, and rape. People seemed to be happy and proud to say, "Though we have moved late, we are better off than in the Soviet Union or Eastern Europe, except for Yugoslavia."

On the whole the book is simply and clearly written and reasonably accurate. It offers delightful reading with attractive pictures especially of Soong Ching-Ling, Ting Ling, and Mao Tun taken in the early 1930s.

S. Y. TENG

Indiana University
Bloomington

OBOLER, REGINA SMITH. *Women, Power, and Economic Change: The Nandi of Kenya*. Pp. xiv, 348. Stanford, CA: Stanford University Press, 1985. $38.50.

This book, a revised version of a doctoral dissertation, is "a case study of the impact of colonialism, capitalism, and a cash economy on sex and gender roles among the Nandi, a semipastoral and patrilineal people of western Kenya." Specifically, Oboler concentrates on "the roles of women and men in production, and on women's and men's respective relations to property." In my view, Oboler has fulfilled satisfactorily her stated objective in eight well-argued and very detailed chapters.

It is appropriate at this juncture to discuss briefly Oboler's research techniques and the highlights of the book's contents before assessing the scholarly worth of this publication.

Oboler conducted field research for 18 months in Nandi District between April 1976 and December 1977. She devoted most of her time to one community, Kaptel Sublocation, in the district's north-central section. Kaptel has 2200 people. Oboler selected Kaptel as her research site because the population was "homogeneously Nandi" and is representative of the society as a whole. Oboler collaborated with her husband in field research, and had the help of two assistants, a man and a woman who were "both Nandi in their early twenties, English-speaking, and the Kenyan equivalent of high school graduates." To facilitate fieldwork, Oboler and her husband studied Kiswahili,

Kenya's national tongue. Besides participant observation and language learning, Oboler employed the following anthropological research techniques and data sources, among others: systematic interviews, questionnaires, census data, tape recordings, recording of daily activities of selected informants, and photography.

After introducing her rationale for the research project and the choice of research locale, Oboler presents the historical background of Nandi society in the initial chapter. She offers a general discription of gender roles and a detailed exposition of marriage in Nandi culture. The succeeding chapters consider the themes of colonialism, neocolonialism, and economic change, production and rights in family estate, and a theoretical discussion of sexual stratification and socioeconomic change. Oboler concludes that "Nandi women, though less powerful than men, are not powerless." "A good marriage in Nandi," according to Oboler, is "an active give and take between husband and wife," whereas in a bad marriage, a wife still has remedies by which she can have her complaints voiced openly before the whole community. Women, says Oboler, have "a high level of autonomy" in their daily existence in Nandi society because they possess "very definite rights in property." According to Oboler, the reason for this is that the "traditional system had built into it both security in the form of house property and institutions that allowed women significant access to and control of economic resources." Oboler concludes pessimistically that "in Nandi, as elsewhere, new socioeconomic conditions have undermined women's rights in and access to property in many ways. This process is tipping the sexual balance of power still further toward the side of the men."

Oboler's book is a substantive, significant, and pioneering contribution to the growing literature in women's studies in anthropology. It fills in a serious gap in the study of the role of women in African society in the face of the impact of colonialism, capitalism, and the cash economy. Oboler's detailed description of research techniques will undoubtedly be useful as a model for future researchers in the area. Her findings and conclusions will benefit government development agencies and planners and all those concerned with the advancement of human dignity everywhere. The find printing and the inclusion of many excellent photographs in the text enhance the value of this publication.

Oboler and Stanford University Press are to be congratulated for publishing this book of high quality and enduring value.

MARIO D. ZAMORA
College of William and Mary
Williamsburg
Virginia

SPIEGEL, STEVEN L. *The Other Arab-Israeli Conflict: Making America's Middle East Policy, from Truman to Reagan.* Pp. xvi, 522. Chicago: University of Chicago Press, 1985. $24.95.

This volume is another case history in the thesis Toynbee discussed in his 1923 opus, *The Western Question*—that the problems of Ottoman Empire successor states stem largely from decisions made for them by the West. Whether or not "Israel would have come into being if Roosevelt had lived," its existence has constrained as well as colored global concern for the Middle East. Much as Truman stands accused of responding to Jewish or Zionist pressure in recognizing the new state, contrary to the advice of his foreign policy experts, policies and acts of succeeding presidents are examined in corresponding context.

Spiegel portrays all of them as guided by global goals, with attention to the Middle East commensurate with the course of events there. However, persons asserting the excessive role of domestic pressure groups, especially in election years, can find among his massive data substantiation for their anxieties. Except for Carter, fear of Soviet aggression was a constant catalyst. Access to Middle East petroleum was not a main factor until 1970, although it had prompted Defense Secretary Forrestal to oppose the creation of Israel. Only the experts, such as those in the State Department—who to Spiegel are, pejoratively, bureaucrats—consistently argued that Arab states were as significant as Israel to American status and welfare in that region.

Despite Camp David euphoria, conditions in the Middle East continue to preclude optimism. For me, two of Spiegel's conclusions stand out: "American leaders have consistently assumed that they knew better than other involved statesmen how to provide for the peace and security" there; and "because of . . . concentration on the Arab-Israeli dispute, administrations consistently ignored the potential impediments to U.S. policy arising from other sources in the area." Finally, "battling for the hearts and minds of the American elite has been the true subject of the Arab-Israeli war for Washington."

For 429 pages of concise text there are 59 pages of notes, mostly references, including no fewer than some 60 identified principal interviewees. Predictably, the ratio of Arab sources is regrettably small. A 4-page chronology is helpful. The omission of a bibliography, other than in the notes, frustrates quick and easy reference.

For generalists in international affairs as well as for Middle East specialists, Spiegel has provided a volume valuable as history, and a reference work for years to come. Also, the University of Miami's Graduate School of International Affairs deserves thanks for sponsoring this volume and best wishes for the future of its Middle East Studies Monograph series.

DONALD E. WEBSTER

Claremont
California

WICKREMERATNE, L. ANANDA. *The Genesis of an Orientalist: Thomas William Rhys Davids in Sri Lanka.* Pp. xxvii, 246. Columbia, MO: South Asia Books, 1985. No price.

History and historiography in Sri Lanka are deeply political. The ethnic conflict that fractured society and polity in the early 1980s is fueled by interpretations of history going back thousands of years. Most members of the majority Sinhalese Buddhist community accept as a fact a set of myths that represent Sri Lanka as having been an essentially Sinhalese and Buddhist society and polity for at least 2000 years, and that assert fundamental, primordial differences of language, race, and culture between the Sinhalese Buddhist community and other communities, notably the Tamil, which is identified as Indian.

As ethnic conflict sharpened in the 1970s, a small band of progressive Sri Lankan historians attempted to combat the problem by investigating and revealing the process through which such myths became enshrined as history. An important part of the story lay in the way in which nineteenth-century European orientalists, notably Max Muller, developed and propagated a racial-cum-cultural interpretation of human society and history. Races or cultural groups became the basic units of historical analysis. And Muller's myth of Aryanness was successfully appropriated for—and later by—the Sinhalese, and juxtaposed to the putatively Dravidian—non-Aryan—Tamil culture.

This is however not the story that Wickremeratne tells. Belonging to the more conventional nationalist school of Sri Lankan historiography, he sets Rhys Davids within an analytical and normative framework that celebrates what has been called the rediscovery of Sinhalese and Buddhist history and culture in the nineteenth century, as a prelude to nationalism and independence. Rhys Davids, an associate of Max Muller, is presented as a man, almost forgotten by history, who made a major contribution both to the translation of Pali scripts and to the interpretation of the Buddhist religion to the West. It is not that Wickremeratne is uncritical of the man himself. Rhys Davids spent the first six years of his career in the Ceylon Civil Service, before being dismissed on charges that, if unfairly pressed, were in a formal sense justified. Returning to Britain, and never to visit the East again, he then built a long and remunerative career as an expert on Pali and Buddhism because he was astute enough to see the emerging market for interpretations of Eastern culture and religion—this despite Rhys Davids's acknowledged ignorance of Buddhism after his enforced return from Sri Lanka. If Wickremeratne had been more than allusively critical of the basis of Rhys Davids's expertise, he might perhaps have been led to question rather than celebrate the contributions of Rhys Davids to contemporary Sri Lankans' understanding of their own history.

MICK MOORE

University of Sussex
Brighton
England

WOLF, MARGERY. *Revolution Postponed: Women in Contemporary China.* Pp. viii, 285. Stanford, CA: Stanford University Press, 1985. $24.95.

A bleak woodcut of Qiu Jin, one of modern China's first female revolutionary martyrs, stares out from the cover of Margery Wolf's new book on women in the People's Republic of China, while the title proclaims her regretful conclusion: for Chinese women, revolution has so far been postponed.

Margery Wolf is the author of numerous highly regarded books and articles about women and family life in China, all characterized by considerable sensitivity to women and their point of view. An anthropologist, Wolf's previous work was based on her fieldwork in Taiwan over the last 25 years. *Revolution Postponed* is her first book about the Chinese mainland. It draws on data collected in 1980 and 1981 under circumstances of considerable constraint, which are described in frank and sometimes angry detail in Chapter 2. Her deep familiarity with Chinese family life in Taiwan surely helped Wolf use her time in China so effectively—six government-selected sites in about eight months—and gives her a comparative perspective quite rare among scholars who work on society in the People's Republic.

Wolf is not alone in her critical assessment of the failure of the Chinese Communist Party to achieve the liberation of women proclaimed in its revolutionary rhetoric. But even in the general context of recent scholarship emphasizing the strengths of tradition in revolutionary China, Wolf's picture of what she sees as the Party's unconsciously sexist willingness to "break the promises" made to women in favor of other goals is gloomier than most. Unwilling to accept that no more than hard realities dictated Party choices, Wolf coldly measures the Party's failures against its own rhetoric—and, perhaps unconsciously on her part, against the accomplishments of women's movements elsewhere in the world.

Although the first chapter of *Revolution Postponed* quickly surveys the intertwined women's and Communist movements of the first half of this century, the rest of the book concentrates on China since 1949. Wolf discusses marriage, domestic life, and the painful issues of family planning in detail, carefully comparing women in the work place and at home, in cities and countryside. Her ideas on rural-urban differences are particularly interesting.

Like all Margery Wolf's work, *Revolution Postponed* is engagingly written and easy to read, ideal for the nonspecialist. Scholarly debates are handled in a deft and unobtrusive manner, and the notes provide an introduction to the best of the literature on Chinese women. Some may find Wolf too hard on the Chinese authorities and others will be glad to see them held to account, but all should learn from her lively and sympathetic portrait of Chinese women today.

SUSAN NAQUIN
University of Pennsylvania
Philadelphia

WOLPERT, STANLEY. *Jinnah of Pakistan.* Pp. xii, 421. New York: Oxford University Press, 1984. $24.95.

Wolpert's work now replaces Bolitho's as the standard, one-volume biography of Mohammed Ali Jinnah, the founder of Pakistan. It is meticulously researched and voluminously footnoted, but as a one-man endeavor it cannot match the documentation of Shariful Mujahid's *Quaid-i-Azam Jinnah*, backed by the resources of the Quaid-i-Azam Academy in Karachi.

What one misses in Wolpert's study is any explicit theme or novel interpretation, let alone illustration of the theory of charismatic leadership or nation building. The narrative is straightforward and chronological, enlivened by a sometimes too colorful use of dramatic adjectives and mixed metaphors. It gives the reader a narrow searchlight for Indian history of the first half of the twentieth century in the manner of the old British histories that were based on papers in the India Office Library. Wolpert is as sympathetic to his subject as Jinnah's rather dry, reticent, and lawyerlike character permits. His portrayal of the sidetracking by Mahatma Gandhi in 1920 and later by Nehru of Jinnah's hopes of inheriting the leadership of a united Congress Party in a united, independent India has already been set forth by S. K. Majumdar in *Jinnah and Gandhi*. Those who wish to speculate about history in the conditional— what would have happened if—can have a field day here.

What a social scientist would like to read, instead of the minute accounts of embarcations by train and ship and the endless and familiar negotiations between Muslim League, Congress, and the British, is some analysis of the role of a minority—and heterodox minority subsect at that—politician in the early stages of a nationalist movement. Compare, for instance, the role of Christians in early Arab nationalism. How was it that the orthodox, Sunni bulk of Indian Muslims opted for the leadership of this highly modernized, not to say Anglicized, lawyer over much more indigenous alternatives like Maulanas Mohammed Ali and Abul Kalam Azad? Or, conversely, why did Nehru's Marxist preference for "mass contact" with the ordinary, poor Muslim fail against Jinnah between 1937 and 1947? Only a broader, comparative perspective that Wolpert, like most historians, eschews can attempt to answer these questions.

But this is not Wolpert's intent. We should be thankful for a full-dress biography, objective but inevitably from the Pakistani point of view, to help balance the enormous propaganda value to India of the recent film *Gandhi*.

THEODORE P. WRIGHT, Jr.
State University of New York
Albany

EUROPE

BANAC, IVO. *The National Question in Yugoslavia: Origins, History, Politics.* Pp. 452. Ithaca, NY: Cornell University Press, 1984. $35.00.

Comprehensively researched and elegantly written, Ivo Banac's impressive new study develops the argument that the national question in the interwar Kingdom of Yugoslavia was exacerbated by the adoption of a centralist and inegalitarian form of government. While there were groups among both Slovenes and Croats, as well as Serbs, who were eager for a unification of South Slav peoples in one unit, the dominant political force in Serbia—the Radical Party— viewed the new kingdom as the realization of age-old dreams of Greater Serbia rather than as a partnership of equal peoples in a historically new community. The Radicals therefore beat back efforts to establish Yugoslavia on a federal basis, imposed its Serbian dynasty on the ethnically diverse and historically heterogeneous peoples of the country, disenfranchised Yugoslav citizens of German, Hungarian, and Jewish extraction, and handled currency conversion in a manipulative manner with the result that those in the ex-Hapsburg lands lost 20 percent of their currency holdings outright. Banac also documents the tactics whereby Belgrade squeezed out non-Serb officers from the army and navy and imposed a Serb-staffed bureaucracy, operating according to Serbian traditions and procedures, on the non-Serb population. Taxation differed from region to region, as did electoral representation. In the elections of 1920, for example, the city of Belgrade received one deputy for every 2737 registered voters, while Zagreb received one deputy for every 4954 voters.

In Kosovo and Montenegro, incorporation into the Kingdom of Serbs, Croats, and Slovenes was resisted by force, and a virtual state of war prevailed in those regions for several years—in Montenegro's case, until the mid-1920s. Many of the residents of Kosovo and Macedonia—regions viewed by Belgrade, respectively, as Old Serbia and Southern Serbia—were driven out of the country, and Belgrade encouraged Serbs to colonize these regions. Authorities seized some 154,287 acres of land in Kosovo by November 1940, turning more than a third of it over to new settlers, most of whom were Serbs.

Banac's book is much more than merely an account of the methods by which the centralized system was imposed on the country. He also outlines, one by one, the diverse and often evolving ideologics of the major organizational forces from the Radicals to the Democrats, to the Frankists, the Croatian Peasant Party, the Montenegrin Greens, and so forth, tracing the sundry splits and recombinations that altered the political landscape over the years. While focused on the first two and a half years of the Yugoslav kingdom—from 1918 to 1921—Banac's account takes in the historical sources of mutual Serb-Croat perceptions and of the competing national ideologies, and it comments on the legacy of the policies adopted in those first two and a half years.

Balanced in its analysis, this volume is a masterpiece of historical writing and sure to become a standard reference work on its subject.

PEDRO RAMET
University of Washington
Seattle

BLOCH, SIDNEY and PETER REDDAWAY. *Soviet Psychiatric Abuse—The Shadow over World Psychiatry.* Pp. 288. Boulder, CO: Westview Press, 1985. $25.00.

This carefully organized, erudite account constitutes an exhaustive compendium of events related to world medical politics from the years 1977 to 1983. These two eminent authors successfully undertake to describe the deviate manner and process in which the Soviet government subverted professional objectivity to quell dissent.

The crux of the thesis is the definition of political abuse and mental illness. In chapter 1, we find this question is most complex when we are not guided by a blatant distortion due to a gross psychotic condition. Bloch and Reddaway tell us that the simple forthright question, What is mental illness? becomes more complex where the diagnostic process becomes closely intertwined with social factors. If and when individuals are not in concert with the culture or are not identified with a recognized subculture, they are often defined as mentally ill. This point was exploited to the fullest by the Soviets in their purposeful internment of those who disagreed with the party line. Well-authenticated cases are documented to a remarkable degree in this book; highlighted are the Soviet-bloc nations that supported all the Soviet Union's rationalizations for denying allegations of abuse named by the World Psychiatric Association.

Chapter 2 discusses the Honolulu Congress, held in 1977. At the congress the lines of opposition to the Russians' use of psychiatric hospitalization to silence political dissidents were clear, although the resolution defining them was passed by only a small majority. This chapter presents accounts of the unbelievable personal courage of some of the individual members of the congress's Working Commission. Their efforts prevented the escalation of unbridled abuse in case after case, with some individuals being allowed to emigrate even after they were on the brink of reinternment in a special political mental hospital.

Through the mechanism of the Honolulu Congress's Review Committee, a legal subcommittee, the Russians were constantly trying to sidetrack the effort to expose the abuse by bringing up procedural objections. Nonetheless, the committee proved its worth by its ability to focus the attention of the world professional family on the incontrovertible and shocking truths about the Soviet Union's psychiatric abuse.

The very best work in this excellent book is found in chapter 6, "Dialogue or Confrontations?" The movement to expel the Soviets from the prestigious World Psychiatric Association was filled with enough intrigue to hold the reader fascinated, and the text that covers it is more like a mystery novel than a documentation of real-life events. The preponderance of evidence emerges slowly, like an ominous fog of death, over free thinking and scholarship to the point of total suffocation that requires even the most reluctant to take a stand. The Soviets, of course, resigned from the World Psychiatric Association to defuse the criticism. Their attempts to habituate the world psychiatric community to their psychiatric practices were about as successful as the young maid who, at three months, acknowledged she was a little bit pregnant. Six years later the Soviets had definitely lost their medical masquerade and thousands of would-be victims prevailed. It is hoped that society in general was rescued from a collapse due to man's inhumanity to man.

One cannot speak too highly of the six excellent appendixes as well as the more than 15 pages of notes and references. The copious verification regarding Soviet abuse is almost overwhelming. This book is without a doubt an important work. It should be widely read and pondered as to whether there will ever be an end to human bondage.

K. G. SUMMERSETT

Newberry
Michigan

PUGH, PATRICIA. *Educate, Agitate, Organize: 100 Years of Fabian Socialism.* Pp. xiii, 330. London: Methuen, 1985. $33.00.

RADICE, LISANNE. *Beatrice and Sidney Webb: Fabian Socialists.* Pp. x, 342. New York: St. Martin's Press, 1984. $25.95.

These books commemorate the centennial of the Fabian Society. The Pugh volume traces the society's history from 1884 when a small band of Fabians, in spite of periods of apathy and their tendency to preach, were making themselves heard as "communicative learners." Their astonishing successes were accomplished through a variety of activities, including timely publications. The Fabian Research Bureau's decision in the late 1930s to focus on the future of British colonies was both prescient and timely and gave the British Labour Party a colonial policy. The society's contributions were summed up well by its general secretary in 1960: "The objective study of facts, however unpalatable; intellectual honesty in the face of prejudice and pressure; frank speaking when the timid and calculating prefer silence and equivocation."

An organization's chronological account of successes and failures rarely makes exciting reading and the Pugh book is no exception. Lisanne Radice in many ways has an easier and more satisfying task. She skillfully captures the extraordinary fusion of mind and intellect of the "Webb partnership"; Beatrice and Sidney Webb together worked, researched, wrote, and published an array of monumental works ranging from *The History of Trade Unionism* (1894) to *A Constitution for the Socialist Commonwealth of Great Britain* (1920). Meanwhile, Sidney Webb's service on the London City Council resulted in educational reforms and scholarship schemes for needy pupils. The Webbs's crowning educational success was the founding of the London School of Economics. In his 1923 presidential address to the Labour Party Conference, Sidney Webb, while introducing the now famous phrase "inevitability of gradualness," emphasized that socialism was rooted in political democracy and that "every step towards our goal" was dependent upon gaining "the assent and support of at least a numerical majority of the whole people."

Radice also mentions other characteristics of the Webbs such as their profound ethnocentrism. "Foreign travel brought out the worst in the partnership,"; the Irish were considered charming but detestable; the U.S. House of Representatives was "doomed to impotence varied by disorder"; Koreans were seen as "unsavoury mortals" and a "horrid little race"; and the Japanese tea ceremony was thought to be a "silly business" leading to nothing but "a sip of tea." Disillusionment led the Webbs in the early 1930s to visit the Soviet Union; their trips resulted in several publications, including *Soviet Communism: A New Civilisation?* Radice minces no words in describing it as "monumental in conception, in scope, and in error of judgment." Radice has written a challenging account of a remarkable couple who made a major contribution to modern Britain.

     PAUL W. VAN DER VEUR
Ohio University
Athens

UNITED STATES

BALLARD, ALLEN B. *One More Day's Journey: The Story of a Family and a People.* Pp. xv, 288. New York: McGraw-Hill, 1984. $17.95.

This book concerns a timely subject, the long and close relationship between black communities in urban Philadelphia and rural South Carolina. Its author is qualified in several ways to deal with the subject: his ancestors were members of black communities in both areas; he is a native Philadelphian; he is a social scientist—professor of political science and former dean of the City College of New York; and he has authored other works on black Americans. According to the book's own jacket and the promotional newsletter enclosed in the review copy, such noteworthy authors as Alex Haley, Ralph Ellison, and John A. Williams, as well as Nell Irvin Painter, an eminent historian, have recommended it as an important book on the making of black Philadelphia.

The migration of blacks from both rural and urban areas of the South to large urban centers in the East, Midwest, and West constitutes one of the most important demographic shifts in the history of the United States. It occurred over a fairly long period of time and was associated with major changes in American social, technological, and economic institutions related to the cost of labor: slavery, ethnic class structure, mass manufacture, mechanization of agriculture, and unions. Even a first-time study of the involvement of a few particular communities in the great migration might be expected to relate to a broader analytical perspective such as this. But Ballard is satisfied with tried-and-true references to prejudice, racism, black-white confrontation, self-help, and the usual list of black heroes and black protest organizations. In fact, as Ballard notes, this book certainly is not the first scholarly work on the relationship between black communities in Philadelphia and South Carolina, and for that reason especially, he should have attempted a more intellectually adventurous analysis.

Good description is worthy of scholars, too. In fact, it is more durable and useful in the long term than almost all theory. Ballard, as a trained social scientist, surely knows how valuable carefully documented description can be. In addition, he had easier-than-usual access to important sources of descriptive information: elderly relatives in both areas as sources of oral history, and the letters of ancestors and relatives that had been saved over the years. He refers to his access to these sources, but he rarely uses quotations from them to bolster his description of events, and there is no appendix in which his readers might enjoy selections of relevant oral history and correspondence. Much of the description in the book does not really focus on the particular communities; rather, it is a broad description of the black struggle in America, which is readily available from many secondary sources.

A good scholarly work can be an appropriate place to display art. I enjoyed Ballard's frequent use of verses from black poems, spirituals, and sermons to introduce his themes and to illustrate them. But he does not identify the spirituals clearly enough so that the interested reader can look into them for further meaning and enjoyment. Even his identification of poems and sermons is less than complete. This point is part of my last and greatest complaint.

There are no footnotes or endnotes in this book. The only scholarly notation, if that is what it is, consists of unnumbered lists of incompletely described source materials for each chapter. Because the sources are not numbered and there are no numerical superscripts in the text, it is difficult if not impossible to discover the sources of most statements in the book. It would not make much difference if the book were a novel, or even so well written as to draw the average reader into its subject matter. But neither is the case, and the book is not really accessible to the scholar or to the general reader.

Ballard seems to have been concerned mostly with blending a history of his own family into what is generally known about the history of black communities in Philadelphia and the history of the black movement in America. The book fails, however, because he was careless in documenting the research upon which it is based, not because his purpose was narcissistic.

RONALD PROVENCHER
Northern Illinois University
DeKalb

DANIEL, PETE. *Breaking the Land: The Transformation of Cotton, Tobacco, and Rice Cultures since 1880.* Pp. xvi, 368. Champaign: University of Illinois Press, 1985. $22.50.

Urbanites are well aware of the changes that have taken place in their immediate environment, but few are aware of the revolutions that have taken place in agriculture. Political revolutions are noisy; the revolutions in agriculture have taken place in near silence, but their effect on human beings have been dramatic. Rooted in changed modes of production, these changes have converted agriculture from an individual pursuit to a large-scale capital undertaking. Scientific agriculture and machinery greatly increased efficiency and production, but with them came a displacement of population, and the displaced have been asked to accept the cultural environment of the city that is as strange to them as to the uprooted immigrant. Herein lies the importance of this highly factual but quite as highly dramatic narrative.

Our image of the South is one of the numerous myths we hold. It is not a section where no changes have taken place. Pete Daniel develops in detail the changes that have taken place since the Civil War in the production of cotton, tobacco, and rice. These have been kaleidoscopic. Only three features of Southern farm life appear to have been ever present—drought, floods, and overproduction. There were also ingenuity, diligence, and hard labor along with poverty. For the field hands there were meager wages and a few simple pleasures such as fishing. Sharecroppers scraped to pay debts and, in spite of arduous labor, often lost their holdings. At an ever faster pace their place was taken over by machinery, and they were left to wander almost aimlessly to the nearest town or to the big cities of the North to find menial jobs.

The most rapid mechanization took place in the rice fields. Farmers from the wheat and corn fields of Iowa and Indiana brought with them scientific farming, improved management, and binders and thrashers. The changes in cotton culture came more slowly, culminating after World War II in the coming of the cotton picker. Thousands of hands were displaced. The nature of tobacco growing defied the introduction of machinery for a longer time, but there, too, it finally made its way.

In all three areas, change was slow but persistent. In turn, machinery, new kinds of fertilizer, and improved seeds led to great increases in production. New machinery demanded large capital investment and made it possible for a few hands to cultivate increasingly larger farms. The faster these changes took place the faster came the erosion of the traditional independence of the individual farmer and the small communities. Farmers became more and more buffeted by the conditions of the market, the necessity of loans, and other forces far beyond their control.

Government programs, conceived in response to desperate conditions, suffered from the presence of contradictory aims. Government intrusion aimed at improving methods of production and at the same time improving the condition of the workers in the fields. The more efficient agriculture became, the greater the overproduction that led to acreage allotments. The small farmer and the tenant farmer were the victims. There was callous uprooting of people who had known no other life for generations.

Daniel questions the assumed blessings of modernization. Perhaps the Amish farmer adhering to old methods and content with his simple plow and horse and buggy and who lives near the highly mechanized modern farm with its efficiency is to be envied.

Modernization has exacted a high price. The large capital required to buy machinery, the almost inevitable heavy indebtedness, the vagaries of markets, and the shifts in government policies do not make for equanimity.

PAUL A. VARG

Michigan State University
East Lansing

EDEL, MATTHEW, ELLIOTT D. SCLAR, and DANIEL LURIA. *Shaky Palaces: Homeownership and Social Mobility in Boston's Suburbanization.* Pp. xiv, 459. New York: Columbia University Press, 1984. $40.00. Paperbound, $18.00.

This is a book of disturbing paradoxes. Although touted as a work of history, none of the authors identifies himself as a practitioner of this specialized craft—and the finished product reflects this lack of professional credentials. Similarly, although eschewing what they consider the simplistic interpretations that have been offered in the past to explain suburbanization in favor of more sophisticated analysis, Edel and his colleagues are themselves guilty of employing such vague and emotionally laden terms as "capitalist class" and "working class." And last, despite—or perhaps because of— an impressive display of statistical information, the reader gets very little feel for what it was, or is, like to be a resident of the Boston metropolitan area.

The book is divided into two parts. The first, "Up the Down Escalator: The Worker as Howeowner," argues that the American dream of home ownership has served mainly to burden people of limited means—namely, all but the rich—with a depreciating asset. Over the long run and in the region as a whole, residential real estate proved to be a poor economic investment for the typical family; not only did other types of investment yield higher returns, but in many parts of the region the value of housing actually declined. Furthermore, home ownership hindered physical mobility and trapped many families in communities with poor educational facilities that destroyed aspirations.

In the second part, "Lawns for the Pawns? The Homeowner as Worker," Edel, Sclar, and Luria seek to uncover the historical roots of what they call the "suburban compromise." Rather than seeing a capitalist plot to turn working men into conservative property owners or a free-enterprise success story, the book views suburbanization as a product of many forces, the most important of which was the pressure exerted by the lower classes for a better living environment. It is refreshing to have such a multidimensional approach adopted, but the presentation is lifeless and there are too many gaps in the historical record that require leaps of faith by the reader.

Like home ownership, this book is not meant for everyone. General readers will find the content and style heavy going; specialists in urban studies will find it provocative and challenging, if not always convincing.

MARK I. GELFAND

Boston College
Chestnut Hill
Massachusetts

GLENNON, ROBERT JEROME. *The Iconoclast As Reformer: Jerome Frank's Impact on American Law.* Pp. 252. Ithaca, NY: Cornell University Press, 1985. $24.95.

This biography of Jerome Frank, who lived from 1889 to 1957, highlights his careers as a private attorney, lawyer in government agencies of the New Deal, and judge on the U.S. Court of Appeals, Second Circuit. Glennon's principal thesis is that Frank significantly influenced many of the decisions of the Vinson and Warren Supreme Courts, particularly in the areas of civil liberties and criminal procedure.

In 1930 Frank published *Law and the Modern Mind,* a sweeping critique of traditional jurisprudence. This work, an example of so-called legal realism, depicts law as essentially illogical, unpredictable, and largely dependent upon the individual jurist's prejudices, personality, and past experiences. Only by abandoning narrow legal guidelines and adopting interdisciplinary techniques can the jurist shape the law to meet modern society's needs. Glennon asserts that Frank spent the rest of his life attempting to reconcile legal realism with his own experiences as an attorney and appellate judge.

Frank's first opportunity to apply the tenets of legal realism to American society came in 1932, when he began to serve as general counsel to the Agricultural Adjustment Administration (AAA) in Washington, D.C. He negotiated marketing codes and agreements, drafted key legislation, lobbied Congress, and defended New Deal programs in political speeches. As Frank perceived AAA policy, any profits from a marketing agreement that exempted an industry from antitrust laws should be apportioned among farmers, consumers, and businessmen. Frank thus sought to carry the economic and social reforms of the New Deal further than the Roosevelt administration wished, and as a result, he was "purged" by AAA administrator Chester Davis.

Frank's New Deal service did not end with his expulsion from the AAA. With Roosevelt's blessing, he became special counsel to the Reconstruction Finance Corporation, where he concentrated on railroad reorganization plans. He also drafted portions of the National Recovery Act, helped create the Federal Surplus Relief Corporation and the Commodity Credit Corporation, and served as an adviser to Harry Hopkins, Henry Wallace, and Harold Ickes. Later, as chairman of the Security and Exchange Commission, Frank directed the reorganization of the New York Stock Exchange.

Glennon's last three chapters detail Frank's tenure, from 1941 to 1957, on the U.S. Court of Appeals, Second Circuit. These chapters, unfortunately, pose some puzzling problems. One obvious deficiency lies in Glennon's presentation of evidence to buttress his principal thesis. Glennon cites quantitative data indicating that the U.S. Supreme Court agreed with Frank in 70.6 percent of his cases—the highest degree of support for Second Circuit judges. Glennon then concedes, however, that such evidence "demonstrate[s] a correlation rather than a cause-and-effect relationship" and suggests that although Frank's opinions "prodded justices, judges, and lawyers alike, . . . no formal influence can be traced." He also states that his thesis "does not argue exclusivity; . . . other forces certainly contributed to Supreme Court action even when that action clearly followed the urgings of Frank." A Supreme Court justice's quoting of Frank by name, Glennon asserts, "may indicate no more than the justice's use of Frank's writing as a convenient tool for fashioning his own opinion." After plowing through this morass of scholarly hedging, one wonders if Frank exerted any influence at all on the Supreme Court. A brief, carefully focused analysis of various issues and events that possibly shaped the justices' thinking and an extensive condensation of these chapters would have strengthened Glennon's thesis.

Glennon further dilutes the validity of his thesis in his assessment of Frank's role in *U.S.* v. *Rosenberg*. After devoting three-fourths of chapter 5 to detailed discussions of many of Frank's opinions, Glennon disposes of the Rosenberg case in a mere three pages. He contends that Frank upheld the Rosenbergs' death sentences because he was a fervent anticommunist and as a Jew he feared a public backlash if he exhibited leniency toward the Jewish defendants. Glennon, unfortunately, does not document these explanations with citations from Frank's voluminous personal papers. He argues further that Frank "unequivocally accepted the rule of law and the canons and traditions of his chosen profession" and could not "ignore the clear mandate of the Supreme Court." This reasoning is not consistent with Frank's life-long devotion to legal realism and his legal crusades for basic personal liberties. Although he briefly acknowledges the irony of Frank's Rosenberg opinion, Glennon's criticism is muted: "Frank's position, though consistent and defensible, did not reflect great moral courage."

In conclusion, this book promises much more than it delivers. Glennon asks many rhetorical questions but fails to provide satisfactory answers. On the whole, this work reads more like a draft of a seminar paper than a polished publication. There is far too much repetition of factual and summary material. Jerome Frank apparently exerted extraordinary influence upon the American legal system; sadly, this book fails to capture the significance of his contributions.

DAVID E. ALSOBROOK
Carter Presidential Materials Project
Atlanta
Georgia

RUBIN, BARRY. *Secrets of State: The State Department and the Struggle over U.S. Foreign Policy*. Pp. ix, 334. New York: Oxford University Press, 1985. $25.00.

Barry Rubin set for himself the task "to give both the policy community 'insider' and the interested observer a picture of how the policy makers and policymaking system have actually functioned." His thesis is that American foreign policy often fails because some goals are undefined and no clear way of reaching other goals is ever formulated. Rubin blames Congress, presidents, and the State Department bureaucracy for failing to establish goals, to have clear lines of authority and accountability, or to persevere in following a coherent course of action over a long period of time.

Rubin's history of the State Department focuses on the growth of rival policymaking organizations, for example, the National Security Council, the Department of Defense, and the Central Intelligence Agency. He suggests that presidents tend to follow a pattern in dealing with these organizations.

As they enter office they hope to have the secretary of state as their principal consultant and advisor on foreign affairs. Few recent presidents have kept this resolve.

The State Department's Foreign Service was used to making long studies and writing analytical papers with different courses of action that could be followed, leaving the final decision up to the president. Franklin Roosevelt and presidents who followed him found this procedure cumbersome and too difficult to follow in situations they thought demanded immediate decisions and actions. They began to rely more and more on their White House staff and outside advisors.

In hopes of speeding along the foreign policy process, the National Security Council was established, in 1974, as a coordinating body; however, because the council's chairman had the ear of the president, the council soon became a policymaking body. The result was to make life difficult for the secretary of state and his subordinates. The Foreign Service officers were experts and knowledgeable of the area they served, but presidents have a tendency to listen to those closest to them and the ones who tell them what they want to hear. Henry Kissinger, for instance, was extremely sensitive to what President Nixon wanted to hear and colored events to meet the president's desires.

The secretary of state sometimes resigned in disgust when he was left out of the decision-making process. Rubin describes why Secretary Cyrus Vance left office; the cause was the failure of Zbigniew Brzezinski and President Carter to follow his advice that any attempt to rescue the hostages being held by the Iranian extremists was bound to fail.

Rubin argues that the fragmentation of policymaking and management responsibility has led to many confusions and failures of American foreign policy. One has to agree with Rubin that fragmentation of responsibility has hindered effective policymaking and implementation.

Another factor that makes life difficult for the secretary of state and his subordinates is the dispersion of functions that require agencies other than the State Department—the Central Intelligence Agency and the Departments of Defense, Agriculture, and Commerce, among others—to deal directly with foreign representatives. An example of this dispersion is found in the handling of intelligence information. The Central Intelligence Agency collects and analyzes intelligence information; the Defense Department has its own Defense Intelligence Agency; and the State Department has an Intelligence and Research Bureau. The complication of the business of international relations is not limited to intelligence. The Department of Agriculture helps Third World nations improve their food supply by furnishing technical information; the Commerce Department seeks business opportunities for American investors in foreign nations; and the list goes on.

Rubin hints at, but does not directly confront, the question, Have our presidents and secretaries of state been at all familiar with the acronym "PODSCORB"? This acronym is used as a memory device to recall the primary functions of management, which are planning, organizing, directing, staffing, coordinating, reporting, and budgeting. In each of these functions are embodied certain principles that Rubin claims are violated by our presidents and secretaries of state: unity of command, goal setting, and communications within the organization and external to the organization. Rubin points out many faults in the management of the State Department, but makes no reference to any principles of management. His critiques do not provide useful suggestions for improving managerial and bureaucratic structure of our foreign policy institutions.

This book will be of great interest to students of public administration and business management. It provides examples of how not to administer complex organizations, but it might have done more to be constructive.

ARTHUR GALLANT
Benjamin Franklin University
Washington, D.C.

SARKESIAN, SAM C. *America's Forgotten Wars: The Counterrevolutionary Past and Lessons for the Future.* Pp. xiv, 265. Westport, CT: Greenwood Press, 1984. $29.95.

Sam Sarkesian has had the good idea to write a book about "forgotten wars": the counterrevolutionary wars fought by a nation that won its independence in revolution. He has not written of all those wars, though he has developed case studies of the most instructive and important: the Second Seminole War, the Philippine-American War, the punitive expedition into Mexico, and the war in Vietnam, 1965 to 1970. Each war is examined in terms of three subjects: what Sarkesian calls the "state of the nation," America's military posture at the time, and the "nature of the conflict," which means, for example, looking at the Philippine war in the context of Manifest Destiny and looking at the expedition into Mexico as "bandit chasing." Despite some reservations on my part, I feel the results are quite valuable.

One strength of this book is that Sarkesian does not imagine that all elements in his comparisons are, or can be made to be, congruent. Nor does he fall into the trap of believing that he can quantify his conclusions, despite a good bit of statistical data about federal expenditures, gross national product, the size of military personnel, and so forth. For the most part he eschews jargon, writing a clear, unadorned prose. He documents his argument adequately, though almost entirely from secondary accounts. While he offers up some conclusions and "guidelines for American policy," he wisely does not press the guidelines very far. He is thoughtful, sympathetic to the problems of the nation and of its military, never forgetful of the rightful claims of the opponents of that military. He is not, I think, quite right in his description of the massacre and punitive expedition at Balangiga in 1901, but this is the fault of his source.

My reservation arises from the fact that Sarkesian limits the bibliography wholly to American titles. One of the problems Americans have faced in understanding counterrevolutionary movements is that we have viewed them in isolation—our own isolation—rather than in a comparative framework. This does not matter greatly when Sarkesian is dealing solely with a discrete series of events, a specific war, or a minor campaign, but it means that his theoretical framework, and the conclusions, have little resonance. It seems to me impossible to understand America's counterrevolutionary response in any theoretical way if one does not also know the literature on the British and French empires, empires that had a far more extensive experience with liberationist, counterrevolutionary, and revolutionary movements. The Seminole War does not differ markedly from the Maori Wars in New Zealand, the punitive expedition to Mexico hardly at all from Governor Jervois's punitive expedition up the Perak River in Malaya, or the Philippine-American War much from any number of British conflicts in southern Africa. Sarkesian's methodology, sound within its confines, nonetheless reflects the larger American problem: the apparent belief that America's forgotten wars are unique. Until we fully understand that he who only his own country knows, knows not his country, we will remain locked in the castle of our exceptionalist historiography.

ROBIN W. WINKS

Yale University
New Haven
Connecticut

SOCIOLOGY

GOULDNER, ALVIN W. *Against Fragmentation.* Pp. 333. New York: Oxford University Press, 1985. $27.95.

This book, substantially completed by Gouldner before his death in 1980, represents his final effort to explain both the power and appeal, and the limitations, of Marxist dialectic. A former work, *The Two*

Marxisms, had promised an additional three volumes in this field: on "post-Marxist" Marxists, the technical and sociohistorical origins of Marxism, and Marxism's rationality and limits. *Against Fragmentation* collapses these three treatments into one volume and culminates with a plea for social theory to develop a "holistic rationality" of the kind that eluded Marx.

The three sections of the book form a kind of dialectic of their own. The first, "Marxism and the Intellectuals," poses the question that haunts Marxism: if social being determines consciousness, how could Marx and Engels reject their bourgeois origins and identify with the working classes? The section concludes that Marxism does indeed live on two levels: a revolutionary materialism suspicious of theory and intellectuals, and a commitment to the power of ideas to change the world, which opens it up to intellectuals, of whom Marx was clearly one. A second section, "The Ecology of Marxism," traces outside influences, culminating in Marx's rivalry with Mikhail Bakunin, that forced Marx to define his positions in opposition to them.

The third section—"Against Fragmentation," hence the title of the book—attempts to explain the appeal of Marxism in light of the dichotomies revealed in the earlier part of the work. Gouldner's answer stresses Marx's creativity in binding together previous intellectual traditions, Marxism's underlying emotional appeal, and particularly Marx's use of Hegelian concepts of developing reality, in which the proletariat's role is legitimized by its struggle for the reunification of the whole of society.

This effort to show Marxist social theory as unifying disparate elements of reality slips into a discussion of social theory generally and a call to develop a sociology that would account for the whole of society. Talcott Parsons and Max Weber are briefly criticized for failure to develop such a sociology; like Marx, they were caught between the need to provide a comprehensive picture of totality and a desire to highlight part of reality that they felt had been neglected.

While the earlier chapters provide useful insights into the appeal of the Marxist synthesis, this final section remains unconvincing. Gouldner would surely have elaborated on it had he lived. As it stands, critics may suggest that Gouldner has proved the impossibility of such grand theory rather than its possibility. The book as a whole, however, is a worthy final work of a great scholar.

WALTER E. ASHLEY

Pace University
New York

POPENOE, DAVID. *Private Pleasure: Public Plight.* Pp. viii, 162. New Brunswick, NJ: Transaction Books, 1985. $19.95.

Private Pleasure: Public Plight, by David Popenoe, chairperson of the Department of Sociology at Rutgers University, is a social and cultural analysis of community life in the metropolitan areas of three nations: the United States, Sweden, and England. As a careful reading of this volume substantiates, Popenoe's comparative analysis has substantially benefited from his repeated visits to England and Sweden.

This volume is divided into three parts. Part 1 provides a historical overview of the urbanizing process in the United States, Sweden, and England, with particular emphasis appropriately given to England's evolution from a rural to a largely metropolitan society. The following section examines the usual physical form of the metropolitan communities in the three nations, utilizing as case examples Seattle, Stockholm, and Birmingham. As Popenoe underscores, Seattle's urban sprawl is largely due to America's love affair with the automobile and the American penchant to reside in single-family detached housing. Stockholm's urban development is relatively compact, reflecting the crucial role of governmental planning in Sweden. Birmingham's physical form represents a midrange instance between the usual sprawl of the American metropolis and the compact nature of Sweden's metropolitan areas.

Part 3 consists of a perceptive examination of the characteristic life-styles and social structures of the metropolitan areas of the three nations. Swedes prize the efficiency and orderly character of their metropolitan areas, which are, however, marked by a large degree of impersonality and a lack of social interaction. The lives of metropolitan Americans, while free from work, are largely centered on their homes and churches. English metropolitan life is characterized as comfortable—although somewhat materially deficient—open, and friendly.

The main thesis of this book is that metropolitan citizens in all three nations have become more private in orientation and less public spirited. In short, Popenoe argues that metropolitanization has hastened the decline of community. My sense, however, is that the kinds of problems confronting the metropolitan areas of the United States, Sweden, and England, like personal alienation and estrangement, are nationwide in scope and are due to the dynamics of rapid socioeconomic change.

This is a good work that deserves the attention of all serious scholars of metropolitan areas. It represents a truly bona fide comparative approach to our study of the phenomenon of metropolitanization.

NELSON WIKSTROM
Virginia Commonwealth University
Richmond

ROSEN, KENNETH T. *Affordable Housing.* Pp. xiii, 183. Cambridge, MA: Ballinger, 1984. No price.

This book seeks to examine the strengths and weaknesses of public policy toward private housing in the light of rising shelter demands, a chronic depression in market-offered supplies, and uncertain availability of credit. Despite a four-decade commitment by Congress to decent and affordable housing, results have been disappointing. In Kenneth T. Rosen's view there are a number of reasons for such an outcome, notably the federal government's embrace of high interest rates to curb inflation and later—under Reagan—its diminished contributions, both as lender and guarantor, to credit supplies in favor of free-market forces. The result has been chronic cyclical instability in the credit supply, a special bane of first-time home buyers. In addition, this instability has adversely affected housing starts. The thrust of Rosen's book is an attempt to explain what a reconstituted housing policy should consist of, given the demographic, supply, and credit requirements affecting housing in the 1980s.

Rosen sees housing demand in the present decade as arising primarily from population growth, the need to replace unsuitable and lost dwellings, and satisfying special demands attributable to mobility or affluence such as second homes and resort homes. The younger age groups in the population will, in Rosen's judgment, provide strong demand for new—mainly rental—housing into the 1990s. However, the traditional definition of a family and the kinds of housing needed will change in the wake of more single-person households. The lower cost of renting, together with rising net disposable income and high levels of unmarried females in the work force point to a bullish projection about household formations and hence housing demand. Rosen hedges on specific rates of new formations, however, because of the unknowable state of the economy's health at future points in time.

In addition to renters, many people will purchase housing. Traditional mortgage lending practices over the past 80 years point to a consistent rise in the proportion of residential housing costs met by borrowing—as much as 95 percent in 1980. It also reveals a significant shift away from traditional sources of lending—such as savings and loans, mutual savings banks, and commercial banks—to newer sources, many specially created for mortgage credit. Rosen estimates that, depending on interest rates, price levels, and the like, an imbalance of as much as 50 percent could evolve between credit availability—in short supply—and demand during the next decade. Rent and land-use controls, according to Rosen, affect housing supply limitedly but in the main adversely. The former dissuades landlords and builders from conserving or augmenting supplies of decent housing; the latter limits the supply of lower-priced housing and/or the density of populations.

The most incisive chapters in the book trace the effects of deregulating the economy and of inflation on traditional sources of housing financing. With inducements strong to invest elsewhere than in commercial banks and savings and loan associations, the national government has been obliged during the past decade to devise new policies to assure adequate funds for housing. The description of those policies—pass-through certificates, improved liquidity possibilities, superceded state usury limits, and counter-cyclical efforts—gives a guardedly positive verdict about their efficacy. Current problems confronting the primary actors are explored in some detail, with the conclusion that better coordination among them is inescapable in order to lessen chronic volatility in the market place. Continuing positive involvement by the national government in the funding of middle-class housing seems assured.

This book is an adequate, if on the whole a rather brief, treatment of the middle-class housing problem and government's role in relation to it in the 1980s. The level of written analysis is sometimes likely to bewilder a layperson lacking special knowledge in this field—indeed, the treatment of the array of government agencies and programs tied into the housing problem makes it difficult for the expert to sort out clearly who does what in relation to whom and why. While recognizing the merits of brevity in this book, it is unfortunate that this dimension is not covered with more detail or clarity. I also found it difficult to determine where Rosen sensed that the money to close the credit gap discussed in chapter 3 was going to come from. The credit gap and the reforms for restructuring credit discussed in later chapters are sometimes difficult to relate to each other, particularly in terms of how specific defects of the former are dealt with by specific features of the restructured system.

HARRY W. REYNOLDS, Jr.
University of Nebraska
Omaha

STARK, RODNEY and WILLIAM S. BAINBRIDGE. *The Future of Religion: Secularization, Revival and Cult Formation.* Pp. vi, 571. Berkeley: University of California Press, 1985. $29.50.

This ambitious book combines new and revised chapters to present a major sociological theory regarding religion.

It is an old book. Stark and Bainbridge prefer certain nineteenth-century sociological definitions of religion to newer overly broad definitions. They opt for a substantive definition many believe too Western to be serviceable in the study of Eastern religions. An older positivism prevails. Only quantifiable experience has high status in their empiricism. The debate with R. Wuthnow is typical: qualitative empirical evidence is merely "suggestive" while the quantitative variety is "conclusive"; their conclusion that the data confirm only one value system rather than the four Wuthnow claims tempts them to the dubious conclusion that the other three do not exist, that "a large number of these respondents must not have one." The book also seems old in assuming a view of human nature that is individualistic and needs-oriented. The interpretation of religious behavior as a market system derives naturally enough from these anthropological assumptions in the English-language world.

But it is a new book, too. Against much post-Enlightenment conventional wisdom—although not all functional theories—secularization is regarded as not only a threat to existing religion, but a major stimulus of fresh religious activity in sects—revival—

and cults—innovation. Many data show that American belief in the supernatural is strong despite secularization. Thus, there is no Bible belt in terms of belief in the supernatural, but there is an unchurched belt in the West. Cult activity concentrates where church membership is weak, and sect activity where the churches are salient but secularized. These facts should not surprise us. Religion offers compensators, such as eternal life, the most general of which require supernatural beliefs to be plausible. Secularizing ideologies and social forces cannot provide such compensators, as shown by the vigor of religion in militantly atheistic nations.

For me, the criticism of other scholars usually seemed more casual than convincing. Non-U.S., quantitative confirmation for their findings is confined to Western civilization. Vast areas of sociologically relevant religious experience are sacrificed for the sake of quantitative comparability. But this book is a landmark in one stream of sociology of religion. It brilliantly illumines many American developments and sets an agenda for much additional research.

HARRY E. YEIDE, Jr.

George Washington University
Washington, D.C.

TILLY, CHARLES. *Big Structures, Large Processes, Huge Comparisons.* Pp. xii, 176. New York: Russell Sage Foundation, 1984. $14.50.

The last decade has witnessed a remarkable resurgence in interest in historical sociology. Charles Tilly's *Big Structures, Large Processes, Huge Comparisons* will generate still more momentum for this resurgence because it perceptively reviews and critiques past and present research in the area and proposes an important theoretical and methodological agenda for future studies.

Books this short rarely contain so much insight. Tilly incisively blends theoretical and methodological analysis with descriptive and prescriptive discussion. The first half of the book is largely a theoretical indictment against what Tilly refers to as eight "pernicious postulates" that contemporary historical sociologists have inherited from their nineteenth-century predecessors. These false principles include beliefs that

— societies can be studied as autonomous and distinct entities;
— "big structures and large processes" can be understood by studying individuals in isolation from groups;
— all social change can be explained by formulating coherent, general theoretical models;
— large-scale social changes occur in a series of stages;
— social differentiation causes social change and advancement;
— social order emerges only where social integration exceeds differentiation;
— social disorder causes deviant behavior; and
— conflict precipitated by constituted authorities is legitimate, while conflict precipitated by individuals is illegitimate.

Tilly contends that these myths concerning "big structures and large processes" emerged because many nineteenth-century social scientists—for example, Comte, Spencer, and Tönnies—developed conjectural histories based on prevailing popular opinions without researching and comparing concrete historical events.

The second half of the book presents a detailed methodological classification of the ways in which historical sociologists can carry out "huge comparisons." Here, Tilly reviews four approaches for doing macrohistorical research: (1) individualizing comparisons, which compare specific historical instances of a phenomenon to grasp the peculiarities of each instance; (2) universalizing comparisons, which strive to establish the uniformities in a phenomenon by comparing various historical instances; (3) variation-finding comparisons, which try to uncover the variations in a phenomenon by examining the differences among historical instances; and (4) encompassing comparisons, which compare different historical instances occupying different locations within a system to determine the relationship of the instances to the system. Tilly reviews and critiques the research of four social scientists whose work exemplifies these research approaches—Reinhard Bendix, for individualizing comparisons; Theda Skocpol, for universalizing comparisons; Barrington Moore, for variation-finding comparisons; and Stein Rokkan, for encompassing comparisons.

There are admittedly several conspicuous shortcomings in this book. Problems emerge when comparing Tilly's appraisal of nineteenth-century historical sociology in the first half of the book with his prescriptions for doing historical research in the second half. For example, at one point Tilly criticizes Durkheim's theoretical conclusions only later to praise Durkheim's use of methods. I suspect Tilly would regret the implication that good historical methods can lead to bad findings. More frustrating are Tilly's occasionally superficial methodological classifications of Bendix, Skocpol, Moore, and Rokkan's highly sophisticated and variegated research. Nevertheless, Tilly's failures are minor when compared to his successes. At worst, the book is still ambitious and provocative; at best, it is shrewd, seminal, and even path-breaking. Historical sociologists will be discussing and debating this book for many years to come.

       RICHARD A. WRIGHT

McPherson College
Kansas

ECONOMICS

BEHREND, HILDE. *Problems of Labor and Inflation.* Pp. 250. Dover, NH: Croom Helm, 1984. $29.00.

WEITZMAN, MARTIN. *The Share Economy.* Pp. vi, 167. Cambridge, MA: Harvard University Press, 1984. $15.00.

Problems of Labor and Inflation is a collection of essays written by Hilde Behrend over a 25-year period. Despite Behrend's efforts, the book fails to reach a reasonable level of cohesiveness. The two problems addressed in the title are not examined jointly, and one of them—inflation—is not even discussed until three-fourths of the way through the book. As a result, the book fails to present an overall perspective of the labor-market difficulties facing modern industrial economics. Two other weaknesses undermine the usefulness of the book. First, Behrend claims that the book reflects an interdisciplinary approach to labor-market issues, combining economic and psychological perspectives. The analysis fails, however, to incorporate the advances made in economics in the past 20 years and consequently the book contains only a rudimentary presentation of the economic approach to labor markets. Second, the book provides no rigorous evidence to support the assertions made on the state of industrial relations. This lack substantially reduces the persuasiveness of the arguments presented. In spite of these limitations, the book does present a useful enumeration of the problems arising in the field of industrial relations and may be of interest to specialists in that field.

Unlike Behrend's book, which primarily poses problems without offering solutions, *The Share Economy* by Martin Weitzman purports to provide a solution to the major macroeconomic problems of our time. Weitzman presents an exhilarating vision of a profit-sharing economy in which problems like inflation and unemployment are forever banished by simply having firms pay workers variable wages. While the economic implications of profit sharing are not new, Weitzman's contribution is to focus on the macroeconomic implications of widespread profit sharing. Economists have long advocated that greater wage flexibility will reduce the impact of economic downturns on employment, and Weitzman has presented an effective method for accomplishing that goal. However, not stressed by Weitzman is the fact that in a share system workers' wages, like profits, will vary with the business cycle.

Essentially, in a share system workers reduce the risk of losing a job by increasing the risk of pay cuts. Workers' preferences toward these two risks may provide part of the answer as to why profit sharing is still not widespread. This omission is typical of the lack of balanced presentation that is the book's primary drawback. Like the patent medicine salesman, Weitzman offers to cure too many of the economy's ills with only one prescription, and the reader becomes suspicious. Nonetheless, the share system suggested by Weitzman deserves further consideration and this book provides an easy introduction for economist and layperson alike.

MICHAEL D. BRADLEY
George Washington University
Washington, D.C.

BORDO, MICHAEL D. and ANNA J. SCHWARTZ, eds. *A Retrospective on the Classical Gold Standard, 1821-1931.* Pp. xi, 681. Chicago: University of Chicago Press, 1984. $65.00.

The world of money is the most abstract form of social and economic affairs and hence the most difficult to understand. While money facilitates and measures exchanges, it is also a commodity and a store of wealth. As such, its value and its usefulness can fluctuate, seemingly unconnected to its relationship with the real commodity world. This imparts to money an almost mystical quality, a mystification further intensified by the difficulty in tracing its actual meaning.

It was once widely held that adherence to a gold standard would stabilize international monetary relations and through these the world economy. Each nation would peg its currency at a fixed gold value and guarantee convertibility into the metal upon demand. This provided for stable exchange rates between currencies and an adjustment mechanism for shifts in trading patterns. Imports, for instance, would cause an outflow of gold and a reduction in the domestic money supply. This deflationary process would alter the terms of trade, making imports dearer and exports more attractive. The resulting inflow of gold would then set off an inflationary process. The seesaw motion was seen as a means to regulate the international and domestic economies and to control governments from pursuing independent monetary policies, with inflationary policies leading to a gold drain and vice versa. But it presupposed that countries would respect the mechanism despite any inflationary or deflationary consequences.

The highly technical papers printed in this volume were originally presented at a conference organized by the National Bureau of Economic Research in 1982. While they are of interest primarily to specialists, the essays also provide a commentary on the controversy that still surrounds the gold standard.

There is considerable debate over whether an actual transfer of gold made the standard operational or whether capital flows and commodity and interest rate arbitrage were sufficient to integrate the international economy. This issue is further complicated because it is possible to see one or the other process dominant during different eras within the classical gold standard period and to notice differences depending on the country or countries selected for closer examination. The degree of strict adherence varied from case to case, and the lack of allegiance did not automatically foretell negative consequences. At times the standard is presented more as an institutional trapping than a functional device.

The extremely complex picture offered in the papers highlights a common problem within economics: the greater the collection of data and the more specific the analysis, the more difficult it becomes to say anything conclusive. No overall conclusions are drawn except to say that either the gold standard is not an absolute requirement of international relations, or that while attractive it may no longer be feasible.

The author of the summary paper, in fact, would wistfully "recommend repealing World

War I," as only then could the standard be reintroduced. This desire is perhaps based more on fond remembrances than a careful reading of the papers, but such also is the stuff of fable.

GARY ROTH
Hofstra University
Hempstead
New York

CLINE, WILLIAM R. *Exports of Manufactures from Developing Countries.* Pp. xv, 229. Washington, DC: Brookings Institution, 1984. $26.95. Paperbound, $9.95.

GRUNWALD, JOSEPH and KENNETH FLAMM. *The Global Factory: Foreign Assembly in International Trade.* Pp. xvi, 259. Washington, DC: Brookings Institution, 1984. $29.95. Paperbound, $10.95.

William Cline in his excellent book provides a wealth of new data for the 1970s on the growth of exports of manufactured goods from less developed countries to industrial ones. He includes materials on traditional and new products, penetration ratios, geographical diversification, substitution among developing-country suppliers, and substitution for Japanese exports. The significance of the United States as a market for the exports of developing nations is clear. Exports of manufactures are important to the economic development of the Third World.

Cline, applying quantitative methods, examines the outlook for rising protectionism in the 1980s. His model shows that high import penetration triggers protectionism. He concludes, however, that "no widespread surge in protection appears to await exports of manufactures by developing countries [in the 1980s]"—assuming that no protracted global recession occurs to provoke autarkic policies in industrial nations. Cline believes that developing countries should diversify their manufactured-goods exports and increase them at a limited rate so as not to stimulate protectionism in developed countries. Nontariff barriers are a far more crucial facet of protectionism than tariffs.

Joseph Grunwald and Kenneth Flamm's *Global Factory* also deals with the export of manufactured products from less developed countries and the concerns in industrial nations. It focuses on the complementary international intra-industry trade in manufactured goods: the transferring of labor-intensive assembly operations to developing countries, while component production remains in the industrial nation. Grunwald and Flamm argue that when such trade is carried out within a multinational enterprise—as much of it is, especially in the case of nontraditional manufactures—it probably serves to reduce political resistance to imports.

Items assembled abroad for U.S. firms have in recent years reached one-sixth of total U.S. imports of manufactures and about one-fourth of U.S. imports of manufactures from developing countries. Semiconductors figure importantly in this coproduction activity, as they have a high value-to-weight ratio—making for low transportation costs—and because technological change has been rapid—meaning costly automated equipment becomes quickly obsolete. Thus, manufacturers have located labor-intensive assembly in less developed countries. Foreign assembly—principally in Malaysia, the Philippines, Korea, and Singapore—now dominates this phase of the production of semiconductor devices for the U.S. market.

In contrast to countries in Asia, Mexican assembly for the American market emphasizes television receivers and other electrical supplies; Haiti's main assembly imports are apparel. Grunwald and Flamm's book analyzes the impact of coproduction on the American, Mexican, Haitian, and Colombian economies and includes policy recommendations to improve the positive impacts of such production sharing.

The book might have been strengthened had Grunwald and Flamm interviewed parent companies of the multinationals engaged in foreign assembly for import, discussing with them the pros and cons of intrafirm transactions versus subcontracting. Parents and affiliates of multinationals often have different perceptions. Such information might add to the recommendations on developing-country policies.

In the conclusion of Grunwald and Flamm's study there is a brief mention of robots. Assembly has always been labor-intensive, because machines have been inflexible. Robots can be programmed to do different tasks that involve high precision. They can handle short production runs. They may represent a viable domestic alternative to the international division of labor involved with new products. Grunwald and Flamm recognize, however, that whether assembly takes place in less developed countries, or whether automation occurs in America, there will in the future be a sharp decline in the number of manufacturing jobs for unskilled workers in the United States.

Grunwald and Flamm's volume is an outstanding book of interest to students of economic development, multinational enterprise, and U.S. economic and, particularly, trade policy. I recommend it with enthusiasm.

MIRA WILKINS
Florida International University
Miami

LUBIN, NANCY. *Labour and Nationality in Soviet Central Asia.* Pp. xix, 305. Princeton, NJ: Princeton University Press, 1985. $32.50.

Changes in ethnic balance in Soviet Central Asia favoring the indigenous population have provoked increased speculation about the area's potential restiveness.

Nancy Lubin examines one important implication of this demographic trend, namely, the potential for political tension in Uzbekistan due to problems in manpower utilization. She studies the population growth in Uzbekistan against the background of economic development, examining the size and composition of Uzbekistan's working-age population and its absorption into the economy. There are serious dislocations in certain sectors and geographic areas in terms of manpower supply that affect the Central Asians much more than the Europeans. The indigenous nationalities continue to be concentrated in the traditional rather than modern sectors and are thus only partly included in the processes of urbanization, industrialization, and modernization. The combination of growing economic strains and relatively low participation in the economy's modern sectors are cited as conditions that might favor political unrest along ethnic lines.

Looking to the political implications of the growing labor imbalances, Lubin scrutinizes the hiring policies and preferences for different types of work among the different nationality groups, and the incomes among different sectors and among the population working in social production and private economy. She then examines the role of culture and tradition, pointing to different standards and aspirations that determine behavior in the labor force among different nationalities.

While tension within the labor force is growing, a number of economic and cultural factors alleviate the political and economic pressures. The government has been able to contain and defuse the sources of tension. By providing preferential hiring for the indigenous nationalities, the government has lessened the sense of discrimination; by tolerating the existence of thriving private economies, it has managed to reduce the ethnic tension and disaffection in the economic sphere. Lubin concludes that, despite the growing pressures, the delicate balance will most likely be maintained in the near future by the two-sided economic and social policies of the government, as well as by the ambiguities in Central Asian society itself.

Lubin's book is meticulously researched and well documented by a wide range of sources, including unpublished materials and interviews. Lubin shows herself to be an acute observer and critical analyst capable of finding useful information in any type of source. She has produced a book that is an extremely valuable contribution to the study of the socioeconomic change in Soviet Central Asia.

MICHAEL K. LENKER
University of Pennsylvania
Philadelphia

SMITH, V. KERRY, ed. *Environmental Policy under Reagan's Executive Order: The Role of Benefit-Cost Analysis.* Pp. ix, 266. Chapel Hill: University of North Carolina Press, 1984. $25.00.

MILBRATH, LESTER W. *Environmentalists: Vanguard for a New Society.* Pp. xv, 180. Albany: State University of New York Press, 1984. $29.50. Paperbound, $9.95.

In February of 1981, President Reagan signed Executive Order (EO) 12291, directing that changes be made in the way the federal government analyzed the desirability of its own regulations. The order has been widely perceived as setting the stage for a fundamental reversal of Washington's regulatory role. V. K. Smith has edited a book the essays of which discuss the impact of EO 12291, in three contexts.

First, just what was new and revolutionary in the order? R.N.L. Andrews agrees with W. N. Grubb, D. Whittington, and M. Humphries that the principal novelty of the EO was that while the federal government had used benefit-cost analysis since 1934, the trend until 1981 was to widen the scope of benefits considered. Thus, for example, environmental quality was considered, in its way, on a par with national income as a regulatory benefit. EO 12291 reinstated the exclusive focus—where not prohibited by law—on national income. In this sense it is a return to the Water Control Act of 1934. The effect is thus implicitly to vest private rights in existing standards; the burden is on a proposed regulation that might disrupt business growth. Hence the asymmetry—with which the Supreme Court disagreed—in the treatment of regulation, where detailed defenses were required, and deregulation, assumed valuable in all cases.

Second, how have the agencies coped with the new order? As Grubb, Whittington, and Humphries note, less than 1 percent of regulations required full EO 12291 analyses. In their examination of a score of analyses conducted under the EO, they conclude that there has in some cases been an improvement in quality, but that there is a distressing tendency toward elementary mistakes and to ignore any benefits of the regulation while focusing sharply on costs borne by industry. A. Fisher describes in detail how the Environmental Protection Agency has responded to the new way of doing business, and in particular has broadened its conception of the costs of regulation. She also includes a comparison of the procedures of the Environmental Protection Agency and the Department of Transportation. A. Fraas, of the Office of Management and Budget, describes the role of this agency and stresses the difficulty of good analysis.

A number of essays present more sustained discussions of this last point. A. M. Freeman III considers two questions. First, when can the results of past analyses—of different geographical areas, for example—be transferred to current problems? Second, when, indeed, is it worthwhile to gather more information? C. F. Runge distinguishes two sorts of analytical uncertainty: "scientific uncertainty"—we do not know precisely what impacts even perfectly enforced regulations will have—and "regulatory uncertainty"—the impact of a regulation on the behavior of economic agents is hard to predict. Both these discussions illustrate that while it is easy to ask tendentious questions—as Fraas does in his appendix—still, some answers can be forthcoming if only the questions are taken seriously.

Finally, some attempt is made to evaluate the impact of EO 12291 and of the governmental use of benefit-cost analysis generally. R. W. Crandall argues that in environmental matters the relevant actors are so diverse, the data so imperfect, and the standards so unrelated to the real problems that the prospects for improvements are slight. As against this, P. R. Portney provides some "back-of-the-envelope" calculations of the costs and benefits of regulatory oversight; he concludes that it is plausible to regard it as potentially valuable. It is difficult to know where to come down.

V. K. Smith provides an introductory survey of the volume, and of benefit-cost analysis, generally. There is some indication that the authors did not trouble to read each other's contributions; had they done so, I feel the book would have been much improved. As it is, one comes away with a real sense of the difficult issues involved in benefit-cost analysis of environmental concerns, but without a clear feeling—which may perhaps be impossible in any case—for the overall impact of EO 12291.

If President Reagan received a popular mandate for change, and if EO 12291 is an expression of that mandate, then the future of environmentalism appears bleak. L. W. Milbrath's short book—about half of which is devoted to appendixes—is designed to do two things: first, in the manner of the prophets of old, to convince us that something is fundamentally wrong with our worldview; and second, to point out the existence and character of an emerging, and better, substitute "social paradigm."

In achieving those goals, the book is only partly successful. Milbrath is too much the scholar to raise the passion necessary for prophecy, and his characterization of the "dominant social paradigm" and its inability to deal with modern problems is not wholly convincing. The fact that nuclear war is absent from the Bible, for example, does not mean that a biblically based ethic is powerless to guide our reflections in this matter.

Does an alternative exist? Milbrath discusses at length the result of surveys conducted in 1980 and 1982 in three nations— the United States, West Germany, and the United Kingdom, though whether the latter included more than England is not clear from the text. The surveys focused on attitudes toward the present economic structure, environmental concerns, and political action. Milbrath finds that a surprisingly large proportion of the public—19 percent in the United States, 29 percent in Germany, and 24 percent in England—has beliefs that differ sharply from the "dominant paradigm" and fall into what he calls the "vanguard": roughly, pro-environment; having non-material values, a nonexploitative view of resources and species, and a preference for avoiding risk; unwilling to rely on a price system to allocate resources; and strongly advocating social change. Beyond this, it is impossible to assess the efficacy of this "new paradigm," and, as Milbrath remarks, "only time will tell whether [the environmentalists] will be listened to as they try to lead society in a new direction."

PHILIP A. VITON
Ohio State University
Columbus

OTHER BOOKS

AARON, HENRY J. and GARY BURTLESS, eds. *Retirement and Economic Behavior*. Pp. xv, 352. Washington, DC: Brookings Institution, 1984. $31.95. Paperbound, $11.95.

ABBOT, PHILIP and MICHAEL B. LEVY, eds. *The Liberal Future in America: Essays in Renewal*. Pp. vi, 207. Westport, CT: Greenwood Press, 1985. $29.95.

ADAMS, JOHN. *The Contemporary International Economy*. Pp. xi, 548. New York: St. Martin's Press, 1985. Paperbound, no price.

ALBERT, GEOFFREY P. *The American System of Criminal Justice*. Pp. 149. Beverly Hills, CA: Sage, 1984. Paperbound, no price.

ALTHEIDE, DAVID L. *Media Power*. Pp. 288. Beverly Hills, CA: Sage, 1985. $28.00. Paperbound, $14.00.

AMBLER, JOHN S., ed. *The French Socialist Experiment*. Pp. x, 224. Philadelphia: ISHI, 1985. $27.50. Paperbound, $12.95.

ARESTIS, PHILIP and THANOS SKOURAS. *Post-Keynesian Economic Theory*. Pp. xii, 235. Armonk, NY: M. E. Sharpe, 1985. $30.00.

BADASH, LAWRENCE. *Kapitza, Rutherford, and the Kremlin*. Pp. xi, 129. New Haven, CT: Yale University Press, 1985. No price.

BAHL, ROY. *Financing State and Local Government in the 1980s*. Pp. xiii, 258. New York: Oxford University Press, 1984. $24.95. Paperbound, $11.95.

BAXTER, CRAIG, ed. *From Martial Law to Martial Law*. Pp. xiv, 455. Boulder, CO: Westview Press, 1985. $35.00.

BEISNER, ROBERT L. *Twelve against Empire: The Anti-Imperialists 1898-1900*. Pp. xxviii, 310. Chicago: University of Chicago Press, 1985. Paperbound, $9.95.

BERNSTEIN, PAULA. *Family Ties, Corporate Bonds*. Pp. x, 176. New York: Doubleday, 1985. $14.95.

BESAG, FRANK P. and PETER L. BESAG. *Statistics for the Helping Professions*. Pp. 375. Beverly Hills, CA: Sage, 1985. $24.95.

BETHLEN, STEVEN and IVAN VOLGYES. *Europe and the Superpowers: Political, Economic, and Military Policies in the 1980s*. Pp. xii, 164. Boulder, CO: Westview Press, 1985. Paperbound, $20.00.

BLALOCK, H. M., Jr. *Causal Models in Panel and Experimental Designs*. Pp. x, 287. Hawthorne, NY: Aldine, 1985. $49.95. Paperbound, $24.95.

BLALOCK, H. M., Jr. *Causal Models in the Social Sciences*. Pp. x, 448. Hawthorne, NY: Aldine, 1985. $49.95. Paperbound, $24.95.

BLECHMAN, BARRY, M., ed. *Preventing Nuclear War: A Realistic Approach*. Pp. 197. Bloomington: Indiana University Press, 1985. $22.50. Paperbound, $17.50.

BLISHCHENKO, I. and N. ZHDANOV. *Terrorism and International Law*. Pp. 287. Moscow: Progress, 1984. Distributed by Imported Publications, Chicago, IL. $5.95.

BLUME, WILBUR T. and PAUL SCHNELLER, eds. *Toward International Tele-Education*. Pp. xv, 256. Boulder, CO: Westview Press, 1985. Paperbound, $19.50.

BODY, PAUL. *Joseph Eotvos and the Modernization of Hungary, 1840-1870*. Pp. 134. New York: Columbia University Press, 1985. $18.00.

BOTTOMORE, TOM, ed. *Finance Capital*. Pp. vi, 466. Boston: Routledge and Kegan Paul, 1985. Paperbound, $15.95.

BRAHAM, RANDOLPH L. *Jewish Leadership during the Nazi Era*. Pp. xiv, 154. New York: Columbia University Press, 1985. $20.00.

BRAUN, AREL. *Small-State Security in the Balkans*. Pp. xi, 334. Totowa, NJ: Barnes and Noble Books, 1983. $23.50.

BROWN, ARCHIE, ed. *Political Culture and Communist Studies*. Pp. xii, 211. Armonk, NY: M. E. Sharpe, 1985. $30.00. Paperbound, $14.95.

BROWN, JAMES and WILLIAM P. SNYDER. *The Regionalization of Warfare.* Pp. xi, 291. New Brunswick, NJ: Transaction Books, 1985. Paperbound, no price.

BRUBAKER, TIMOTHY H. *Later Life Families.* Pp. 144. Beverly Hills, CA: Sage, 1985. $19.85.

BRUGGER, BILL, ed. *Chinese Marxism Influx 1978-84: Essays on Epistemology, Ideology and Political Economy.* Pp. 218. Armonk, NY: M. E. Sharpe, 1985. $30.00. Paperbound, $14.95.

BRUTENTS, KAREN. *The Newly Free Countries in the Seventies.* Pp. 280. Moscow: Progress, 1983. Distributed by Imported Publications, Chicago, IL. $5.95.

BUCHOLZ, ARDEN. *Hans Delbruck and the German Military Establishment: War Images in Conflict.* Pp. xiv, 191. Iowa City: University of Iowa Press, 1985. No price.

CALVERT, PETER. *The Concept of Class: An Historical Introduction.* Pp. 254. New York: St. Martin's Press, 1985. Paperbound, $12.95.

CARLTON, DAVID and CARLO SCHAERF, eds. *Reassessing Arms Control.* Pp. xix, 211. New York: St. Martin's Press, 1985. $27.50.

CHANNELS, NOREEN L. *Social Science Methods in the Legal Process.* Pp. x, 276. Totowa, NJ: Rowman and Allanheld, 1985. $39.95.

CHUBB, JOHN E. and PAUL E. PETERSON, eds. *The New Direction in American Politics.* Pp. xv, 409. Washington, DC: Brookings Institution, 1985. $26.95. Paperbound, $9.95.

CURTIS, MICHAEL, ed. *Introduction to Comparative Government.* Pp. x, 512. New York: Harper & Row, 1985. $25.50.

DeROSE, FRANCOIS. *European Security and France.* Pp. xvi, 143. Champaign: University of Illinois, 1985. $19.95.

DEUTSCHER, ISAAC. *Marxism, Wars and Revolutions: Essays from Four Decades.* Pp. xxix, 276. New York: Schocken Books, 1985. $25.00. Paperbound, $8.95.

DONNELLY, JACK. *The Concept of Human Rights.* Pp. 120. New York: St. Martin's Press, 1985. $22.50.

DUIGNAN, PETER and L. H. GANN. *The United States and Africa: A History.* Pp. xiv, 450. New York: Cambridge University Press, 1985. $29.95.

EASTBY, JOHN. *Functionalism and Interdependence.* Pp. xiii, 118. Lanham, MD: University Press of America, 1985. $21.00. Paperbound, $8.50.

EDWARDS, GEORGE C., III and STEPHEN J. WAYNE. *Presidential Leadership: Politics and Policy Making.* Pp. xiii, 480. New York: St. Martin's Press, 1985. $39.95.

FLYNN, GREGORY and HANS RATTINGER, eds. *The Public and Atlantic Defense.* Pp. xviii, 398. Totowa, NJ: Rowman and Allanheld, 1985. $45.00.

FOLTZ, WILLIAM J. and HENRY S. BIENEN, eds. *Arms and the African: Military Influences on Africa's International Relations.* Pp. xv, 221. New Haven, CT: Yale University Press, 1985. $22.50.

FREUDENBURG, WILLIAM R. and EUGENE A. ROSA, eds. *Public Reactions to Nuclear Power: Are There Critical Masses?* Pp. xiii, 370. Boulder, CO: Westview Press, 1984. $36.00.

GARDINER, JOHN A. and THEODORE R. LYMAN. *The Fraud Control Game.* Pp. xvi, 266. Bloomington: Indiana University Press, 1985. $24.95.

GIANAKOS, PERRY E., ed. *George Ade's "Stories of 'Benevolent Assimilation.'"* Pp. v, 82. Detroit, MI: Celler Book Shop, 1985. Paperbound, $7.50.

GIBSON, LAY JAMES and ALFONSO CORONA RENTERIA, eds. *The U.S. and Mexico: Borderland Development and the National Economies.* Pp. xvii, 262. Boulder, CO: Westview Press, 1985. Paperbound, $25.00.

GIROD, ROGER, PATRICK de LAUBIER, and ALAN GLADSTONE, eds. *Social*

Policy in Western Europe and the USA, 1950-80. Pp. xi, 117. New York: St. Martin's Press, 1985. $25.00.

GOLDMAN, SHELDON and THOMAS P. JAHNIGE. *The Federal Courts as a Political System.* Pp. viii, 263. New York: Harper & Row, 1985. Paperbound, no price.

GOREAU, ANGELINE. *The Whole Duty of a Woman: Female Writers in Seventeenth-Century England.* Pp. viii, 344. New York: Doubleday, Dial Press, 1985. Paperbound, $12.95.

GRACHEV, ANDREI. *In the Grip of Terror.* Pp. 150. Moscow: Progress, 1982. Distributed by Imported Publications, Chicago, IL. $2.95.

GRAHAM, OTIS L., Jr. and MEGHAN ROBINSON WANDER, eds. *Franklin D. Roosevelt: His Life and Times.* Pp. xii, 483. Boston: G. K. Hall, 1985. $27.50.

GRUENWALD, DONALD, ed. *"I am honored to be here today...."* Pp. x, 309. Dobbs Ferry, NY: Oceana. $30.00.

HAYHOE, RUTH. *Contemporary Chinese Education.* Pp. 287. Armonk, NY: M. E. Sharpe, 1985. $17.95.

HELLER, MARK, DOV TAMARI, and ZEEV EYTAN, eds. *The Middle East Military Balance, 1984.* Pp. 316. Boulder, CO: Westview Press, 1985. $35.00.

JELLISON, CHARLES A. *Besieged: The World War II Ordeal of Malta, 1940-42.* Pp. xii, 288. Hanover, NH: University Press of New England, 1985. $19.95.

JODICE, DAVID A., comp. *Political Risk Assessment: An Annotated Bibliography.* Pp. xii, 279. Westport, CT: Greenwood Press, 1985. $35.00.

JONES, HOWARD, *The Course of American Diplomacy: From the Revolution to the Present.* Pp. xiv, 639. New York: Franklin Watts, 1985. $24.95.

KAUFMANN, HUGO M. *Germany's International Monetary Policy and the European Monetary System.* Pp. v, 154. New York: Columbia University Press, 1985. $20.00.

KEEBLE, CURTIS, ed. *The Soviet State: The Domestic Roots of Soviet Foreign Policy.* Pp. vii, 244. Boulder, CO: Westview Press, 1985. $45.00. Paperbound, $17.95.

KEETON, GEORGE W. and GEORG SCHWARZENBERGER, eds. *The Year Book of World Affairs 1984.* Pp. vii, 377. Boulder, CO: Westview Press, 1984. $42.00.

KEGLEY, CHARLES W., Jr. and EUGENE R. WITTKOPF, eds. *The Nuclear Reader: Strategy, Weapons, War.* Pp. xx, 332. New York: St. Martin's Press, 1985. $27.50.

KHOROS, VLADIMIR G. *Populism: Its Past, Present and Future.* Pp. 294. Moscow: Progress, 1984. Distributed by Imported Publications, Chicago, IL. $8.95.

KREGEL, J. A., ed. *The International Oil Market.* Pp. vii, 180. Armonk, NY: M. E. Sharpe, 1985. $30.00. Paperbound, $14.95.

KREPON, MICHAEL, *Strategic Stalemate.* Pp. xvi, 191. New York: St. Martin's Press, 1984. $25.00.

KUHN, RAYMOND, ed. *The Politics of Broadcasting.* Pp. 305. New York: St. Martin's Press, 1985. $25.00.

MANOR, JAMES, ed. *Sri Lanka in Change and Crisis.* Pp. 229. New York: St. Martin's Press, 1984. $25.00.

MATHISEN, TRYGVE. *Sharing Destiny: A Study of Global Integration.* Pp. 185. New York: Columbia University Press, 1984. $26.00.

McARTHUR, BENJAMIN. *Actors and American Culture, 1880-1920.* Pp. xiv, 289. Philadelphia: Temple University Press, 1984. $29.95.

McKINLAY, JOHN B., ed. *Issues in the Political Economy of Health Care.* Pp. ix, 294. New York: Methuen, 1985. Paperbound, $12.95.

MIKHAILOV, N. *Panorama of the Soviet Union.* Pp. 264. Moscow: Progress, 1985. Distributed by Imported Publications, Chicago, IL. $11.95.

MUELLER, DENNIS C., ed. *The Political Economy of Growth.* Pp. vii, 285. New Haven, CT: Yale University Press, 1985. $27.50. Paperbound, $9.95.

NAGLE, JOHN D. *Introduction to Comparative Politics: Political System Performance in Three Worlds.* Pp. 360. Chicago: Nelson-Hall, 1985. Paperbound, $18.95.

OREN, NISSAN, ed. *Images and Reality in International Politics.* Pp. 247. New York: St. Martin's Press, 1985. $22.50.

OREN, NISSAN, ed. *When Patterns Change: Turning Points in International Politics.* Pp. 269. New York: St. Martin's Press, 1985. $22.50.

O'ROURKE, DAVID K. *A Process Called Conversion.* Pp. 191. New York: Doubleday, 1985. $13.95.

PETERSON, PAUL E. *The New Urban Reality.* Pp. xv, 301. Washington, DC: Brookings Institution, 1985. $31.95. Paperbound, $11.95.

PORRITT, JONATHAN. *Seeing Green: The Politics of Ecology Explained.* Pp. xvi, 252. New York: Basil Blackwell, 1985. $24.95. Paperbound, $6.95.

RONCAGLIA, ALESSANDRO. *Petty: The Origins of Political Economy.* Pp. xi, 118. Armonk, NY: M. E. Sharpe, 1985. 25.00.

RUSSETT, BRUCE and HARVEY STARR. *World Politics: The Menu for Choice.* Pp. xiv, 617. New York: W. H. Freeman, 1985. $22.95.

SCHWEBER, CLAUDINE and CLARICE FEINMAN, eds. *Criminal Justice Politics and Women.* Pp. 133. New York: Haworth Press, 1985. $19.95.

SMIRNOV, A. D. et al. *The Teaching of Political Economy.* Pp. 334. Moscow: Progress, 1984. Distributed by Imported Publications, Chicago, IL. $8.95.

SOROKIN, PITIRIM. *Social and Cultural Dynamics.* Pp. xxvii, 704. New Brunswick, NJ: Transaction Books, 1985. Paperbound, $19.95.

SPANIER, JOHN. *American Foreign Policy since World War II.* Pp. xi, 353. New York: Holt, Rinehart & Winston, 1985. Paperbound, no price.

SPIDCHENKO, KONSTANTIN, *USSR: Geography of the Eleventh Five-Year Plan Period.* Pp. 229. Moscow: Progress, 1984. Distributed by Imported Publications, Chicago, IL. $6.95.

SPINNEY, FRANKLIN C. *Defense of Facts of Life: The Plans/Reality Mismatch.* Pp. xviii, 260. Boulder, CO: Westview Press, 1985. $35.00. Paperbound, $16.00.

STORING, HERBERT J., ed. *The Anti-Federalist.* Pp. viii, 374. Chicago: University of Chicago Press, 1985. Paperbound, $9.95.

SULEIMAN, EZRA N., ed. *Bureaucrats and Policy Making.* Pp. 292. New York: Holmes and Meier, 1985. $37.50. Paperbound, $16.95.

TARASOV, KONSTANTIN and VRACHESLAV ZUBENKO. *The CIA in Latin America.* Pp. 280. Moscow: Progress, 1984. Distributed by Imported Publications, Chicago, IL. $3.95.

THOMAS, CAROLINE. *New States, Sovereignty and Intervention.* Pp. x, 177. New York: St. Martin's Press, 1985. $27.50.

TURNER, CHARLES F. and ELIZABETH MARTIN, eds. *Surveying Subjective Phenomena.* Pp. xvi, 617. $47.50. New York: Basic Books, 1985.

TURNER, JONATHAN H. and DAVID MUSICK. *American Dilemmas: A Sociological Interpretation of Enduring Social Issues.* Pp. x, 375. New York: Columbia University Press, 1985. $40.00. Paperbound, $15.00.

WALLACE, RICHARD CHEEVER and WENDY DREW WALLACE. *Sociology.* Pp. xxii, 677. Newton, MA: Allyn & Bacon, 1985. No price.

WARD, MICHAEL DON. *Theories, Models, and Simulations in International Relations: Essays in Honor of Harold Guetzkow.* Pp. xvi, 625. Boulder, CO: Westview Press, 1985. $35.00.

WATSON, RICHARD A. *Promise and Performance of American Democracy.* Pp. xiii, 692. Somerset, NJ: John Wiley, 1985. $25.95.

WORONOFF, JON. *Japan's Commercial Empire*. Pp. 415. Armonk, NY: M. E. Sharpe, 1985. $14.95.

WORSLEY, PETER. *The Three Worlds: Culture and World Development*. Pp. xiv, 409. Chicago: University of Chicago Press, 1984. $28.00. Paperbound, $12.95.

INDEX

Aarhus Psychiatric Hospital, 146-47
Action for Mental Health, 20
Almshouses, 19
American Law Institute, 91, 102
American Psychiatric Association, 90, 128
Asylums, 14-17

Bardach, Eugene, 122
Baxstrom v. *Herold*, 116
Bemis, Merrick, 16
BLITCH, CAROLYN L., *see* BOWERS, WILLIAM J., coauthor
BLOOM, JOSEPH D., *see* ROGERS, JEFFREY L., coauthor
Bowers, William J., 10
BOWERS, WILLIAM J., DANIEL J. GIVELBER, and CAROLYN L. BLITCH, How Did *Tarasoff* Affect Clinical Practice? 70-85
Brown v. *Board of Education*, 31

California, psychotherapists in, 70-85
Canada, recidivism in, 113
  see also Ontario
CARE AND TREATMENT OF THE MENTALLY ILL IN THE UNITED STATES: HISTORICAL DEVELOPMENTS AND REFORMS, Joseph P. Morrissey and Howard H. Goldman, 12-27
Chicago, defendants pleading insanity, 109
Civil commitment, 28-41, 42-55, 56-69, 145-47
CIVIL COMMITMENT OF THE MENTALLY ILL: AN OVERVIEW, Mark J. Mills, 28-41
Community Mental Health Centers Act (1963), 20
Community mental health movement, 20-22, 23, 26, 146
Community programs for the mentally ill, 94-95, 140
Connecticut, insanity acquittees in, 106-8, 110
Crimes, seriousness of, 97

Dangerousness
  mental illness and, 34-36, 37, 39, 52-54, 71, 88, 95, 98
  of offenders, 150-51
Deinstitutionalization, 14 n.5, 21-23, 32
Denmark, forensic psychiatry in, 149, 151
Dixon v. *Attorney General of the Commonwealth of Pennsylvania*, 117
Durham, Mary L., 10
DURHAM, MARY L. and GLENN L. PIERCE, Legal Intervention in Civil Commitment: The Impact of Broadened Commitment Criteria, 42-55

Eckerman, William C., 129

Female mentally disordered offenders, 132
Finland, forensic psychiatry in, 149
Fukunaga, Kenneth, 109

Geller, Jeffry, 24-25
GIVELBER, DANIEL J., *see* BOWERS, WILLIAM J., coauthor
GOLDMAN, HOWARD H., *see* MORRISSEY, JOSEPH P., coauthor
Grave disability, 36-37, 46-47, 51-55

Herstedvester Detention Center for Criminal Psychopaths, 151
HOW DID *TARASOFF* AFFECT CLINICAL PRACTICE? William J. Bowers, Daniel J. Givelber, and Carolyn L. Blitch, 70-85

Iceland, forensic psychiatry in, 149
Illinois, insanity defense in, 102
INDEXING CIVIL COMMITMENT IN PSYCHIATRIC EMERGENCY ROOMS, Steven P. Segal, Margaret A. Watson, and L. Scott Nelson, 56-69
Insanity acquittees, 106-9
  hospitalization of, 109-12
  in Oregon, 86-99
Insanity defense, 87-89, 91-92, 99, 115-26, 148
  frequency of acquittals via, 104
  frequency of use of, 103-4
  perceptions of, 118-19
  reform of, 119-21
  research on, 100-114, 121-26
INSANITY DEFENSE: PROBLEMS AND PROSPECTS FOR STUDYING THE IMPACT OF LEGAL REFORMS, THE, Henry J. Steadman and Joseph P. Morrissey, 115-26
Involuntary Treatment Act (Washington State, 1979), 46-55
Involuntary Treatment Act (Washington State, 1973), 44-46

Jackson v. *Indiana*, 134
Joint Commission on Mental Illness and Health, 20
Juveniles, in forensic facilities, 132

INDEX

Kenno, Charles K., 128-29
Kerr, Charlotte A., 9
KERR, CHARLOTTE A. and JEFFREY A. ROTH, Populations, Practices, and Problems in Forensic Psychiatric Facilities, 127-43

Lanterman-Petris-Short Act, 57-58, 67, 117
LAW AND PSYCHIATRY: SCANDINAVIA IN THE 1980s, Leif Öjesjö, 144-54
LEGAL INTERVENTION IN CIVIL COMMITMENT: THE IMPACT OF BROADENED COMMITMENT CRITERIA, Mary L. Durham and Glenn L. Pierce, 42-55
Lister, Eric, 24-25

MANSON, SPERO M., see ROGERS, JEFFREY L., coauthor
Maryland, recidivism in, 112
Massachusetts Mental Health Act of 1970, 117
Media coverage, and the insanity defense, 103
Medicaid, 22-23
Medicare, 22
Mental hygiene movement, 17-20
Michigan
 insanity acquittees in, 106-8, 110
 insanity defense reform in, 119-20
Mills, Mark J., 9
MILLS, MARK J., Civil Commitment of the Mentally Ill: An Overview, 28-41
Missouri, insanity acquittees in, 106-8
Moral treatment, 14-15
Morrissey, Joseph P., 9, 10
MORRISSEY, JOSEPH P. and HOWARD H. GOLDMAN, Care and Treatment of the Mentally Ill in the United States: Historical Developments and Reforms, 12-27
MORRISSEY, JOSEPH P., see STEADMAN, HENRY J., coauthor

National Association for Mental Health, 128
National Committee for Mental Hygiene, 18
NELSON, L. SCOTT, see SEGAL, STEVEN P., coauthor
New Jersey, insanity acquittees in, 106
New York State
 insanity acquittees in, 106-11
 insanity defense in, 101-2
 recidivism in, 112-13
Norman, William Barry, 129
Norway, forensic psychiatry in, 149

Öjesjö, Leif, 10
ÖJESJÖ, LEIF, Law and Psychiatry: Scandinavia in the 1980s, 144-54

Ontario, insanity acquittees in, 106-8
Oregon
 insanity acquittees in, 86-99, 106, 108
 recidivism in, 113-14
OREGON'S PSYCHIATRIC SECURITY REVIEW BOARD: A COMPREHENSIVE SYSTEM FOR MANAGING INSANITY ACQUITTEES, Jeffrey L. Rogers, Joseph D. Bloom, and Spero M. Manson, 86-99
Outpatient mental health care, 147

Parens patriae, 9, 10, 16, 35-36, 44, 51, 53
Pasewark, Richard A., 9, 10
PASEWARK, RICHARD A., A Review of Research on the Insanity Defense, 100-114
Pierce, Glenn L., 10
PIERCE, GLENN L., see DURHAM, MARY L., coauthor
Police power, 9, 10, 16, 44, 51, 53, 90
POPULATIONS, PRACTICES, AND PROBLEMS IN FORENSIC PSYCHIATRY FACILITIES, Charlotte A. Kerr and Jeffrey A. Roth, 127-43
Professionalization, 136
Psychiatric emergency-room clinicians, 56-69
Psychiatric facilities, forensic, 127-43
Psychiatric Security Review Board, 86-99, 113, 141
Psychotherapists, impact of *Tarasoff* on, 70-85

Recidivism, criminal, 99, 107, 112-14, 153
REVIEW OF RESEARCH ON THE INSANITY DEFENSE, A, Richard A. Pasewark, 110-114
Rogers, Jeffrey L., 9
ROGERS, JEFFREY L., JOSEPH D. BLOOM, and SPERO M. MANSON, Oregon's Psychiatric Security Review Board: A Comprehensive System for Managing Insanity Acquittees, 86-99
Roth, Jeffrey A., 9
ROTH, JEFFREY A., see KERR, CHARLOTTE A., coauthor
Roth, Loren H., 37-38

Scheidemandel, Patricia L., 128-29
Segal, Steven P., 10
SEGAL, STEVEN P., MARGARET A. WATSON, and L. SCOTT NELSON, Indexing Civil Commitment in Psychiatric Emergency Rooms, 56-69
SHAH, SALEEM A., Preface, 9-11
Sheldon, Robert B., 129
Social Security Disability Insurance, 23
State Care Act (New York State), 19

State mental hospitals, 19-20, 23, 25-26
Steadman, Henry J., 9, 25
STEADMAN, HENRY J. and JOSEPH P. MORRISSEY, The Insanity Defense: Problems and Prospects for Studying the Impact of Legal Reforms, 115-26
Stone, Alan A., 37-38
Supplemental Security Income, 23
Sweden
　civil commitment in, 145-46
　forensic psychiatry in, 148-50, 154

Tarasoff v. *Regents of the University of California*, 70-85

Three Ratings of Involuntary Admissibility (TRIAD), 56-69
Transinstitutionalization, 14 n.5, 19, 23-24

Vitek v. *Jones*, 134

Washington State, civil commitment in, 40, 42-55
WATSON, MARGARET A., *see* SEGAL, STEVEN P., coauthor
World Health Organization, 153-54
Wyatt v. *Stickney*, 117
Wyoming, insanity defense in, 102, 105-6

CHICAGO

THE CULTURAL REVOLUTION AND POST-MAO REFORMS
A Historical Perspective
TANG TSOU

"Tsou offers us a strong paradigm for the study of contemporary Chinese politics. Because Tsou attacks head-on some dominant themes in modern world political history, a wide range of scholars will be interested in his thesis and want to engage it in debate. All China specialists will have to reflect on it."
—James R. Townsend, University of Washington
CLOTH $29.95   400 PAGES

GENDER JUSTICE
DAVID L. KIRP, MARK G. YUDOF, and MARLENE STRONG FRANKS

"[The authors] ask that we reconsider the accepted paradigm that 'equality' directly results from treating women indistinguishably from men. Instead, they fluently argue that the paradigm more applicable to true gender justice is liberty....A challenging book, complex and disturbing....For those deeply interested in the politics of public policy pertaining to sexual equality, it will open radically new avenues of thought."—*Kirkus Reviews*
CLOTH $19.95   256 PAGES

DISCRIMINATION, JOBS, AND POLITICS
The Struggle for Equal Employment Opportunity in the United States since the New Deal
PAUL BURSTEIN

"A highly original study of the struggle for equal opportunity in employment since the New Deal. With complex and compelling arguments that shed new light on the reason, timing, and way that Congress prohibited discrimination in employment, Paul Burstein convincingly challenges conventional wisdom on the genesis of Civil Rights legislation."—William Julius Wilson, University of Chicago
PAPER $12.95   258 PAGES
LIBRARY CLOTH EDITION $30.00

JUDGES AND THE CITIES
Interpreting Local Autonomy
GORDON L. CLARK

Clark analyzes four court disputes in depth, showing that the concept of local autonomy has very different meanings and implications in each of them. "A landmark volume."—Julian Wolpert, Princeton University
CLOTH $25.00   264 PAGES

Now in Paper

THE HARDEST DRUG
Heroin and Public Policy
JOHN KAPLAN

"An exceptionally clear and accurate summary of what we know about the drug and its effect on people and on crime rates, and a balanced account of our efforts to treat addicts and curb trafficking."—James Q. Wilson, *The New Republic*
PAPER $9.95   262 PAGES
STUDIES IN CRIME AND JUSTICE SERIES

THE UNIVERSITY OF CHICAGO PRESS
5801 South Ellis Avenue, Chicago, IL 60637

The Pacific Century
Economic and Political Consequences of Asian-Pacific Dynamism

Staffan Burenstam Linder. Spectacular economic growth in the Pacific Basin is forcing a shift in the world's political and economic center of gravity, a shift away from the Atlantic to the Asian-Pacific region. This book is designed to give the general reader a firm grasp of the new Pacific dynamism and to clarify its impact on the global marketplace. The author first describes the factors that have produced the phenomenon—huge increases in production, international trade, and overall economic achievement. He then speculates on the consequences of the shift to Pacific primacy: how it will influence political and economic strategies in other sectors, encourage new economic partnerships, and pose a threat to certain national economies. Warning that protectionism is not the answer to the threat, the author concludes by showing how non-Pacific nations can use Pacific growth to their benefit. Cloth, $18.95; paper, $7.95

P'eng Te-huai
A Political Biography

Jürgen Domes. In 1978 the Chinese Communist Party posthumously rehabilitated Marshal P'eng Te-huai—veteran of the Long March, leader of China's forces in the Korean War, and Minister of Defense from 1954 to 1959. An outspoken critic of Mao's development policies, P'eng was branded a "traitor" during the Cultural Revolution and sent to prison, where he remained until shortly before his death in 1974. P'eng has subsequently been rehabilitated and is now considered an important contributor to the cause of Chinese communism. This study reconstructs P'eng's biography within the framework of political and socioeconomic developments in China, and uses P'eng's life and career as a means of investigating the typology of intra-party conflict in the CCP, the evolution of anti-Maoist doctrine, and the ways in which personal images are manipulated in the People's Republic of China. $25.00

Stanford University Press